WESTERN POLICY
AND
EASTERN EUROPE

FOUNDATION FOR FOREIGN AFFAIRS SERIES

WESTERN POLICY AND EASTERN EUROPE

Edited by
DAVID S. COLLIER
and
KURT GLASER

Published in cooperation with
Foundation for Foreign Affairs, Inc.

HENRY REGNERY COMPANY
CHICAGO

FOUNDATION FOR FOREIGN AFFAIRS SERIES, NUMBER 10

The Foundation for Foreign Affairs, 154 East Superior Street, Chicago, Illinois 60611, is a non-profit corporation devoted to the promotion of a wider understanding of international relations—political, economic and cultural. Books in the Foundation for Foreign Affairs Series are published in the interest of public information and debate. They represent the free expression of their authors and do not necessarily indicate the judgment and opinions of the Foundation.

Contents

31811

Part Three

EASTERN EUROPE AND WORLD POLICY

Part Four

IN SUMMARY

Introduction

THE CHAPTERS IN this book, the third of its kind, have been adapted from papers delivered at a conference of European and American scholars on Western policy and Eastern Europe, held in Chicago from March 25 to March 28, 1965. The sponsors of this conference were the Foundation for Foreign Affairs, Chicago, and the Studiengesellschaft für Fragen mittel- und osteuropäischer Partnerschaft of Wiesbaden. Although the chapter topics were selected and assigned with a view to balanced coverage of the field of interest, each contributor was entirely free in the selection and presentation of material; the opinions expressed are those of the authors and not necessarily the views of the Foundation or the Studiengesellschaft.

The first of this series of conferences, dealing with the Berlin problem and the future of Eastern Europe, was held in Chicago in March, 1962. At that time, the Berlin wall was still relatively new, and the political and legal problems it raised occupied the center of attention for those concerned with European affairs. While this first conference did not result in any immediate and tangible effects on American or West German governmental policies, there is no doubt that it contributed to deeper understanding of mutual problems on both sides of the Atlantic. The participants—scholars, journalists and even practical politicians representing several European countries in addition to the United States and the German Federal Republic—became fully aware that the problem of German partition and reunification and the problems of Eastern Europe are closely linked and that the reunification of Germany and a solution of the Berlin problem are hardly likely to be achieved without steps toward a new order in Eastern Europe—and vice versa.

During the three years since the first conference, the Berlin wall has not by any means dwindled in importance; but the public has come to take it for granted, and attention has been distracted by new crises in Africa, Southeast Asia and other parts of the world. The latter are, of course, manifestations of the same worldwide confrontation of militant communism and constitutional democracy, a conflict that both intensifies and feeds on the problems generated by that other great confrontation—the affluence of scientific civilization vis-à-vis the poverty of primitive societies. Insofar as Berlin is concerned, things have not really changed since 1962: the problems of the divided city, of access routes through the Soviet Zone and of reuniting divided Germany remain the same. So do the problems of Eastern Europe, where some countries now enjoy a little more freedom than they did three years ago, but where the peoples still exist under the yoke of one-party systems.

The second conference, held in September, 1963, in Wiesbaden, analyzed the achievements and potentialities of the Common Market and of West European integration, both in terms of their significance as steps toward a united Western Europe and of their impact east of the Iron Curtain. Although this conference, like the first, brought together diverging points of view, it demonstrated two facts of the highest political significance. One is that Western Europeans, however great their interest in further economic and even governmental integration of the free part of the continent, are not likely to become so engrossed in their own problems as to forget their fellow Europeans currently under Soviet hegemony. The other is that the attractive forces of the Common Market and of democratic capitalism are so great as to make increasingly impossible the ideological and institutional consolidation of communist societies within a field of influence that extends across East-Central Europe and perhaps even into the Soviet Union. Since it has been demonstrated that the magnetism of the Free World cancels out that of Marxist ideology, the most that the Kremlin and its satraps can manage is to maintain an uneasy status quo, a status quo that becomes increasingly hollow and sterile as force and opportunist incentives are employed to shore up a failing ideology.

Because the achievement of Western aspirations depends on taking advantage of a situation already evolving in favor of the Free World, it was decided to devote the third conference to examining developments in Eastern Europe in some detail and to analyzing the attitude of East European peoples and their governments toward a future united Germany and toward a united Europe in which Germany plays an important role. Such an analysis was possible only with a simultaneous reappraisal of changing Soviet policies in Europe, the Soviet-Chinese conflict and the stresses and strains that beset Marxist-Leninist ideology today, since all these problems are highly interdependent.

The sponsors of this conference, and certainly the participants as well, are quite aware that conferences of scholars for the exchange of knowledge and opinion seldom make immediate contributions to world politics or directly influence the history of nations. They may, nevertheless, help to overcome one of the greatest enemies of humanity and world peace: lack of knowledge and unwillingness to understand other peoples. Since the operational ranges of foreign policies are limited by public opinion and since, in the history of democratic states, public opinion has more than once figured as a source or stimulant of policy changes, there is little doubt that scholarly conferences held in an attitude of open-mindedness ultimately produce results, especially when their findings are made available to the educated public. It is in this spirit that this book is offered.

David S. Collier
Foundation for Foreign Affairs, Inc.

Kurt Glaser
Southern Illinois University

January, 1966

Part One

EASTERN EUROPE TODAY:
WHAT KIND OF EVOLUTION?

CHAPTER I

Eastern Europe: Social Change, Intellectual Restlessness, Political Uncertainty

JOHN C. CAMPBELL

THE HALLMARK of the communist system in Stalin's day was rigidity. Whether one holds the man, the institutions or the doctrine responsible, the fact of the "monolith" was fairly close to the official boast. That rigidity and conformity might not have lasted long in any event. But it was Stalin's death in 1953 that opened the way for change, both in the Soviet Union itself and in the satellite states of Eastern Europe.* More than a decade has now passed, a period in which the latter area has witnessed the emergence of new intellectual currents, social forces and political attitudes, together with the reappearance of some that are quite old and were merely temporarily absent from the scene.

The thaw of the early post-Stalin years and the striking events to which it led in Poland and Hungary in 1956 are now history. The hopeful glow of the Polish October has faded, and the Hungarian outburst for freedom was stifled by armed force, leaving but a mem-

* The countries under consideration here are Poland, Czechoslovakia, Hungary, Rumania and Bulgaria. Albania, which has joined the Chinese camp, is a special case. Sovzone Germany is dealt with in other contributions to this volume. Yugoslavia, despite its rapprochement with the U.S.S.R., retains its independence. The term "satellite" is used here as one of convenience, without judging the degree of dependence, which has varied from time to time and from one country to another.—*Eds.*

ory of the few glorious days when the nation could speak with its own voice. Yet if 1956 was not a beginning, neither was it by any means an end. The forces in East European society that broke through the surface of Stalinist uniformity almost from the moment of Stalin's demise—forces of social change arising inexorably from the system itself, intellectual questioning of its doctrine, a human yearning for free self-expression and the familiar strains of national feeling and identification—were not buried with the hopes of 1956. They have continued to play their part. If they helped to destroy Stalinism, with an assist from Khrushchev, that did not make them necessarily compatible with the Khrushchevism that replaced it. Equilibrium, which communist leaders have sought in attempting to thread their way between the dangers of "dogmatism" on the one side and "revisionism" on the other, has not been found. There is instead a shifting disequilibrium, subject to many influences and fully controlled by none.

Some of the impetus for change has come from outside: from developments in the Soviet Union, from the conflict with China, from Yugoslavia and from the West. Some—and this is our present concern—has come from within. Any inquiry into the social and intellectual forces now perceptible in Eastern Europe and their influence on the future of these nations invites speculative, rather than categorical, responses. We do not have the kind of evidence that makes proof of this or that point self-evident. Even if hordes of Western journalists, poll-takers and sociologists were offered full and free scope to go hither and yon and poke about wherever they pleased, we should probably still be far from firm conclusions. There is, obviously, no single mold for either internal evolution or relations with the Soviet Union. The East European regimes do not fit any except the most general common definition. Some are closer to Moscow than others. Some are closer to their own people than others. All have differing mixtures of the various elements and tendencies distinguishable in their makeup.

A further element of uncertainty lies in the fact that a new generation has grown up under the communist system. Some impression may be gained of its feelings, ideas and beliefs, but nowhere can they be measured, and the pattern is never the same. Most of the present political leaders have been on the scene (though not always with a continuum in high office) since World War II. Will their successors come from the cadres of the Communist parties or from today's skeptical, nonconformist youth?

Among the points of special interest is, first, what has been called the erosion of ideology. What is happening to the authority of Marxism and its use as an instrument of the system? Second, what are the effects of the revival of nationalism and of the open doors to the West? Third, what is the interaction between two separate but related trends, the growth of autonomy and freer choice for individual states within the communist bloc and the liberalization of the internal order of each of them? Such broad questions go beyond the limits of this paper, to say nothing of the limits of present powers of prediction, but they should be posed as a means of giving purpose and perspective to the discussion.

Let us look separately at four individual countries: Poland, Czechoslovakia, Hungary and Rumania. (Bulgaria is omitted because new trends there are much less perceptible.) It will then be possible to judge what broader generalizations across national boundaries may be permissible.

POLAND

Poland has gone through the experience of an exhilarating assertion of national feeling, with high hopes for a tolerable compromise between the realities of international politics and the desires of the people followed by years of growing disillusionment and increasing alienation of the population from the regime. The Gomulka leadership, which used and depended on popular support in 1956 to ward off collapse and to assert Poland's right to run its domestic affairs without Soviet interference, has settled for a bureaucratic system of rule in which the sources of power do not go beyond the reconstituted United Workers' (Communist) party. The party has by now largely rid itself of those elements that might be termed revisionist or liberal. The revival of police methods, the still doctrinaire approach to economic questions, the underlying hostility to the Catholic church, the increasing restrictions on free expression, the general bleakness of the leadership and especially of Mr. Gomulka himself—all these factors have turned the people to apathy, skepticism and an attitude of "What's in it for me?"

Poland gave promise of inspiration and leadership among the communist states of Eastern Europe after 1956. In some ways it is still more open and more liberal than the rest. Yet it has lost much of its unique character and position. The regime is without question Polish, since Soviet control has not returned, but it has been losing the qualities that come from contact with the people and at least semi-acceptance by them. On this score its "national communism" has lost its luster.

Perhaps this reference to national communism only confuses matters. Poland's cultural life grows not out of Marxism or any theoretical or political system but out of the Polish experience, out of the genius of the few and the humanity of the many. But the essence of thought and artistic expression, as aspects of a nation's cultural life, lies in their communication; and in Poland the channels of communication are under the surveillance and control of the state authorities. Literary or artistic expression has no real content if it is mere sycophancy or conformity to the "line" of a political authority; nor can it, at the other extreme, play a positive role if it has no real relevance to the conditions under which the nation must live and try to survive. The tragedy of Poland's intellectuals is that their scope for exerting a creative influence on their nation's destiny has been so narrowed. As long as it was possible for a philosopher to reinterpret Marx as he wished, for an economist to work out the pattern of a specifically Polish road to socialism or for scholars to take up, renew or deepen an acquaintance with the Western world and seek its relevance to Polish life, then their minds and their talents could be put to the service of the people. But the regime made its choice against taking such risks to itself. One after another, literary discussion clubs and publications were forced to close.

The *cause célèbre* of "the thirty-four" is a striking example of the pass to which things have come. The letter delivered to Prime Minister Cyrankiewicz in March, 1964, by the leading figures in Polish cultural and scientific life, some of them individuals of world renown, was a sincere and passionate appeal for maintenance of the minimum of freedom from governmental interference and censorship necessary for them to continue their work with honesty and dignity. That news of it got out and provoked unrest within the country, as well as embarrassing questions from outside, was immaterial to the real issue in Poland—whether the regime intended to carry through a Zhdanov-like policy against prominent persons who were neither plotters nor opposition elements but respected representatives of Polish letters. Perhaps it would be premature to say that the issue has been decided. Most of the thirty-four held their ground under great pressure, for the regime left no doubt that in its view this was not a literary but a political struggle. Gomulka himself, in a speech to the Union of Polish Writers in September, 1964, that could only widen the gulf, left no doubt of his position that the task of literature was to play its part in the "battle for a socialist metamorphosis of the nation's mentality."[1]

Yet it is at this point that a longer perspective seems called for. While in many respects Poland has gone backward toward forms and methods reminiscent of the Stalinist system, no one, neither Gomulka nor whoever succeeds him, can repeal the events of 1956 or the effects they had on Polish life. Poland has passed through a many-faceted experience during the last decade, including continued contact with the West, open questioning of the sacred cows of Marxism-Leninism-Stalinism-Khrushchevism, a flowering of the humanities and the social sciences, adaptation of the educational system to Polish needs and a quiet strengthening of the motive force of Polish nationalism. When other East European nations are reaching for the benefits of a "Polish solution," allowing them to be rid of direct Soviet domination of their internal affairs; when "liberalization" is belatedly making its appearance in those countries; when the Kremlin itself shows signs of compromising with Soviet writers instead of whipping them into line by "administrative measures"—at such a time it is difficult to see Poland as a kind of permanent anachronism in that part of the world. It may be true that neither the middle-aged nor the younger generation of Poles has any further hope that the Gomulka regime—which is little more than a balance of contending groups with Mr. Gomulka and his cronies firmly holding the balance wheel—can somehow be a transition to something better,[2] or that any faction of the Communists offers a preferable alternative. Yet the very cynicism of the younger generation and its apparent indifference to politics may have significance for the future.

Social change is not easily perceptible because its currents run under the surface and the political attitudes to which it gives rise may not appear for many years. But we do know some things about population trends, about the economy, about the mood and thinking of the youth that seem to point in directions other than what may be suggested by the barren orthodoxy of the present political leadership or the disillusionment and frustration of the intelligentsia.

Poland's population, reflecting the cataclysmic changes of the war and postwar periods, is now largely homogeneous—Polish in ethnic nationality and Catholic in religion. It is infertile soil for Marxism and for Russian influence; and though for obvious geographical and political reasons both will continue to set limits on Poland's evolution, the question is what kinds of Polish ideas, attitudes or institutions are in germination beneath the surface of the present system. It is a young population, ever more removed from the concerns of the prewar era and even from those of the early years of communist rule.

Polish youth seems to find little but emptiness and frustration in its present environment. Marxism, even in its revisionist form made popular by Leszek Kolakowski and others just a few years ago, repels rather than attracts. The economy, despite undeniable progress, offers no dynamic prospect and cannot escape the shadow of a serious unemployment problem. While university students vaguely favor the general idea of socialism, they are apathetic to its concrete manifestations and scornful of its practitioners in their own country. There is a spirit of skepticism that finds expression in contempt for communist doctrine and all party or political activities, in the vogue of jazz, abstract art or avant-garde theater, or in a nihilism that rejects any kind of ideological system or political faith.

This independent-minded youth, not the officially sponsored youth organizations, may well provide the future leadership of Poland. Representative of what is becoming a new middle class, it can gather strength in today's Poland because it is indispensable to the modernization and growth desired by all. There is a kind of negative equilibrium in which the influence of leading intellectuals and of the Church, though both are on the defensive, continues to temper the power of the regime. A new generation, benefiting from that equilibrium as well as from continuing contact with the West and with new forces stirring in other communist countries, seems bound to make its energy and abilities and its fresh views felt in nearly all aspects of society: in the economy, the educational system, the arts, the professions and eventually in the political system itself. The Polish road to socialism, little more than a slogan when first announced and now scarcely mentioned officially, may develop into something quite different in content from the road Gomulka followed in 1956–58 or the one he follows today. The Poles will hardly be left behind in the evolution that, despite periodic halts and retreats, has been transforming Eastern Europe since 1953.

CZECHOSLOVAKIA

What has happened in Czechoslovakia, which for so many years seemed the most tractable of all the satellite countries, to challenge the communist leadership on so many fronts? In the past two years, previously unheard of ideas are being publicly expressed even—or one should say especially—within the Communist party itself. One thing that has not happened, namely, the continued advance of the economy, is perhaps most significant. The grudging support or toleration that the hard-headed Czechs gave to their regime after the communist seizure of full power in 1948 was conditioned by fear and hopelessness on the one hand and by the relatively favorable economic situation on the other. When the economy began to sputter and run down, the regime could no longer contain the pressure of criticism and discontent against the whole gamut of its policies, political as well as economic.

Antonín Novotný and the other communist leaders had long clung to virtually Stalinist policies. While asserting loyalty to Moscow they had lagged well behind the Soviet Union in adapting to new conditions, to say nothing of what was happening in neighboring Poland and Hungary. The regime held off making any concessions, fearing—rightly—that any breach in the dike of party authority and control could release a flood. But eventually there was no choice, because the spirit of criticism was reaching right into the party itself. Official economists began to write on the breakdown of the system of centralized planning and direction of the economy. Marxist philosophers showed a new spirit of independent inquiry. The publications of writers and journalists, taking advantage of official condemnation of the personality cult, called for a full accounting of what had happened in the Stalin years, automatically inculpating the men in power then, who still held power over a decade later. Most disturbing of all was what can only be called an outburst of Slovak nationalism within the ranks of the Communists.[3]

At a time when the purge trials of the Stalin period were being reviewed and reversed in one East European state after another, the Czech communist leadership found that it could not put off the issue any longer. The ghosts of Rudolf Slánský, Vlado Clementis and others who had been executed would not stay quiet in their graves. The main difficulty for the Prague leaders was that those prominent Slovak Communists who had been condemned with Clementis as "bourgeois nationalists" were still alive, and powerful voices among the Slovak communist leadership and rank and file were demanding their rehabilitation. At this point, in mid-1963, Prague began to give way. Those purged in the trials of the early fifties were cleared. A number of prominent Stalinists were removed from leading positions. In September, 1963, Prime Minister Široký was thrown to the wolves. The danger was not one Novotný and the party apparatus could take lightly. The Slovak question had gravely weakened the first Czechoslovak Republic and contributed to its ultimate collapse. The same forces, notwithstanding the communist labels on the chief actors, held the threat of pulling the state apart again. Nationalism posed a more deadly threat to Novotný and company than it did to Gomulka in Poland, for the simple reason that Czechoslovakia had never been, and had not become under communist rule, a homogeneous national state.

The link between Slovak disaffection and general dissatisfaction with the regime was apparent in the forms taken by the campaign against control, censorship and "dogmatism." The leaders of that campaign have been intellectuals: historians, philosophers, economists, novelists, poets, journalists. The revisionism of the historians, Czech and Slovak, has included a reinterpretation of the anti-German uprising in Slovakia in 1944. Whether the accepted revision, which is now being written under the auspices of the Academy of Sciences in Bratislava, will correspond to historical truth is another matter; what is important in the present context is the new image of the revolt as a great achievement of the Slovaks under Slovak leadership.

Similarly, the campaigns for revision of the Slánský trial and against control and censorship were led by literary periodicals, by *Literární Noviny* and *Plamen ("The Flame")* of Prague, but especially by *Kulturný Zivot ("Cultural Life")* of Bratislava and even at times by *Pravda,* the organ of the Slovak Communist party. It was the Slovak Writers' Union, in April, 1963, that first openly demanded punishment for all those guilty of the crimes of the Stalin era and the Slovak Journalists' Union that pressed the demands further. Czech writers and journalists also played their part. Their demands for greater freedom to write have supported Slovak nationalism (within a communist context, of course, not "bourgeois" nationalism or separatism) and in turn have been supported by their Slovak colleagues.

Literature in Czechoslovakia has passed through a period of thaw that, although less daring, has been somewhat comparable to the liberalization in Poland and Hungary in 1955 and 1956. Several novels of openly anti-Stalinist political character have appeared. Regardless of their literary merit, they have performed an important service by exposing and condemning the system that had terrorized and stifled the people over a period of many years. A few express disillusionment with the whole world of ideology and politics, seeking something beyond the barren confines of socialist realism. The literary periodicals, however, give the best picture of the running dispute between communist conformity and liberalization. An ideological plenum of the Central Committee of the Communist Party of Czechoslovakia in December, 1963, laid down the lines of battle on two fronts, against dogmatism and revisionism. It was the latter that was obviously the main danger in the eyes of the leaders, who sought to reassert party control and to prescribe the norms to which writers and artists were to conform. Ever since, the official philosophers, ideologists and the press have been calling for adherence to the line: literature and art must advance the cause of socialism, and the party must be their judge.

More than once *Rudé Právo*, the party newspaper, has thundered against revisionists and denounced them by name. More than once editors and authors, usually indirectly, have fought back and tested the regime at every turn. The struggle has been carried on at writers' congresses, in editorial offices, in the halls of the Academy of Sciences. Editors have lost their jobs. Officers of the writers' organizations have been changed. Criticism of the regime has been contained, as it was not in Poland or Hungary in 1956, but it is there nonetheless. Having been compelled to forsake the system of total repression, the communist leadership may well be unable to return to it.[4]

It is especially where its own survival demands concessions, in the economic field, that the regime has had to give way. The plain fact is that Marxism on the Soviet model, with a centrally planned and controlled economy, has failed in Czechoslovakia. Highly placed economists, such as Ota Sik, Director of the Institute of Economics at the Academy of Sciences, recognize this and are trying to find a system that will work. The recently unveiled "new model" may not work either, but it has the virtue of placing much of the authority for production decisions in the hands of those who manage individual enterprises and have some knowledge of consumer demand—a change made by Yugoslavia over a decade ago. The orthodox advocates of central planning and management are still vocal and may force a compromise, but the regime cannot afford to be dogmatic any longer.

An interesting point about these economic reforms is that they tend to dilute central authority in day-to-day practice, although the few people who run the society at the top can always assert their power to change the system if they choose to do so. Whether it will represent some real shift of power from party representatives to industrial managers is a question we cannot answer now. That is a real possibility; for if one looks at what lies behind the new reforms, one is struck by an evident change in the basic purpose of production. If the motive is to reach a certain point on the scale of industrialization, to meet a fixed rate of annual growth, to meet the demands of the Soviet Union for armaments and heavy goods or the demands of developing economies inside and outside the communist bloc, or just production for the sake of production, then maybe the old system is the best. But if the purpose is to provide goods for the Czechoslovak people, to meet their demands as consumers and to raise living standards, then the choice must be for something closer to a market economy.

The second of those purposes is what evidently moves the Prague leaders today, though they are still narrow-minded party bureaucrats. Much as they may prefer the familiar ways of the past, they have the job of governing Czechoslovakia; and in the present state of affairs both at home and within the "socialist camp" they cannot perform that job without at least minimal tolerance and support from their own people. In this respect the trend toward liberalization in domestic affairs and the trend toward greater national autonomy within the bloc run parallel, a situation that has not always existed in Czechoslovakia in the past.

The party writers in the Czechoslovak press continue to talk of the urgency of waging the ideological war with the capitalist world and with bourgeois influences at home. They express concern over "negativist criticism," "radical skepticism" and "nihilism" and "a whole tangle of non-Marxist and non-partisan views which creates a favorable situation for political adventurism."[5] Their shrill tone betrays what must be real and increasing anxiety over the failure of the people, especially the youth, to take ideology seriously. There is an intrinsic difficulty, not overcome by the regime, in denouncing the errors of the personality cult of the Stalin period while preaching a Leninism that is indistinguishable in people's minds from the official dogma and slogans of that period. The attempt to maintain the system intact, while making concessions to what can only be called revisionism in the economic and other spheres of public policy, rests largely on hackneyed appeals to party unity, party discipline and the struggle for socialism. In a rapidly changing situation, in which the regime has already shown its inability to immunize itself from public pressures, this is a far from infallible strategy of defense.

HUNGARY

Hungary, in the past few years, has been in many ways the most striking example of "liberalization," as it was before October, 1956. While János Kádár has remained in the driver's seat all the way, his policies have changed remarkably since the early period of stern repression after the revolt. He has relaxed the pressures on the ordinary citizen, allowed a measure of freedom of expression, provided more consumer goods and leisure time, encouraged non-Communists to carry on in responsible jobs without fear of persecution and permitted thousands to travel abroad. Under the slogan "All who are not against us are with us," he has made a tacit armistice with the people. These have not been fundamental concessions, as total power still rests with the party and the regime, but the contrast with the Rákosi period is so marked that one can feel in the atmosphere a sense of relief that things are not nearly so bad as they might be. "Kádárism," a Hungarian has pointed out, "presents a choice of evils, for the question is no longer whether the nation should cooperate with its rulers, but what form that cooperation should take and how much of Hungary's interests and integrity may be preserved. . . ."[6]

What is the explanation? Some outside observers say that the Hungarian people have demonstrated their basic strength, that the regime has been forced to take account of their desires. Some even say that the present situation is the result of the very fact that Hungary had a revolution, that although the vital aims of national independence and greater democracy could not be achieved, the revolt had the effect of showing how strong public feeling was and thus set limits that could not be overstepped in restoring communist rule. The regime itself has a different explanation. It congratulates itself on the abandonment of the crimes and errors of the personality cult period. It affirms that it has found better ways to build socialism and that the people, except for a few reactionary remnants, are marching foward with it toward that goal. Toleration of non-Communists, whether they be writers who ignore their proper social role as the Communists see it or technicians and managers who cooperate with mental reservations, represents no concession to bourgeois ideology. This is merely a stage, say the party spokesmen, in the creation of the new socialist order. Perhaps it is nearer the truth to say that both regime and people have shown a keen sense of political realism. The latter are sick of ideology; the regime is wise enough not to insist too much.

The revolt of 1956 was largely prepared by the intelligentsia and fought by the students and workers. Let us look at each of these groups and see what its role has been under the new dispensation.

The teachers and writers who were imprisoned after the revolt have now all been released, even Istaván Bibó, the political philosopher of a new democratic and socialist "third road" who kept on expounding his thoughts to the world after the revolt had been crushed. At first the writers adopted a policy of silence, expressing their contempt for the regime by refusing to write at all. Now they are producing again, not as converts to Kádár's road to socialism or as its bitter opponents, but as individuals who have something to say to their readers and are finding that they are permitted to say it, within limits that are fairly well recognized on both sides. Hungarians can read the works of Lászlo Németh, whose play, *The Journey,* represented a sort of compromise with the regime but not a surrender. They can once more read stories by Tibor Déry, Gyula Háy and others, communist writers who were in the forefront of the revolution and paid for it with prison terms. These authors are even using themes that spring from Hungary's experience under communism and from the events of 1956, as they must if they are to write honestly about the contemporary scene; but they are writing as literary artists, not as political pamphleteers.

Those who go too far with experimental literature are soon called to order. Two provincial literary weeklies, *Alföld* and *Jelenkor,* published essays and articles that party authorities condemned as containing views that were incorrect and petty bourgeois, some representing a throwback to the conservative traditions of populism, others a dallying with modernism, all hostile to Marxism-Leninism and the policy of the party. Both journals then fell into line and promised to "improve" their editorial work in the future and to promote socialist literature. "There can be no room in our periodical," wrote *Alföld,* "for the anti-Marxist notion of a predestined conflict between the 'people' and the 'government' and for the distorted offshoots of the third-road theory." That one sentence revealed quite clearly what the political limits on literature were and also what was in the minds of those writers who were not mere creatures of the regime.[7]

Hungarian youth is an enigma. A large number of those who played so big a role in 1956 left for the West. But many now in their twenties still carry the searing effects of that experience. Some are doubtless indifferent, nihilistic, bitter in their non-commitment, like their counterparts in Poland and Czechoslovakia. The party line and the official youth organization have no appeal. Students are attracted by much that is Western, not just by the surface manifestations but by thought that goes beyond the political and ideological formulas of the day. Yet the atmosphere of 1955–56 is absent. Youthful intellectual energy seems to be directed to the sciences, to technology, to managerial training and to the arts, avoiding their political implications. Many have flocked into the Socialist Workers' (Communist) party, but as opportunists rather than as devoted Leninists or loyal bureaucrats.[8]

The regime itself recognizes that all is not well. An article in a magazine intended for Western readers refers to the fact that "the angry young men of Hungary want more freedom to develop their personality and more liberty and that they hate hypocrisy."[9] The explanation given is that their revolt is against the mistakes of the Rákosi era, against the slow pace of development, against the failure of men to fulfill the promise of an ideal, not against Marxism or the system itself. It may be just as great a distortion to say that they are in revolt against socialism and yearn for the kind of freedom enjoyed in the West. Perhaps the most instructive point is that while the regime recognizes that teaching the young to parrot slogans and to clap in unison is no longer a guarantee of their support, their restrained bitterness and impatience today lead to questions that go deeper than why Marxist-Leninist theory was allowed to be sullied by Stalinist practice.

As for the workers, whose participation in the revolt of 1956 and the resistance that followed its suppression gave the lie to the communist claim to be the party of the proletariat, they have not been won to the system but are living with it as best they can. No longer pushed to the extreme by the ever-mounting norms of output that marked the earlier senseless rush to industrialize, they exert a steady pressure for better wages, more leisure and a greater share of the goods available for consumption. In a period of continued industrial growth, real wages of industrial workers have been rising, despite failures in agriculture. The workers do not constitute a revolutionary element—or counterrevolutionary, from the communist viewpoint— in today's society, but two factors must be kept in mind: they are not interested in socialist ideology or in the world communist movement; they are interested in their own welfare and in being Hungarian.

Nationalist feeling in Hungary, which so deeply colored the whole affair of 1956, remains a very important part of today's picture. The Kádár regime, which can never be entirely free of the stain of its origin as a Soviet agency imposed on the Hungarian people in their moment of agony, is most cautious in dealing with nationalism. Naturally it takes some credit for paying attention to popular desires. Naturally, too, it displays some concern for the Hungarian minority being persecuted by the Rumanian authorities in Transylvania. Yet this is all very restrained. The Hungarian communist regime is more vocal and explicit in its condemnation of nationalism than any other communist regime in Eastern Europe. The "nationalism to be found in some social strata," as one party ideologist put it, continues to exist as a bourgeois and anti-socialist poison that should not be underrated.[10]

Kádár has taken on some of the color of nationalism, though never in defiance of Moscow and without claiming to have found a specifically Hungarian road to socialism. Still, the very fact that he is the leader of Hungary, at a time when nationalism is on the rise throughout Central and Eastern Europe and when "national communism" is appearing whether its existence is recognized or not, places limits on the degree to which he, or any successor of his, can ignore popular feelings and follow an abjectly pro-Soviet policy.

RUMANIA

Rumania's record in the past two years has been one of notable success in the assertion of independence from Soviet control over its economic development and certain aspects of its foreign policy, a success surprising to outside observers and probably to many Rumanians as well. It may be attributed in large measure to the skill shown by top strategists of the communist regime, who were able to calculate and time their moves so as to take advantage of the Soviet-Chinese dispute, exploit the Albanian affair, assert their economic independence, curry favor with the West and avoid reprisals from Moscow. Gheorghe Gheorghiu-Dej had no open dispute with Khrushchev. He capitalized on the Hungarian revolt of 1956, playing the Soviet game at the time and being rewarded two years later by the withdrawal of Soviet troops from Rumania, after which he used Hungarian "disloyalty" as a pretext for a nationalistic policy that left no doubt of the dominant ethnocentric character of Rumanian rule in Transylvania. The statement by the Central Committee of the Rumanian Workers' (Communist) party in April, 1964, following the dispute over the role of the Council for Mutual Economic Assistance (COMECON), was a virtual declaration of independence, indicating that, within the general framework of its treaty obligations and its status as a socialist country, Rumania would make its own decisions in its relations with its neighbors, the Soviet Union, China and the West. The Kremlin let that statement pass without public comment. In Bucharest, meanwhile, the Rumanian-language edition of *Problems of Peace and Socialism,* which gives the Moscow line in many languages all over the world, has been printed with the notable omission of all the key articles on questions involved in the Soviet-Chinese dispute and in Rumania's quarrel with COMECON.

These developments, as noted above, owe much to the political maneuvering of the Rumanian leaders. How much they owe to developments within Rumanian society is difficult to assess. There is no doubt of the popularity of all moves of an anti-Russian or anti-Hungarian character, since they are directed against Rumania's traditional enemies. Yet actual liberalization in the government's treatment of the Rumanian people has been conspicuous chiefly by its absence. Although political prisoners have been amnestied and some relaxation of tension has taken place, the ruling group is still generally hated and distrusted. Its methods remain tough in contrast to those in Poland or Hungary. De-Stalinization did not go much beyond renaming streets and towns and blaming already purged rivals as the real Stalinists (though Gheorghiu-Dej himself exercised power all through the Stalinist period). Much more notable were the measures aimed at removing the heavy hand of Soviet cultural influence: the closure of the Gorky Institute and of Cartea Rusa, the large

Soviet bookstore in Bucharest; the elimination of Russian as a compulsory language in the schools; and the revision of Rumanian history to play up the Rumanian role and play down that of Russia and the Soviet Union. Even the hitherto proscribed subject of Rumania's eastern frontiers has been raised indirectly by publication, under the auspices of the Rumanian Academy, of some obscure writings of Karl Marx on the subject of Russo-Rumanian relations in his day.

This appeal to nationalism has been accompanied by a broadening of relations with the West, evident in cultural exchange agreements with France, the United States and other countries, and in arrangements for increased trade and investment. The main motive is economic, to get from the West essential machinery and other goods to carry through ambitious plans for industrialization, regardless of what Rumania's fraternal socialist partners think or do about it. A related consideration, surely, is the desire to establish relationships of greater strength and confidence with the non-communist world in order to create a stronger bargaining position with the Soviet Union. Finally, some weight may be given to the historic ties with Western nations, which affect the outlook of Rumanians both inside and outside Communist party ranks.

Rumanian culture, writes a contemporary poet favored by the regime, has been created by the people in the course of their whole existence, especially in those historic struggles that brought national independence in the nineteenth century and national unity and socialism in the twentieth. He does not need to mention that the national liberation movement of the last century was directed chiefly against Russia. Significantly, there is no mention at all of Slavic influence throughout Rumanian history, one of the main themes of a few years ago; no credit is given to Russia for assisting in the development of the culture of the new socialist society, but due notice is given to the ties with world literature, music and art. Rumanian culture has "a strongly specific character—a bright reflection of the national genius."[11] The more the Rumanians evoke the names and works of the great figures of their own past—Eliade Radulescu, Alecsandri, Eminescu, Titu Maiorescu, Iorga, Enescu, Brancusi—the more they are bound to stress their ties to Europe and the Western world. Many of these men previously were severely criticized, especially Iorga, a man of world reputation and known anti-communist views who is now praised for his great qualities of patriotism and humanism.[12] A cautious literary opening to the West took place in 1964, when a conference of writers met publicly to discuss their attitudes on Kafka, Joyce and Proust and to touch on the whole subject of "bourgeois" literature in ways not possible before. Translations of Western works, both classical and contemporary, are being printed and sold in huge numbers.

How much these trends of nationalism and links with the West will be translated into political terms is an open question. They have certainly contributed to the decrease of concern with ideology. That concern, incidentally, was never so great in Rumania as in other East European states. Being a Communist, for a Rumanian, has meant opportunities, power, protection or a job. Today, at a time when membership in the Rumanian Workers' (Communist) party is higher than ever, well over one million, the dedicated Communist is a rare phenomenon. The new generation, as far as one can determine, is taken up with the challenges of technical accomplishment growing out of the industrial progress that continues to be made. That progress has been more striking than in the other East European states because Rumania's starting point was so far behind theirs. There is now an entire new group of educated and technically trained people, professionals who are interested in accomplishment and in rewards.

There is no firm evidence that the antagonism between the regime and the people has been measurably reduced by the changes of the past few years. The safest conclusion is that it has not. Yet the trend toward nationalism, in both the political and the cultural fields, and toward the assertion of independence from the Soviet Union seems bound to have its influence on the domestic scene. The example of Yugoslavia, where the relaxation of Stalinist internal policies was delayed until some time after the break with Moscow in 1948 but then became unmistakable, suggests that it will.

CONCLUSIONS

The satellite states of Eastern Europe have been going through a process of change in the past decade, as has the Soviet Union itself in some degree, involving (1) reforms in the economic system in the direction of more flexible organization, use of incentives and greater consideration of consumer demand; (2) continued growth of a new professional middle class; (3) a limited relaxation of control over intellectual and cultural life; and (4) increased contacts with the outside world, especially the West. In addition, there has been a surge of nationalism, which has affected governmental policies as well as popular attitudes. These trends differ in strength and in character from one state to the next, making generalization difficult. They interact with one another, and all of them tend to weaken the orthodox ideology and create difficulties for the ruling groups.

The changing social structure may provide one key to what is happening, although the lack of statistics and concrete evidence permits only opinions rather than conclusions. Official doctrine describes the society in this way: the socialist revolution is being completed; the old upper and bourgeois middle classes and the *kulaks* have been liquidated (though noxious remnants of their influence can still be found); the proletariat, led by its communist vanguard, has guided this whole transformation and now with the working peasantry and the new socialist intelligentsia forms a classless society that is ready to march forward to communism. In reality, the society is anything but classless. Roughly speaking, four classes can be distinguished: (1) the party politicians and bureaucrats, with their intellectual and opportunist hangers-on; (2) the professional men, managers, technicians and others who make the economic system work, plus those intellectuals who maintain at least semi-independence; (3) the industrial working class, which is growing in numbers but enjoys little in the way of material reward or political influence; (4) the collectivized peasantry (except in Poland), which continues to be exploited.

The relationship between the first two of these groups should be of the greatest import for the future. If they tend to merge, can the party stalwarts absorb the professional and technical men and women into the present power structure, or will the latter impose their ideas, needs and standards? Will some kind of synthesis that bears little resemblance to the picture as we see it today emerge?

Although it is beyond the scope of this paper to try to forecast the political consequences of the currents of social and cultural change, one point should be made: in the politically immature societies of this part of Europe, the intellectual elite plays a more significant role than in the West. At one extreme among current predictions is the belief that these trends cannot be stopped and will flow on inexorably to real national independence for the nations of Eastern Europe and political freedom for their peoples. At the other extreme is the belief that the communist regimes, in close association with Moscow, are able to control them and to stop the process short of any real danger to their own power or to the vital interests of the Soviet Union. Some who make this assumption believe that the changes have been deliberately undertaken or encouraged as a means of deceiving the West, gaining added flexibility for communist strategy and disarming potential opposition to communist rule.

The basic fact of the communist monopoly of political power remains. Moreover, the area is still part of the Soviet security zone, and the Kremlin can bring decisive power to bear if it finds it necessary to do so. Yet within those limits considerable change can and does take place. The dispute with China has weakened Moscow's ideological authority and political control. Not every assertion of an independent line by a government will bring forceful Soviet intervention, as the Rumanian leaders have shown. Not every concession by a government to nationalism or to popular desires for a freer or fuller life can be withheld or withdrawn, except at too high a cost. The regimes, without ceasing to be unrepresentative of the people they rule, do not remain static. The pendulum will swing backward from time to time, but the general forward movement of change goes on.

What characterizes the East European countries today is the uncertainty of their direction, as Soviet leadership and ideology no longer set their course. That uncertainty must permeate the thinking of those in authority, both in the Kremlin and in the capitals of Eastern Europe. Events happen, and it is rarely possible to go back to the way things were before. The opening of the doors to the West is a case in point. They may have been opened on the basis of a close calculation of the balance of advantage to the communist regimes. It may be physically possible to shut them again, as it was possible to build the Berlin wall. But will they be closed? Will this be possible at a time when both rulers and subjects are widening their horizons beyond the limits of the "socialist camp"?

There have been and will be wide differences among the individual states. Poland is still the firmest in its capacity to make its own decisions; Hungary has gone furthest in the attempt at reconciliation between regime and people; Czechoslovakia, long held back, is boldest in its experiments in economics along lines pioneered by the Yugoslavs; Rumania is most spectacular in its assertion of economic independence; Bulgaria has hardly moved at all in any direction, while Albania has moved right off the Soviet reservation.

It is difficult to find any formula or pattern that explains the relationship between the trend toward autonomy, or national communism, and the development of a more liberal or human type of society. But the two trends interact; and the influences of social change, cultural aspiration and the mere passage of time seem destined to contribute to both, if what we have seen in the past few years provides a proper basis for judgment.

NOTES TO CHAPTER ONE

1. *See* speeches of the Polish writer Jozef Lenart at the Fourth Congress of the Polish United Workers' Party, *Trybuna Ludu,* June 18, 1964, and of Wladyslaw Gomulka, *ibid.,* September 19, 1964 (translations by Radio Free Europe).

2. A point emphasized by Zbigniew Rapacki in a recent unpublished essay entitled "La Pologne et les autres démocraties populaires."

3. Edward Taborsky, "Czechoslovakia: Out of Stalinism," *Problems of Communism,* May–June, 1964, pp. 5–14.

4. *See* H. Gordon Skilling, *Communism National and International: Eastern Europe after Stalin* (Toronto: University of Toronto Press, 1964), pp. 106–30.

5. Michal Pecho, in *Nová Mysl,* December 12, 1964 (translation by Radio Free Europe).

6. *Talking to Eastern Europe,* ed. G. R. Urban (London: Eyre and Spottiswoode, 1964), p. 142.

7. *See* László M. Tikos, "Hungary: Literary Renascence," *Problems of Communism,* May–June, 1964, pp. 33–34.

8. Francois Fejtö, "Hungarian Communism," in *Communism in Europe,* ed. W. E. Griffith (Cambridge, Mass.: The M.I.T. Press, 1964), I, 215–16.

9. László Boka, "Impatient Youth," *The New Hungarian Quarterly* (Budapest), Winter, 1964, p. 9.

10. S. Gáspár, in *Népszabadság,* December 4, 1964 (translation by Radio Free Europe).

11. Demostene Botez, "The Building of a Culture," *Rumanian Review* (Bucharest), No. 3, 1964, pp. 4–9.

12. Dan Zamfirescu, in *Luceafarul,* November 17, 1964 (translation by Radio Free Europe).

CHAPTER II

Marxist Cultural Policy in Poland

GEORG W. STROBEL

RECIPROCAL RELATIONS BETWEEN CULTURE AND POLITICS

DIFFERENCES IN THE DEFINITION of culture are not only apparent between the Eastern and Western areas of cultural history, they are also to be found from one national cultural region to another within the Roman or the Byzantine cultural tradition. In the main stream of Polish culture, usage follows French preference for the term "civilization" rather than "culture," a civilization in the fullest sense of the word being the fruit of the cultural process, a cultural system still in evolution and in no way ossified or stagnant. A pupil of the French sociologist Emile Durkheim, Stefan Czarnowski, who until his death in 1937 was probably the most important cultural historian of East-Central Europe, defined the concept of culture as "an entire system of objectivized elements of social acquisition common to a series of social strata, which through their objective character have developed a propensity for territorial expansion."[1]

There is a remarkable similarity between the Marxist concept of culture and that prevalent in Polish and Czech circles. Both postulate the identity of culture and civilization. This fact is particularly relevant to the phenomenon of the socialist cultural revolution, which is intended to help reshape society according to socialist standards. The Polish and Czech concept of culture favors this political objective.

Treatment of culture as a homogeneous entity cannot, however, conceal the existence of a number of contradictory trends in present-day cultural policy and cultural creativity. These contradictions raise definite obstacles to an ideologically oriented cultural revolution. One of these contradictions—and probably the one with the most far-reaching consequences—lies in the existence of a definite cultural content within the intimate religious life of the individual. This cultural sphere tends to escape from Marxist cultural objectives and thus violates the political limits of the ideologically coordinated public culture. In those areas where the Church still exerts appreciable influence within the supposedly monolithic Marxist culture, as among the Polish peasantry and urban petty bourgeoisie, the result is the cultivation of an intellectual-religious culture. This constitutes a subculture that conflicts with the assumptions and objectives of public cultural policy. The existence of such contradictions adulterates the Marxist total culture with elements of Western cultural understanding, a process that cannot but call forth emotional or adaptive reactions. The result in any case impedes the progress of socialist cultural transformation.

This circumstance is all the more significant since Marxism-Leninism considers the broad field of culture to be an active segment of the superstructure and hence a social matter that cannot be left to individual decision. As a weapon of class warfare, culture thus belongs in the political category.

Under communist rule, culture serves as a political instrument. However, this political instrument is subject to influences from quarters that are ideologically foreign to socialist culture. Although the necessity of strict party control over culture and its expressions is proclaimed as a matter of course, the operation of these extraneous influences creates an ideological necessity for such control. The ideological battle is therefore fought with particular intensity in the cultural sector. Party control is invoked, not only to assure the controlling role of Marxism, but also to assure a Marxist-oriented ideological alienation of the culture, that is, the elimination of internal contradictions derived from the historical development of the culture in its native habitat. The objectives of cultural policy are thus downgraded to the status of a dependent function of party goals. An interdependence of cultural and political policy and their interaction in accordance with the currently effective tactical line of the party leadership follow as a natural result.

The basic principles of socialist cultural policy are: (1) the projection of party ideology, (2) popularity of form, (3) closeness to popular tradition and (4) representation of typical productive activities. Although these principles play a much less important role today than before the Twentieth Congress of the Communist Party of the Soviet Union, it should not be concluded that the socialist state and its party intend to let the realm of culture escape from their influence after the expiration of a limited period of greater freedom dictated by political considerations. According to the official doctrine, presently de rigueur, the political and ideological transformation of society is to be introduced and accompanied by a cultural revolution.[2]

It is thus clear that the socialist cultural revolution constitutes one of the main instruments of political rule in the arsenal of the Communist party. Together with other instruments of rule, among them institutionalized tools of control, it is to be employed for the establishment of new social and productive relationships.

Quite apart from goals of cultural policy derived from ideology and politics, the socialist cultural revolution in Poland must contend with distinctive deep-seated and absorbing cultural problems. These stem from Poland's traditional cultural development and the stage of progress that its economic transformation has achieved. Insofar as problems of this kind arise, the similarity between the socialist countries and all modern industrial societies is particularly striking.

At any given stage of political and ideological development the goals of the socialist cultural revolution in different societies should be identical and generalized. These goals are clearly dependent on ideology. The problems of cultural policy encountered in the respective societies are, however, just the opposite: they are markedly independent from ideology and have their roots in industrial society. Their intensity depends on the maturity of the productive system and the material culture of the society in question.

Within a number of specific areas, therefore, socialist cultural development is by no means controlled by ideology alone; it is also determined by certain factors foreign to Marxist doctrine. These factors often prove susceptible to ideological influence. Their interaction with ideology, however, renders the cultural policy problems they raise far harder to solve in East-Central Europe than in analogous Western industrial countries.

In Poland, moreover, socialist cultural policy must take account of a special foreign policy situation giving rise to what can be called foreign policy functions of culture. The operational area of cultural policy in Poland thus extends beyond what is normally considered the range of problems with which socialist cultural policy and its cultural revolution are expected to deal.

THE SOCIALIST CULTURAL REVOLUTION IN PRACTICE

Cultural Functions Dependent on Ideology

As the first of those functions of culture that depend on ideology, the politicizing and ideological awakening of the individual through guided cultural influences is intended to provide the basis for harmonizing social with political and ideological evolution and for arousing a new social consciousness. Although no attempt is being made to enlist the general population in the party, the aim is to transform the hitherto unpolitical average man into a Marxist, or at least a consciously political citizen receptive to Marxist ideas.

To overcome the basic contradiction in Polish cultural development, the conflict between religion and Marxism, the contention that it is quite possible to find a common political platform uniting Marxism and socially critical Left Catholicism has recently been propagated in Poland. Should it prove possible to achieve such a platform, one of the greatest obstacles to the ideologizing of the individual would be overcome.

Evidence of the possibility of such a rapprochement between socially critical Left Catholicism and Marxism is seen in the changing role of religion in the life of the masses of the people, who distinguish between clerical politics and their own religious convictions. It is argued that since the Church is seeking closer ties with the people, it must move closer to the political views of the masses; the function of Left Catholic social criticism is to point the way.[3] The Cuban revolution is cited as a case in point: although Marxist, Castro's movement drew sustenance from the "religious inspiration" of Catholicism and particularly from Catholic social criticism; in the early days of his government, the bearded dictator cited St. Thomas Acquinas more often than Marx.[4]

It is clear that the Communists, despite their basic enmity toward the Church and religion, are employing arguments of this sort to achieve access to Left Catholic and Left Protestant circles. The "Pax movement" offers a suitable instrument for this policy. Elements of the "popular front" tactic are evident in this pragmatic cultural policy.

Steps taken for the purpose of ideologizing and politicizing the individual go hand in hand with efforts to secularize both society and the individual. The popular strength of religion in East-Central Europe and the tactic of courting Left Catholics as "natural allies" of Marxism, however, dictate the avoidance of frontal attacks against religion or the Church as such. Instead, secularization is regarded as a process expressing the objective needs of social progress.

In marking the boundary between the ecclesiastical and secular spheres, emphasis is placed on restriction of the Church to the realm of the supernatural—which Marxists regard as imaginary.[5] The Church's cultural activities are to be progressively curbed in accordance with the policy of continuing secularization, since such activities conflict with the Marxist-Leninist orientation of culture and therefore can have no social importance. They belong entirely to the private life of the individual, and they are in any case hindrances to the ideologizing and politicizing of the personality in the Marxist sense.[6]

When the steps of cultural policy constituting a program of secularization are carried out with tactical skill, they lead to an attitude of religious indifference. This causes the individual to approach a state of mind that brings him closer to Marxism and increases his receptivity for it. Secularization is therefore never to be forced with high-pressure or guerrilla methods, since such tactics would cause antagonism and would damage rather than promote the cause of Marxism. A purposeful socialist cultural policy should therefore permit the trends constituting secularization to ripen gradually, cultivating them with care and discretion; only then can setbacks be avoided.[7]

It is thus apparent that, in one important question of cultural policy at least, a lesson in the methodology of the socialist cultural revolution has been learned from the years of Stalinist compulsion. The choice of the gradual cultivation of religious indifference— a state of mind that lends itself to Marxist cultural infiltration— rather than compulsion and naked force as the preferred approach to secularization should result in practical gains for the socialist cultural revolution.[8]

As an inevitable concomitant of the secularization campaign Christian religious morality is being undermined and a new "socialist morality" is being cultivated. Rejection of religious morality is justified with the argument that "religion usually affects human behavior so as to have a detrimental effect on morals."[9] The social value of religious morality is downgraded, in fact denied altogether.[10] Efforts are being made to achieve a socialist morality that rejects the patent class character of religious morality—only to exchange it for an orientation based on social groups or occupations. "Socialist morality," as a result, is gradually slipping into the same kind of development as the rejected religious morality.

No immediate attempt to achieve a code of socialist morality having universal validity is being made; rather, moral codes are initially being proclaimed for individual occupations or social groups and are later to be synthesized into a general code of socialist morality. The uncertainty that besets these experiments is illustrated by the fact that a moral code issued for Polish military officers in 1963 has since been considered a mere code of professional ethics.[11] "Professional morality," which is intended to serve as a foundation for the new universal socialist morality, is regarded principally as "the adaptation of moral values present in a society to the concrete occupational situation and their modification to fit specific professional tasks."[12] Since the universal socialist morality has not yet been created, the "adaptation of moral values present in a society" means an adaptation of Christian religious morality, thus restoring that morality to a position of influence in precisely those areas where the new universal socialist morality was supposed to emerge. Quite obviously, the Polish Communists have fallen into a vicious circle involving religious and ecclesiastical problems directly relevant to most aspects of the socialist cultural revolution and impeding its achievement in a number of ways.

Fulfillment of the goals of the socialist cultural revolution is to take concrete form in a newly shaped socialist society. The elite of this new society during the transitional period is to be an intelligentsia characterized by its new orientation and by constant expansion. A progressive blurring of the boundary between highly qualified technicians and the intelligentsia is also predicted, since the increasing intellectualization of productive processes is expected to transform the latter increasingly into a technocratic intelligentsia. About half of the Polish intellectuals already represent technical occupations.[13] These developments culminate in the vision of a homogeneous society in which human effort and human talents would be developed to their full potential but in which the cultural elite would be replaced by a collective and primarily technocratic intellectualism.[14]

The trend toward social equalization has been considerably accelerated through the gradual closing of the gap between the socioeconomic status of intellectuals and workers during the years following World War II—in terms of a superficial hierarchy of rank and prestige based on relative income. The former absolute advantage enjoyed by intellectuals over workers, expressed by the income ratio of 1:2.8 immediately before the outbreak of the war, has now dwindled to the ratio of 1:1.2.[15] While the average real wage per hour for workers has risen by 38 per cent over the prewar level, the real income per hour earned by intellectuals has dropped 25 per cent.[16]

The intellectuals have suffered an absolute economic and consequently a social and psychological *déclassement,* which compounds the effects of other tendencies toward equalization and contributes to displacements in the social hierarchy.[17] A single social group, the intelligentsia, is being forced to bear, unilaterally and absolutely, the social and economic burdens of the equalization sought by public policy. The resulting smoldering resentment on the part of the intellectuals operates as an additional obstacle to the furtherance of the socialist cultural revolution.

A major hindrance to the development of socialist culture in Poland and to the achievement of the cultural revolution lies in the historically conditioned Russophobia prevalent in all social strata of the Polish people. Poles sharing this anti-Russian attitude are inclined to reject socialist culture as an alleged branch of Russian culture. Since Soviet culture has been offered to the public as the prototype of socialist culture per se, in utter disregard of actual cultural preferences in Poland, a major objective of the socialist cultural revolution has been the rehabilitation, upgrading and propagation of Soviet culture. The cultural superiority many Poles feel toward their eastern neighbor has contributed measurably to the reserve that even party-line journalists display in dealing with specific phases of socialist cultural policy.

Cultural Functions Independent from Ideology and
Rooted in Industrial Society

Ideologically motivated socialist cultural policy is directed at creating a culture for the broad masses, that is, a mass culture.[18]

Mass culture is expected to "democratize" society, to eliminate the formation of elites and to promote social equalization.[19]

Notwithstanding this specific role of mass culture in the socialist cultural revolution, the fact must be kept in mind that the objective problem of mass culture exists in every highly developed industrial society as a result of reduced working hours and increased leisure time. This problem made itself felt in Western countries far earlier than in East-Central Europe; its intensity is dependent on the relative economic maturity of the society in question and not on any particular ideology.

While Western social thinkers aspire to employ mass culture to develop a nonpolitical orientation of the individual in society and to assure maximum personal development, mass culture is mobilized by the socialist cultural revolution for the systematic de-individualization of the person and the creation of a social collective. Although mass culture employs the same media and techniques in different geographic areas, its purposes vary: Eastern mass culture serves ideology alone, Western mass culture at least theoretically serves human beings.

When achievement of the stage of full communism is accompanied by the culmination of the socialist cultural revolution, the result must necessarily be the downfall of the classical cultural ideal, for this culmination is seen as "the natural end of the formation of elites in culture."[20] A monotonous equalitarian culture would then dominate the scene. Eastern and Western mass culture thus exhibit important distinguishing characteristics, despite their common roots: the enforcement of ideological conformity in the East and a pragmatic, nonideological orientation in the West.

The strong emphasis Communists place on the material side of culture suffices to stimulate the demand for a technocratic formulation of cultural policy objectives, with obvious ideological consequences. Such a development would entail the disappearance of the traditional Western ideals of human virtue and classical education, which would gradually be replaced by a technocratic standard. Overvaluation of the material side of culture rather than the aesthetic and intellectual side, an attitude implicit in Marxist-Leninist ideology, would thus be carried a step further. Only technology, the Marxist contends, is able to solve "all the problems of humanity."[21]

Technocratization is described as the expression of a socialist humanism that is adapted to specific present-day realities. Its historical continuity is demonstrated with dialectical arguments.[22] Under the pretext of the "humanist aspects of technical progress," the "bourgeois" humanism of the West is to be replaced by a "technocratic" socialist humanism.[23]

Foreign Policy Functions of Culture

One of the major objectives of Polish cultural policy is to support the foreign policy of the Warsaw government by consolidating the incorporation of the Oder-Neisse territories in the Polish state. This function has both an objective and a subjective aspect.

The objective phase of this function of culture consists of efforts to build an intellectual foundation for the incorporation, employing various media and techniques of cultural policy. Scholarship plays a predominant role in this undertaking.

The "scientific demonstration" of Polish rights of possession along the Oder and Neisse rivers proceeds on a number of fronts. Historical research and prehistoric excavations are employed for this purpose, as well as a prolific output of publications in the major languages. These publications not only serve to register research results that tend to support Polish cultural objectives, they also ventilate the Polish point of view in general. In so doing, they frequently transcend the objective results of the scholarly findings as such and enter the field of scholarly speculation.

An additional feature of cultural policy in the East German territories under Polish administration is a selective program for the care of monuments that emphasize the cultural ties between these lands and Poland proper. The alleged close connection between these territories and the Polish motherland is "demonstrated" by drawing attention to former cultural ties, which indeed existed but belong to a period of history long before the emergence of national states.

The subjective phase of cultural policy lies in improving the aesthetic, and more particularly the material, welfare of the new settlers in the Oder-Neisse territories to give these settlers a feeling that they really own the territories to which they have been moved. In the field of material well-being, adaptation of the settlers to a standard of civilization far higher than that of the regions from which they came serves to conceal the fact that the cultural and civilizational level of the Order-Neisse territories has in fact declined since their resettlement. The productivity of the new population has like-wise been raised, with the Germans remaining in the area playing the role of cultural catalysts.[24] In this way, a part of the Polish population was enabled to bypass several decades of normal cultural development.

The Oder-Neisse territories have provided socialist cultural policy with a classical field for experimentation and testing of tactics. Even though the socialist cultural revolution did not reach a sufficient intensity to produce the drastic social changes desired by the party, it nevertheless succeeded in creating a largely homogeneous society free of disturbing regionalisms.[25]

The second foreign policy function of culture derives from the association of international cultural exchange with the concept of coexistence. The idea is widespread, and even deliberately propagated, that the ideological struggle—which forms an integral feature of peaceful coexistence as the Communists understand it—is set aside or even abandoned during a period of *détente.* As Adam Schaff has emphasized, the situation in practice is just the opposite: ideological struggle must actually be intensified in the phase of *détente.* Far from disappearing when scholarly and cultural exchanges are undertaken, it actually determines the character of such exchanges. As Schaff puts it, the cultural form of the ideological struggle constitutes "one of the most natural forms of competition between the two systems and of their struggle for men's minds."[26]

The intensity with which a policy of coexistence is pursued dictates the scope of communist cultural infiltration abroad. Increasingly active coexistence brings with it intensified infiltration of socialist culture in the West. The political objectives of international cultural exchange are as follows: (1) advancement and perfection of science and culture in the socialist country and the use of cultural exchange to strengthen the socialist system; (2) demonstration of a high level of scientific and cultural accomplishment so as to raise the prestige of the socialist country and its system in foreign countries with contrary ideologies or in neutral areas: and (3) expansion and intensification of peaceful coexistence as a form of sharpened ideological struggle, employing the media and techniques of cultural policy.

During a time of *détente,* culture is downgraded to the status of a weapon of ideological and political warfare, even though Communists sometimes deny that such a downgrading has taken place. The internal function of socialist culture, that of transforming society, is thus accompanied by a second function of equal political militancy in the field of foreign affairs. Socialist culture becomes the champion of socialist ideology in areas of contrary political and ideological orientation and thus a versatile political instrument of socialism.

PREREQUISITES AND PROSPECTS FOR THE SOCIALIST CULTURAL REVOLUTION

Cultural Planning and Control

Cultural planning addresses itself to problems of a specifically cultural nature as well as to those of politics in general and of economic policy. The interaction of these aspects is characteristic of modern society. Comprehensive cultural planning on a large scale needs to discover the limits within which a precise cultural conception can be managed and its various aspects coordinated—a problem analogous to that of optimal magnitudes encountered in economic planning.[27]

The broader the area cultural planning attempts to cover, the more hypothetical its results are likely to be. In addressing themselves to cultural activities as a whole, cultural planners can only suggest politically defined goals to the purveyors of culture or judge their performance in terms of conformity with such goals. Exact planning of output or results is possible only in those limited areas in which problems and institutions can be quantified. In general, the degree of precision achievable in cultural planning varies in inverse relation to its scope of operations.

One of the principal weaknesses of the socialist cultural revolution lies precisely in the effort to achieve totalitarian cultural planning. This deficiency is aggravated by the fact that for a long time no sociological investigations were undertaken to determine the attitudes and potential preferences of consumers of culture and the possibility of influencing these consumers in the direction indicated by cultural policy.

A problem of major importance is that of the proper number of people to be engaged in cultural pursuits, a problem that is both sociological and economic. In Stalinist times, the fine arts were force-fed through an excessively large network of art schools and academies, coupled with munificent scholarships. Evidence of saturation was disregarded. Although the artist was trained at state expense, his professional activity paradoxically remained a free profession without state subsidy. As a result, many young artists sank into an economic and sociological cultural proletariat, subsisting in large part from the production of "postcard art," drawings on walls and sidewalks, etc.[28] In the face of this surplus of "artists" in relation to actual demand, relief has come, not from the state, but from the Church, which has provided many free-lance artists with paid assignments. The antagonism between socialist and religious culture has been emphasized by the active cultural role of the Church, since the vast majority of painters, sculptors and similar artists are dependent upon its contracts. In addition to its role as a preserver of culture, the Church has emerged as a promoter of culture; this is obviously detrimental to the goals of the socialist cultural revolution.[29]

Social and Economic Upheaval

Since 1945 Polish society has experienced the overthrow of the previous ruling classes and their ideology, a phenomenon that has increased public susceptibility to social criticism and reformism. The promoters of the socialist cultural revolution have taken due advantage of this situation. Among the factors that seem favorable for a cultural revolution, the foremost is the rapid industrialization that is liquidating traditional peasant structures with their patriarchal families and religious morals, substituting the alienation typical of urban life. Amid this economic and social upheaval, the Church has assumed a unique role. Having become increasingly receptive to social change, the Church is no longer totally opposed to the socialist cultural revolution. It shares the interest of state cultural policy in raising the level of material culture. This shift of orientation is observed mainly in the cities; in rural areas the Church still remains a strongly conservative force. This internal contradiction within the Church weakens its influence on cultural policy; for those who migrate from the farms to the cities—a move that approximately five million Poles made between 1945 and 1960—the Church has lost credibility through its equivocal position.

Polish industrialization has been accompanied by a flight from the land, urbanization, migration into the Oder-Neisse territories and increased social mobility. All these factors have contributed to closing the gaps between the various social strata as they existed before World War II and have thus improved the prospects for the socialist cultural revolution. In general, the social, economic and political upheavals that have taken place since World War II have fulfilled many of the prerequisites for a socialist transformation of culture.

Cultural Media

The socialist cultural revolution has been accompanied by a quantitative expansion of cultural facilities, a development reflecting intensive efforts to achieve a mass culture. Although the socialist cultural revolution is making increasing use of those media that are characteristic of mass culture, there is still a tremendous difference between the intensive coverage achieved in the cities and the comparatively sparse coverage of rural areas. This difference is not merely quantitative; it reflects a basic weakness in socialist culture. The rural areas, which it fails to reach, are far more conservative than the cities; it is here that the Church, which despite sporadic accommodation is still fundamentally opposed to the socialist cultural revolution, retains its greatest influence.

A study of the comparative popularity of mass-communication media indicates that those with a relatively high socializing influence enjoy the greatest acceptance.[30] These media occupy a central position in Polish cultural planning and management because their popularity and influence afford the most favorable prospects for infiltration of society with socialist cultural content.

Considered as a whole, the socialist cultural revolution has been initiated under favorable conditions in Poland, particularly where it impinges on matters of social and economic policy. Although organizational deficiencies have been numerous, they have not seriously hampered operations.

The favorable circumstances under which the socialist cultural revolution was launched in Poland do not necessarily augur its success. The effectiveness of measures designed to produce cultural change depends on their ability to overcome institutional obstacles, such as the intellectual influence of the Church and the political inertia and defense mechanisms of the population as a whole. It is therefore necessary to inquire to what extent the specific goals of the socialist cultural revolution have been achieved and to what extent social changes attributable to this revolution may be observed.

EFFECTIVENESS OF THE SOCIALIST CULTURAL REVOLUTION

The degree of success or failure achieved by the socialist cultural revolution is less apparent in patterns and standards of behavior than in the thought and value systems of individuals. The most realistic evaluations can therefore be obtained through investigations, not of population groups at the extremities of the age scale, but of that median group that was exposed to socializing influences at its most sensitive age, from fourteen to twenty-four: the men and women who are now between the ages of twenty and thirty-five. This group, hereafter called the young adult group for the sake of convenience, contains individuals who have already succeeded to important positions in the party, the state and society and constitutes the generation from which future leadership must emerge. In view of the succession of generations that is beginning to take place in governmental, political and economic life in Poland, an examination of the thought and value systems of this age group is especially pertinent to our theme.

A variety of surveys indicate that the attitudes of the members of the young adult group toward their state and toward the party and its ideology in no way correspond to the political objectives of the socialist cultural revolution. It seems obvious, therefore, that measures of cultural policy designed to ideologize society have remained largely ineffective. Willingness to undertake personal commitments or sacrifices for the cause of socialism has proved to be correspondingly low.[31] When confronted with a choice between the demands of socialist cultural policy and traditional bourgeois scales of values, the young adults surveyed showed a clear preference: the majority of them rejected the slogans and value systems implanted by socialist cultural policy.[32]

Even intensively propagated goals and demands of Polish foreign policy have not met with acceptance in the minds of individuals who did not experience the hardships of the war and its aftermath or who were very small children at the time. The German question, for instance, is treated in Polish public life as a political issue of primary importance for the viability of the state. Although all media of mass communication are constantly employed to focus attention on this problem, the public response has been one of relative indifference. In an inquiry concerning phenomena that particularly disturbed interviewees and caused them personal worry, the first five places were taken by exclusively domestic issues involving criticism of the party and its policies. "West German revisionism" appeared in sixth place only, followed by fear of "atom bomb testing."[33]

The political indifference of the young adult population—an indifference that instead of giving way to the socialist cultural revolution is actually becoming more entrenched—is evident in popular ignorance of the history of Polish communism. The numerous cases in which respondents gave strikingly wrong answers or were unable to answer basic questions suggest that teachers have been quietly sidestepping this essential field of "socialist education."[34]

The failure of the ideologization and politicization sought through the socialist cultural revolution is also apparent in and is aggravated by what people read. Seventy-six per cent of the patrons of lending libraries[35] prefer light fiction or adventure stories, either by noncommunist Polish authors or of Western provenance.[36] A survey of favorite authors showed a vast preference for "classical" Polish authors of the late nineteenth century. Not until the thirty-third place does a representative of postwar social criticism appear: Gustav Morcinek, who is in no way typical of socialist literature and whose greatest creative achievements were produced in the thirties.[37]

The political indifference that the cultural policy offensive has failed to overcome is likewise evident in the newspaper reading and cinema and television viewing habits of the young adult group. There is a clear preference for newspapers of the sensational type, equivalent in content to the New York or London tabloids, which are not the official products of party or government offices. Such publications make an effort to appear either entirely nonpolitical or at least far less political than the official party organs.[38] They are, of course, under the same party supervision as all other publications.[39]

A similar preference for the nonpolitical, that is, for escape from the ministrations of socialist cultural policy, is observable in popular choices of films and television programs. By far the most popular telecasts are entertainment films, with a specific demand for "Westerns,"[40] followed by sports programs and variety shows.[41] The preference of young adults for Western films—a preference that is indicative of the failure of the socialist cultural revolution—is illustrated by a survey of the favorite films of 1963, which demonstrated the unpopularity of Eastern films with political or ideological content. Six of the ten most preferred films were American; two were Polish films without ideological content although not entirely unpolitical, while France and the Soviet Union were each represented by one picture. The Soviet production in question was, significantly, a pacifist anti-war film—an attitude hardly reflecting modern "Soviet patriotism."[42] Anti-German films are rejected as "propaganda concoctions" and are considered lacking in credibility.[43]

The attempt to create a new society in Poland by means of the socialist cultural revolution has remained a failure so far. The traditional social strata have lost compactness and become more variegated; equalizing tendencies have closed the gaps between them and in some cases have produced overlaps. As Polish sociologists admit, however, a new social structure has not been achieved.

Wesolowski is of the opinion that while the upheaval of the years immediately after the war led to a disintegration of the class structure of bourgeois society, a process of recomposition soon made itself felt. While the points of departure and detailed characteristics of the latter differed in some respects from bourgeois tradition, the net result has been a restoration of the previous class structure. Wesolowski thus admits that efforts to create a new socialist society have so far achieved only temporary and superficial successes; beneath the surface of social consciousness and political reality things remain much as they were.[44]

Insofar as the sphere of religion and morals is concerned, there is no doubt that the social upheaval since World War II and the hardships of everyday life have combined to promote the process of secularization and the breakdown of traditional morality. It is in this area that the socialist cultural revolution has scored a certain degree of success.[45] Its magnitude will be determined by the kind and intensity of secularization that has been achieved, and by the degree of religiosity that remains a factor in today's society.

One symptom of the degree of secularization is the declining social prestige of the religious profession. In a recent survey, only 8 per cent of the respondents expressed the opinion that the prestige of the clergy had risen since the war.[46] At the same time, however, the interviews indicate that a high percentage of the young adults continue to regard themselves as "believing" Catholics.[47] It is reported that even higher functionaries of the ruling Polish United Workers' (Communist) party (PZPR) are "believing, even though not regularly practicing Catholics," in whose homes sacred pictures alternate with Marxist classics. The children of these functionaries receive a strongly religious upbringing from their mothers.[48] Religious images are also to be seen in state and local government offices, in party headquarters and in public transportation stations.[49] Party officials march in religious processions and emulate the public figures of bourgeois Poland between the two world wars by counting it an honor to carry the canopy over the sacred statue or relic. Party functionaries and industrial managers alike make their official automobiles available to prelates and to wandering friars.[50] The reverence that even higher functionaries of the party accord to the clergy and to religious symbols is symptomatic of the unique state of tension and conflict that continues to beset Polish society despite all efforts toward further secularization.

The fact that the socialist cultural revolution has been largely a failure in Poland is made evident by tendencies indicating the persistence of bourgeois society. Instead of dwindling, the trend of *embourgeoisement* in Polish society is actually growing stronger, thus confirming Wesolowski's theory of recomposition. Instead of the hoped-for politicizing and ideologizing of the individual, mass indifference and disillusionment are found. What the typical Pole wants is "a no-iron shirt, a foreign suit and English tie, modern pointed shoes and thirty-seven hundred zloty in his pocket."[51] The happiness desired by young adults is bourgeois happiness, not that of idealistic fighters for party, ideology and human betterment.[52]

The desires of young adults for material comforts and for satisfaction of subjective needs show a remarkable uniformity that cuts across all lines of social or class origin. Significant differences between the aspirations of urban and rural groups are not observed.[53] It is noteworthy that the personal desires of Polish youth and young adults have been found to be almost identical with those of French men and women in the same age groups.[54]

The Admission of Failure: Cultural Revolution Becomes Cultural Evolution

State and party leaders have been forced to admit that, in spite of intensive activity designed to produce a cultural revolution, the thought and value systems of young adults remain far from those called for by socialist ideology and that members of this generation continue to be more receptive to Western than to Eastern ideas. This is all the more remarkable in view of the fact that the economic upheaval following World War II exposed Polish young adults to social changes that tended to support the objectives of socialist cultural revolution. Twenty years of communism have not achieved the political and ideological metamorphosis of the middle generation of Poles into pioneers and champions of Marxist ideology.

Since the transparent failure of socialist cultural policy is a matter of common knowledge, efforts are being made to reinterpret the reciprocal relations between politics, ideology, culture and social reality. During the Third Congress of the PZPR, in March, 1959, Gomulka extolled the socialist cultural revolution as "one of the most universal and permanent principles of the Marxist-Leninist policy leading to socialist victory," and thus an element of the "fundamental orientation" of the Polish party.[55] This concept was echoed by other officials of the party and the government. Again, at the Fourth Congress of the PZPR, in mid-June, 1964, Gomulka restated the necessity of the socialist cultural revolution but observed that its success would depend upon the quantitative expansion of cultural media.[56]

The qualitative gap between theory and reality has by now grown too wide to be ignored. Communist ideologists have therefore embarked on a search for new conceptions. One of the newer theories holds that the socialist cultural revolution is subject to a distinctive law of development that leads to automatic stoppages—sometimes as a result of the stabilization of socialism. Stabilization of the dictatorship of the proletariat, it is claimed, calms the stormy waves of cultural revolution that are an immediate and spontaneous result of the political revolution. In the intermediate era of transition to socialism through which Poland is currently passing, the concept of a cultural revolution is no longer in order. Instead, attention is being drawn to the phenomenon of cultural evolution.[57] The acceptance of a theory of socialist cultural evolution rather than revolution is clearly an admission of the bankruptcy of the party and its ideology in the face of the will to self-preservation manifested by Polish society— a will strengthened by the manifold contacts this society enjoys with the West.

NOTES TO CHAPTER TWO*

1. Stefan Czarnowski, "Studies in the History of Culture," *Works* (Warsaw: 1938; reprinted 1956), I, 17 ff. This is a collection of articles written between 1932 and 1937. (The definition, as Dr. Strobel suggests, reflects the Marxist assumption that culture emanates from a material base; Czarnowski also seems to confuse a culture with an economic system.—*Eds.*)

2. At the Third Congress of the PZPR, Gomulka described cultural revolution as one of the "universal and permanent principles" leading to a "victory of socialism." See *Shorthand Record of the Third Congress of the Polish United Workers' Party, March 10-19, 1959* (Warsaw: Central Committee of the PZPR, 1959), pp. 102 ff. Various statements confirming Gomulka's view have appeared from time to time.

3. W. Bienkowski, "Problems of the Sociology of Religion," *Culture and Society* (Warsaw), No. 2, 1963, pp. 99 ff.

4. "Cooperation of Believers and Non-Believers in People's Poland," *Life and Thought* (Warsaw), No. 10, 1964, p. 28.

5. T. Pluzanski, "Why Laity?" *Voice of Koszalin* (Köslin), September 24-25, 1960.

6. A. Sikorski, "Marxism and Religion," *Central Problems of Building Socialism in Poland* (Warsaw: 1960), p. 533.

7. M. Sobolewski, "Laity Legislation During the Twenty Years of People's Poland," special issue of *Arguments* (Warsaw), No. 2, 1964, pp. 25 ff.

8. *Ibid.*, p. 26.

9. C. Pazera, "Does Religion Shape Morality?" *Voice of Olsztyn* (Allenstein), December 10-11, 1960.

10. L. Bandura, "Does Religious Teaching Bring About Morality?" *Arguments*, No. 41, 1960.

11. E. Olczyk, "Moral Norms as Viewed by Officers," *Soldier of Freedom* (Warsaw), December 1, 1964.

12. M. Michalik, "On Moral Codes, Moralism and Professional Ethics," *People's Army* (Warsaw), No. 8, 1964, p. 24.

13. J. Szczepanski, "Social Changes in Poland," *Polish Science* (Warsaw), Nos. 5-6, 1964, pp. 145 ff.

14. S. Zolkiewski, "Mass Culture and Contemporary Culture," *New Culture* (Warsaw), No. 29, 1959.

15. Lidia Beskid, "Income and Consumption," *Politics* (Warsaw), May 23, 1964.

16. *Economic Life* (Warsaw), April 12, 1964. *See also* Lidia Beskid, articles on real wages of industry and construction workers in 1960 and 1937 and on real wages of an employed worker in 1960 as compared with 1937, in *Statistical Review* (Warsaw), Nos. 1 and 3, 1964, pp. 81 ff. and 329 ff., respectively.

17. Stefan Nowakowski, "Egalitarian Tendencies and the New Social Hierarchy in the Industrial-Urban Environment of the Western Territories," *Sociological Review* (Lodz), XVII, No. 1 (1963), 35 ff.

18. A. Kloskowska, *Mass Culture—Criticism and Defense* (Warsaw: 1964) and K. Zygulski, "Problems of Mass Culture in Poland," *Culture and Society*, No. 2, 1964, pp. 38 f.

19. B. Suchodolski, "Perspectives of Educating the New Man," *Democratic Weekly* (Warsaw), Nos. 51-52, 1960.

20. S. Zolkiewski, "Mass Culture and Contemporary Culture," *op. cit.*

21. J. Adamski, "Imaginary Antinomy, Real Conflicts," and "The Concept of Humanism," *Cultural Review* (Warsaw), Nos. 20 and 21, 1960, respectively.

*The Editors wish to thank Jerzy Hauptmann for translating the Polish titles in these notes.

22. M. Kacprzak, "On Ancient and Modern Humanism," *University Life* (Warsaw), No. 5, 1960, p. 6 and L. Ludorowski, "For a Universal School of Culture," *Ermland and Masuria* (Allenstein), No. 34, 1957.

23. *See* the report of a conference on "Humanist Aspects of Technical Progress" held at the Breslau Technical College in early December, 1960, in *Cultural Review*, No. 51, 1960.

24. Georg W. Strobel, "Minderheiten in der Volksrepublik Polen," *Berichte des Bundesinstituts zur Erforschung des Marxismus-Leninismus* (Institut für Sowjetologie) (Cologne), No. 22, 1964, p. 89.

25. Stefan Nowakowski, *Adaptation of the Population in the Oppeln Region of Silesia* (Poznan: 1957); J. Burszta and J. Jasiewicz, "Collision of Cultures in the Western and Northern Territories in the Light of Materials from Koszalin Area Villages," *Polish Folk Art* (Warsaw), No. 4, 1962; and *Creation of a New Society in the Western Territories*, ed. Zygmunt Dulczewski ("Western Territories: Studies and Materials," Vol. V [Pozan: Western Institute, 1961])—essays and materials from sociological studies in the Zielona Gora (Grünberg) area.

26. Adam Schaff, "Coexistence and Ideological Warfare," *Cultural Review*, No. 22, 1960.

27. Georg W. Strobel, "Die sozialistische Kulturrevolution in Polen: Verlauf, Methoden und Problem," *Jahrbücher für Geschichte Osteuropas* (Wiesbaden), IX, No. 1 (1961), 100 f.

28. Z. Kicinski, "Balance Sheet of the Fall-Winter Cultural Season," *Ermland and Mazuria*, Nos. 16-17, 1958, and J. Brodacz, "Legal Wilderness: Culture on a Tour," *Politics*, No. 26, 1960.

29. A. Wallis, "Plastic Arts in Numbers," *New Culture*, No. 8, 1959; B. Czeszko, "On Culture and Money," *Cultural Review*, No. 24, 1960; A. Wallis, "Some Sociological Problems of the Plastic Arts Groups," *Sociological Studies* (Warsaw), No. 3, 1962, p. 165; and the same author, *Plastic Arts: Profession and Environment* (Warsaw, 1964), pp. 36 ff.

30. A. Pawelczynska, "Leisure Time of the Urban Population," *Sociological Studies*, No. 3, 1961, p. 231.

31. *New Culture*, October 12, 1958; "Polens junge technische Intelligenz," *Hinter dem Eisernen Vorhang* (Munich), No. 8, 1959, p. 6; and S. Nowak, "Environmental Determinants of the Social Ideology of Warsaw Students," *Sociological Studies*, No. 2, 1962, pp. 150 f.

32. T. Strumff, "Changes in Customs During the Twenty Years," *Arguments*, No. 18, 1964.

33. "The Contemporary Situation in the Eyes of High School Graduates," *Voice of Koszalin*, No. 214, 1964; J. J. Wiatr, *Sociology of the Army* (Warsaw: 1964), p. 313; and E. Skrzypkowski, "Educational Cooperation: Needs and Opportunities," *People's Army*, No. 11, 1964, p. 4.

34. J. Tomaszewski, "From an Examiner's Notebook," *Politics*, No. 38, 1964; J. Zdun. "From the Experiences of Youth Lecturers in the Army," *People's Army*, No. 7, 1964, pp. 65 ff.; M. Jurek, "Propaganda and Accomplishments," *People's Army*, No. 6, 1964, pp. 14 ff.; and L. Turkowski, "Opportunities of Getting Acquainted with Ermland and Masuria—They are Beautiful," *Voice of Olsztyn*, No. 13, 1965.

35. Among urban readers, 26 per cent are patrons of lending libraries. *See* J. Ankudowicz, "The Book in the Small Town," *Modern Farm Community* (Warsaw), No. 5, 1964, p. 55.

36. J. Wojciechowski, "Kraszewski—And What Next?" *Voice of Peasant Youth* (Cracow), No. 10, 1964, pp. 14 f.

37. P. Ziarnik, "Thoughts About the 'List of Most Popular Writers in Poland,'" *Modern Farm Community*, No. 2, 1963, pp. 47 ff.; J. Wojciechowski, *op. cit.;* and J. Burakowski, "What Does the Peasant Read?" *Voice of Olsztyn*, No. 123, 1963.

38. W. Nycz, "Questionnaire Studies of the Interpretation of Social Policy and of Social Interests Among Students," *Bulletin of the Institute for Social Economy* (Warsaw), No. 2, 1964, p. 24.

39. J. Kadzielski, "On the Problem of a Model for the Cultural Revolution (Lodz: Institute of Philosophy and Sociology of the Polish Academy of Science, Branch for the Study of Mass Culture, 1964), pp. 131 ff.

40. L. Solinski, "If Zorro Were Polish . . . ," *Democratic Weekly*, No. 1, 1965.

41. B. Jankowski, "Television and Peasant Youth," *Peasants' Way* (Warsaw), No. 14, 1964; K. Kozub, "Television in the Countryside," *Green Banner* (Warsaw), Nos. 104-5, 1964, and Z. Dolecki, "Thoughts in Front of a Television Set," *Directions* (Warsaw), No. 1, 1965.

42. J. Falewicz, "Film Preferences of the Urban Population," *Culture and Society*, No. 3, 1964, pp. 170 ff.; K. Zygulski, *Film in a Workers' Environment* (Lodz: 1962), pp. 8 f.; and S. Dyksinski and J. Pencula, "Film in the Opinion of a Peasant Viewer," *Modern Farm Community*, No. 11, 1963, p. 98.

43. *Banner of Youth* (Warsaw), October 19, 1964.

44. The views of W. Wesolowski quoted here are from an unpublished manuscript. *See also* J. Szczepanski, *op. cit.*, p. 150.

45. M. Slominska, "Religious Difficulties of School Youth," *Homo Dei* (Cracow), No. 4, 1958; W. Kalkowski, "Peasant Youth in the Eyes of the Clergy," *Binding Tie* (Warsaw), No. 4, 1961; B. Golebiowski, "Church, Laity and Youth," *Modern Farm Community*, No. 2, 1963, p. 89; and S. Wilkanowicz, "Religion and Social Structure," *General Weekly* (Cracow), No. 1, 1960.

46. A. Sarapata, "From Studies on Changes in the Hierarchy of Occupations," *Sociological Studies*, No. 1, 1962, p. 98; W. Wesolowski, "Occupational Prestige—A Value System—Social Stratification," *Sociological-Political Studies* (Warsaw), No. 15, 1963, pp. 23 f.; and T. Strumff, *op. cit.*

47. "The Contemporary Situation in the Eyes of High School Graduates," *op. cit.*

48. *Voice of Koszalin*, No. 93, 1962.

49. *Ibid.*, No. 189, 1964.

50. *Ibid.*, No. 93, 1962.

51. W. Frykowski and M. Piwowski, "The Gentlemen Thieves," *Culture* (Warsaw), No. 40, 1964.

52. W. Nycz, *op. cit.*, p. 26; "Who Is This Man?" *Banner of Youth*, June 9, 1964; M. Kozalkiewicz, "Youth and Contemporary Problems: What Are They Dreaming About?" *Politics*, No. 21, 1964: and Z. Bauman. "Examples of Success of Warsaw Youth," *Sociological Studies*, No. 3, 1961, pp. 103 f.

53. Eugenia Jagiello-Lysiowa, "What Youth Is Dreaming About," *Modern Farm Community*, No. 12, 1959; Z. T. Wierzbicki, *Zmiaca After Half a Century* (Warsaw: 1964); E. Jagiello-Lysiowa. "The Pursuit of a 'New Style of Life,' " *Modern Farm Community*, No. 5, 1964; B. Weber, "The Model of a Young Man in the Concept of the 'New Farming Community,' " *Modern Farm Community*, No. 12, 1962; and F. Jakubczak, "Problems of Emigration and Adaptation in the Reminiscences of the Young Peasant Generation," *Modern Farm Community*, No. 4, 1964.

54. J. Duquesne, *Les 16-24 Ans* (2nd ed.; Paris: 1963).

55. *Shorthand Record of the Third Congress of the Polish United Workers Party, March 10-19, 1959, op. cit.*, pp. 102 f.

56. *Shorthand Record of the Fourth Congress of the Polish United Workers Party, June 15-20, 1964* (Warsaw: Central Committee of the PZPR, 1964), pp. 156 ff.

57. J. Kadzielski, "On the Problem of a Model for the Cultural Revolution," *op. cit.*, p. 164.

CHAPTER III

Ideological Diversities and Crises Within the Communist Area

PHILIP E. MOSELY

THE COMMUNIST-DOMINATED countries of East-Central Europe are displaying many symptoms of ideological crisis. Perhaps it would be more realistic to say that they are undergoing a series of specific and interrelated crises. A third way to describe their situation is to say that numerous contradictions previously concealed from view by Stalinist controls have now come to the surface. Plainly, the former satellites are confronted by many uncertainties, which result in a sense of moral and psychological malaise. These uncertainties are incompatible with the totalitarian political philosophy and the absolutist controls that, beginning in 1944, attached these nations by force to the Soviet power system. Many ideas and aspirations that had supposedly been crushed forever by the ruthless grip of Stalinist apparatus and Soviet hegemony have revived and found a voice within the framework of communist rule. These aspirations are demanding new answers, even though within single-party systems.

The many creeping crises do not present a political challenge to the ruling Communist parties. That challenge welled up spontaneously in June, 1953, in the Soviet Zone of Germany and in October, 1956, throughout Hungary. The grim experiences of those years, as well as the partial disillusionment that followed the Polish "October," made clear the narrow limits of the people's freedom to act politically in order to change the domestic or international framework within which they live their lives. The ruthless Soviet reactions in 1953 and 1956 made clear the Kremlin's determination to uphold its imperial rule, regardless of the grave damage this inflicted on Rus-

44

sian and communist prestige. In turn, the subsequent abandonment of the most arbitrary and restrictive aspects of Stalinism has led to numerous changes within the East European regimes and has thus raised hopes for gradual accommodations that are more attractive to the subject peoples than the grave risks that would arise from any attempt to throw off Moscow's more relaxed exercise of its hegemony.

The intellectual challenges that have arisen within the communist regimes cover a wide range—from disillusionment and apathy to active but modest attempts to make more flexible, efficient and "livable" the operation of this or that part of the system. There is, in these diverse adjustments to post-Stalinist opportunities, no all-embracing political alternative, no sharply opposing program. On the contrary, each little group of innovators seeks to justify its proposals for adjustment by promising greater efficiency and satisfaction in the operation of the present political system.

It is too early to predict how successfully post-Stalinist communism will adjust to this trend toward diversity and empiricism or to say whether a "modern" and flexible ideology will be able to control and direct the thinking of its subjects as effectively as the outwardly monolithic Stalinism of pre-1956 did. Within communism, ideology and the enforced unity of ideology play an indispensable role. By defining and imposing the sole "correct" view of the past, present and future of mankind, communist ideology has traditionally justified both the monopolistic rule of Communist parties over their own peoples and the messianic ambition to expand communist rule to the entire world. By claiming sole possession of wisdom, the ideology justified absolute rule in all its aspects and condemned dissenters or even friendly critics to punishment as "traitors." Within East-Central Europe communist ideology had the special postconquest function of discrediting and repudiating the pre-communist history and cultures of these ancient nations and of justifying imposition of the Soviet domination and the Stalinist pattern upon them. Now, with the spread of less dogmatic definitions of communism, the ruling parties face many uncomfortable uncertainties. Indeed, the trend toward a more empirical and sophisticated approach to ideology has been reflected in a decline in the power and cohesion of Leninist ideology within many nations of the communist-ruled area of the world.

The decline of ideology, which began within Soviet society with a painful reappraisal of the Stalinist past, has proceeded haltingly, with numerous starts and stops. This decline has had three main

sources: de-Stalinization, nuclear bipolarity and the Sino-Soviet conflict.

In its first stage, from 1956 to 1961, de-Stalinization was intended
by Khrushchev and his supporters as a means of bringing about a
renovation and strengthening of the Communist party in order to
overcome the bad effects of prolonged fear and excessive repression
and to equip the party to deal more effectively with the increasingly
complex tasks of governing and developing a modern society and
leading it in a twenty-year transition from "socialism" to "full communism." In harmony with this intention, past injustices and "ex-
cesses" were denounced, the "personality cult" was dethroned and
steps were taken to enhance the active role of the party at all levels.
In accordance with this limited, inner-party purpose, Khrushchev's
speech against Stalin at the Twentieth Party Congress has not been
published in the Soviet Union. The housecleaning was to be done
within and by the party.

In the second stage of de-Stalinization, which began in 1961, the
process of renovation began to reach beyond the confines of the party
into some of the basic problems of Soviet society. Since then Stalin's
activities in many fields of domestic policy and strategy—but not of
foreign policy—have been subjected to bitter denunciation, only
slightly moderated since Khrushchev's dismissal in October, 1964.
The sensitive channel of literature has recently assumed the central
role in a comprehensive assessment of the effects of Stalinism on
Soviet society. *A Day in the Life of Ivan Denisovich* by Alexander
Solzhenitsyn, which depicts life in one of Stalin's prison camps with
a realism not intended by the official doctrine of "socialist realism,"
was published only after long discussions in the highest party circles,
eventually by Khrushchev's own decision. The same theme has been
treated in other works, including the moving memoirs of General
Gorbatov. The misery that shapes the lives of most of the collective
farm peasantry has formed a second major theme, treated in the
works of Solzhenitsyn, Abramov and others. In contrast to the prison-
camp theme, which describes a past stage, the "pro-peasant" writings
report the grimmer aspect of Soviet life as it is lived today.

The increasingly open and frank reexamination of the oppressive
aspects of Soviet life has had a powerful effect on Communists outside
the Soviet Union, including those of East-Central Europe. After all,
for several decades the Kremlin's supporters abroad had zealously
denied or explained away the unsavory features of Soviet life; since

1961 they have been exposed, on the basis of authoritative and shattering Soviet evidence, as nothing more than sycophantic liars. No longer could they hold up Soviet society as the bright ideal and goal toward which they were struggling. Their predicament was reflected in a dramatic call for a reexamination of basic Soviet institutions presented in a memorandum written in August, 1964, by the late Palmiro Togliatti. In it Togliatti raised, but did not answer, the basic question: Was Stalinism merely an aberration, an accident? (But how can such a massive phenomenon be explained by a Marxist as an "accident"?) Or was it an inevitable consequence of the Soviet system? If the latter, what guarantees are there that a similar phenomenon may not develop out of similar causes, in Russia or elsewhere?

In one sense Togliatti was asserting the necessity for each "serious" Communist party to discard the decades-old habit of relying on the Kremlin to dictate policies and leadership to it. In another sense he was urging the Soviet party to hurry up and come to terms with its own need for an ideological renovation from within if it were to justify its continuing claim to be, if no longer a monopolistic leader, at least an effective "first among equals" within the communist movement. Meanwhile, Communists outside the Soviet Union, including many in East-Central Europe, can claim that they saw and experienced the "aberrations" of Stalinism long before they could be acknowledged, even in small part, within the ranks of the Soviet party.

The search for a new, post-Stalinist equilibrium of ideology is continuing within the Soviet ruling group. Here and there slightly more leeway is granted to literature in its discussion of the recent past and the present. With the dismissal of Khrushchev, the neo-Lamarckian dictatorship of Trofim Lysenko over genetics has been destroyed. Party propaganda stresses the growth of "social" organizations—parent-teacher associations, Young Communist *druzhiny* (authorized vigilante units for combatting minor crime of all kinds), various types of cultural initiatives from below—as evidence of the steady transition of the Soviet system from the "dictatorship of the proletariat" into the "all-people's state" of the near future. Even the dismissal of Khrushchev has been treated as the rejection of a milder "personality cult," repeating an earlier process in a lower key. A new Soviet-style "populism" and "humanism," departing from the Leninist dogma of class warfare, seems more attractive to Soviet people than the "ideological hardening" so often stressed in the past.

Whether a communist ideology that has lost a good deal of its absolute self-assurance and self-righteousness will remain an effective binding and directing force has yet to be determined.

The decline in ideological self-confidence expressed in the various stages of de-Stalinization has been indirectly promoted by one of the unforeseen consequences of the emergence of nuclear bipolarity. By one of those unpredictable ironies—perhaps the true dialectic—of "history," the vast leap forward of Soviet nuclear missile power has confronted those who wield it with an insoluble dilemma: the realization that actual use of that power would mean, as Khrushchev sensibly said, attempting "to build communism in a sea of radioactive dust." Oddly enough, the possessors of that vast power have discovered that they share with the very ideological and strategic adversary whom they had hoped to overpower or overawe a deeply held interest: a common and nonideological interest in survival, in avoiding the use of those new weapons each side has developed and accumulated at such high cost. Later than America, but by the same inner logic, the Kremlin has discovered that excessive power in its nuclear form may be too vast to use for any purpose except to deter a threat to its own survival.

Thus, coexistence, or cosurvival, has become a logical and desperately necessary corollary to nuclear bipolarity. Nevertheless, prodded forward by the Leninist tradition of expansionism, the Soviet leaders under Khrushchev and his successors have tried to escape the clear implications of this dilemma by drawing an artificial and unreal distinction between political coexistence of diverse systems and "ideological coexistence," accepting the first and repudiating the second. In rejecting the "coexistence of ideologies," the Kremlin insists that the struggle for world hegemony will inevitably go on but must be waged by "all means short of war," especially nuclear war. This struggle, it says, will lead to the victory of the "socialist camp," whose allegedly superior political, economic and cultural attractions will, it claims, inevitably win over the scores of new, weak and underdeveloped countries to the side of communism. In the meantime—and it may be a very long time—the Soviet leaders insist on remaining the sole judges of what ideas and values will be permitted to be expressed or to circulate within Soviet society. Yet the all-out advocacy of coexistence, even in this truncated form, tends to blunt the sense of ideological dedication and urgency that is supposed to prevail in season and out among Communists. If coexistence is necessary and attractive in Soviet society with its ingrained sense of great-power mission, it appears even more necessary and more attractive among the one hundred-ten million people of East-Central Europe, for whom the role of either auxiliary or victim is equally hateful.

A third stimulus to the decline of ideology in many of the communist-ruled countries is the open conflict between the two major and independent centers of communist power. Several of the central issues in the dispute between Moscow and Peking are the very ones that have fostered a decline in ideological vigor: de-Stalinization and nuclear bipolarity. The Chinese Communists cannot forgive Khrushchev or his successors their attacks on Stalinism, for the Chinese party cannot yet rule and develop its country by non-Stalinist methods. Peking also accuses the Soviet leaders of putting the survival and prosperity of Russia ahead of their "internationalist, revolutionary duty" to face up to all risks, even that of nuclear war, in order to hasten the retreat and eventually the demise of "imperialism." On these issues the Chinese Communists are waging a bitter competition for influence among and leadership over Communist parties in all parts of the world. They offer the developing countries a militant "path to socialism," instead of the relatively gradualist and cautious formula advocated by the Kremlin.

When two powerful Communist parties hurl anathema at each other, each in the name of its own sole "correct" version of Marxism-Leninism, they are, in effect, urging Communists, potential sympathizers and even interested bystanders to serve as a jury to judge the merits of their quarrel. As in the past, the clash between two absolutist dogmas tends to promote the relativization of ideology. Instead of listening to one authoritative and deafening voice within communism, the many bands of partisans or supporters are forced, whether they like it or not, to use their own eyes and their own reasoning. Yet the record of fanatical creeds in the past suggests that, when party programs and party obedience come to possess only relative and temporary—not absolute and eternal—value for believers, the high pitch of ideological faith and unquestioning loyalty gives way in time to moods of uncertainty and drift and worst of all, from the Kremlin's standpoint, to skepticism and apathy.

These factors in the decline of ideology as an organizing and mobilizing force within communism have been felt more deeply and more rapidly within East-Central Europe than within the Soviet Union itself. De-Stalinization has been accepted more willingly in the former satellites than in the Soviet Union. For one thing, the peoples of the Soviet Union had gradually become accustomed to one feature after another of the Stalinist system; they had, in a sense, participated, however unwillingly or unwittingly, in its elaboration. For the peoples of East-Central Europe, even for many Communists, the sudden imposition of the Stalinist system in its full rigor was a sudden and tremendous shock. Since they had had practically no part in elaborating that system, it was far easier for them to shrug off its worst features after 1956. The psychological separation from Stalinism came as a great relief for everyone except a small number of party and secret-police "specialists" in Stalinist methods.

Coexistence, or at least the avoidance of nuclear war, also comes more easily to the East European countries than to the more deeply indoctrinated and isolated people of the Soviet Union. No interest of theirs can be served by nuclear combat or communist expansionism. On the contrary, the very fact of the increasing destructiveness of war has greatly reduced the importance of their territory in Soviet strategy. To Stalin both their homelands and his political control over them were indispensable in the forthcoming "final and decisive" struggle to conquer Western Europe. Today, on the other hand, if there is to be no war, or if that war is to be decided within a few hours by volleys of intercontinental missiles, the advantages the former satellites offer to Soviet strategy are greatly reduced.

In the pursuit of a partial "relaxation of tensions" with the West, the East European countries, except the puppet regime in East Germany, have, if anything, greater needs and greater opportunities than the Soviet Union. Except for the unsettled frontier between Poland and a reunited Germany, these countries have no occasion to fear Western encroachment on their security, territory or independence. Therefore, when the Soviet leaders advocate more active cultural and scientific relations with the West, why should the former satellites lag behind them? Their cultural and social outlooks have developed in far older and more intimate interpenetration with Western and Central Europe than with Russia. In such fields as economics, sociology and psychology their scholars are well equipped to participate on a strong footing in international scientific exchanges. The period of full-blown Stalinist control over their intellectual life was relatively brief and was imposed from without. They have no messianic or expansionist goals toward the West. Any expansion of communism in Europe would actually reduce both their importance and their freedom of maneuver within the communist camp.

When the Soviet Union urges expanded trade with the advanced industrial nations of the West and seeks large credits from them, why should the former satellites hang back? Their economies are in some respects better equipped than that of the Soviet Union to benefit from an expansion of East-West trade. They have relatively more numerous and more experienced businessmen, accustomed to the intricacies of free-enterprise systems. Their smaller and more easily managed economies can adjust more rapidly to the search for new export opportunities. Their far greater dependence on foreign trade gives them an incentive to diversify their search for foreign markets and foreign sources of equipment, a policy that serves to reduce their present overdependence on the Soviet economy. And because this overdependence is neither natural nor always beneficial to the Soviet economy, this search for closer links to the world market can be pressed quite far without running up against strong Soviet resistance or counteraction.

In their basic attitudes toward the Sino-Soviet rift, the communist leaders in East-Central Europe are caught between conflicting motivations. The rift has brought them great advantages. In denouncing Stalinism, the Soviet leaders have, they proclaim, renounced Stalin's habit of appointing and dismissing satellite leaders. Except in East Germany and Bulgaria, the leaders now exude an aura of confidence in their own partial independence and durability. When Peking has accused Moscow of extorting the votes and applause of its puppets by force, Khrushchev and his successors have gone out of their way to deny this charge. While Moscow still asserts its claim to have the strongest and most authoritative voice among the parties, it also parades its support for the equality of all parties. When it urges "consultation," not dictation, as the only proper way to coordinate policies and actions among communist regimes and parties, the party leaders in East-Central Europe have been eager to take the Kremlin at its word.

On the other hand, the former satellite leaderships have shown deep anxiety over the recurrent tendency of the Sino-Soviet conflict to get out of control. They fear that if the political conflict turned into an all-out struggle the Soviet leaders might again demand the abject obedience of its smaller allies. If the Soviet leadership felt its power more directly threatened by Chinese hostility than it has been so far, it might once more intervene directly in the factional disputes within the East European parties in order to reestablish its direct control. This preference for a continuing but rigorously controlled conflict between Moscow and Peking has been expressed most clearly by the Rumanian party, which has taken an unusually active role in the dispute. After attempting to mediate between Moscow and Peking, it proclaimed its independent path to communism in a declaration of April, 1964, and in March, 1965, it refused to attend the Moscow Conference of Communist parties.

In this new and complex situation the East European parties can now look elsewhere than to Moscow and Peking for political advice and ideological nourishment. In particular, the Italian party, which first raised the slogan of polycentrism in 1956, has been exerting a growing influence. It has led the way, among Communist parties, in adjusting its program to new facts of European life. Its leadership now accepts the European Common Market as a progressive step in European life and has asked for the first time to be represented in the European Parliamentary Assembly. The Italian party now goes so far as to argue that capitalism can be "transformed" gradually from within, so that it can "grow over" into a socialist system without a violent revolution and even without a "dictatorship of the proletariat." Some of its spokesmen go so far as to claim that parliamentary democracy, with full democratic freedoms, would be preserved permanently under communist rule! While these views, which now represent the "Far Right" among Communists, may or may not be sincerely held, the fact that they can be discussed as legitimate opinions within international communism injects a new element of flexibility into discussions among and within parties.

The Italian party, which is one of the largest and intellectually liveliest parties, has occasionally exerted an influence unprecedented in Stalin's time on Soviet analyses and decisions. For example, on both political and intellectual grounds the Italian party rejected the standard Soviet view of the European Economic Community long before Moscow was willing even to review its own position. Moscow spokesmen have held, inconsistently, both that this great initiative represents an imperialist plot of the monopolies and that it is bound to fail and is therefore of no importance. Italian communist spokesmen discovered rather early that these views had little appeal within their own country, for the Community was succeeding even better than its advocates had expected and was also bringing many tangible benefits to Italian workers. Since 1961, the whole question has been reexamined in a series of conferences among Italian, Soviet and other communist economists and economic policy makers; and the Soviet analysts have revised their estimates sharply, even though there has not been any startling reversal in Soviet policy toward the Community.

Similar types of interaction have become more frequent and effective between some countries of East-Central Europe and the Soviet Union. After 1955 the superior quality of Czechoslovak, Hungarian and East German shoes and textiles was quickly recognized by consumers in Moscow and other major Soviet cities; even though usually sold without labels, ex-satellite imports are strongly preferred over most Soviet products because of their durability and style. Moscow editorialists have recently been asking whether Soviet factories must lag forever behind their satellite competitors in these qualities. Both supporters and, more recently, critics of Khrushchev's large-scale plans for the production and use of chemical fertilizers have repeatedly drawn attention to the valuable experience to be gained from Sovzone Germany's more advanced agricultural methods and its chemical industry. Soviet analysts have similarly been studying the Hungarian experiment of charging a modest rate for "capital use" (avoiding the "capitalist" term "interest") of permanent installations and equipment (instead of treating them, as in traditional Soviet planning, as a cost-free "gift" from the state budget to the enterprise). There have been rumors that this innovation may be introduced into Soviet management. Czech experiments in decentralized management, using simplified indices of enterprise performance, are cited by the specialized Soviet press in favor of a bolder application of the principles of "Libermanism." The Soviet resort to public opinion polling on a modest scale has been influenced by the more comprehensive types of polling surveys that are regularly carried out in Poland.

The time is gone when the interaction between the Soviet system and its European satellites represented a one-way street, when "the sun rose in the East." Today the former satellites, having regained a substantial measure of autonomy, offer both an area of small-scale and manageable experimentation and a zone of acclimatization for Western ideas and practices. In these two interrelated roles their intellectual and managerial skills have been exerting a modest but perceptible impact on the Soviet search for new paths of empirical innovation.

The gradual turn to empirical tests of effectiveness for policies, as well as for material investments, runs parallel to the decline in the fervor of Marxist-Leninist ideology. After being roundly criticized for "quotationmania," for having "played it safe" by citing passages in Lenin's writings to justify this or that policy, communist economists are now urged to make their analyses as concrete and as close to reality as possible. Instead of juggling abstract categories, sociologists are now beginning to study why young people often avoid the officially sponsored clubs and why many factories suffer from a rapid and wasteful turnover of personnel.

The decline in the active or activating role of ideology has, nevertheless, even deeper sources than the newly recognized need for empirical factualness and policy-oriented research. This broader trend arises directly out of the partial de-Stalinization of Soviet life. After all, the official ideology leaves unanswered numerous questions that are deeply troubling to many Soviet people, especially to the intellectually gifted among them. How, for example, can Marxism-Leninism, even in its Khrushchevian and post-Khrushchevian garb, explain such basic phenomena of our time as the emergence and reign of the Stalinist system, the effects of nuclear bipolarity, the deep rift between the Soviet and Chinese parties or the great economic vitality of the West and Japan?

These and similar questions can be and are asked more freely within the East European countries than in the Soviet Union. In the former satellites the decline of ideological vigor is accentuated by the alien origin of the Stalinist dogma, which was imposed from without and which is often ignored as irrelevant. On the other hand, the decline of communist ideology has not been accompanied by any revival of sympathy for the prewar regimes, except perhaps in Czechoslovakia, where cautious references can be heard now and again to the high level of civic and intellectual freedom attained under the "bourgeois" Masaryk Republic. The younger generation, which has been moving up to new responsibilities, evidently believes all that it has recently heard said by the Communists against Stalinism, as well as most of what the Communists have said for twenty years against the political and social systems between the two world wars.

After ideologies have been imposed and discarded several times within the memory of one or two generations, the prestige of ideology as such, and trust in it, are bound to decline. In its place, intense attention is being given to problems of efficiency, management, material incentives and social organization, all within the general framework of the existing systems. Among the ruling party groups special anxiety has been aroused by a visible, though often denied, gap between the older and younger generations. In the former satellites as well as in the Soviet Union, many young people seem to their elders to be cynical, uninterested in general ideas, which have so often led their elders astray, and content to secure some modest material comforts for themselves after several decades of turmoil. Many younger people complain of the gap between the idealistic professions of communist officials who, in their eyes, have now joined the ranks of the "elders" and their inward corruption by the enjoyment of power and the emoluments that go with it.

In the former satellites, as well as in the Soviet Union, many young people are searching above all for sincerity. They rate the plain unvarnished truth far above the "party truth" that each regime wants them to accept. Apathy toward rhetorical claims to possess the "sole correct truth" is more widespread than active or challenging skepticism, but both apathy and skepticism present genuine dangers to systems that seek to assure their own continuity by enlisting the active, voluntary and unquestioning loyalty of a large part of each new generation.

The decline in the self-confidence of dogmatic communism has left a partial vacuum, which is being filled variously by both Marxist and precommunist trends of thought. Some thinkers, old and young alike, have turned to the rich storehouse of pretotalitarian Marxism to examine a diversity of values that were suppressed under Stalinist rule. Questions of the reconciliation of personal, intellectual and even political freedom with the "building of socialism" are under serious debate, though such discussions are usually confined to trusted circles. The history of prewar Polish socialism, which was ruthlessly rewritten under Stalinist pressure, is gradually being reconsidered; and the powerful current of democratic socialism seems to be reemerging, at least in the intellectual field, as an influence in Polish life. In several former satellites the philosophical and literary influence of Georgy Lukacs has revived, and other writers and thinkers who were persecuted directly or rejected posthumously under Stalinist rule are being rehabilitated.

A more widespread influence has been exerted by precommunist traditions. In Poland the role of Catholicism remains strong, though many believers are concerned over the spread of religious indifference among Poland's increasingly urbanized population. A great weakening of Russian and Russianizing influence is clear throughout the area, except in Bulgaria. In Czechoslovakia the works of Franz Kafka, long withheld from readers as symbols of "decadence," are now accepted—despite the fact that they were written in German—as an authentic national contribution to world literature. A kind of "populism," drawing in part on prewar sociological research and on literature about the peasants and their way of life, is winning strong acceptance among the younger intellectuals.

The strongest element supporting this process of revival is nationalism, which is deeply imprinted in minds and memories throughout this contentious part of Europe. It is easy to play on Polish and Czech fears of a Germany that is again a strong power, but nationalist emotions have also undergone a recrudescence elsewhere. After the Hungarian national uprising of 1956, the Rumanian Communists took advantage of the "unreliable" record of the Magyars to erode many of their cultural and linguistic rights in multinational Transylvania; and the pressure of Rumanization seems to have grown stronger with Rumania's own rejection of Russian cultural hegemony. Within Czechoslovakia the element of Slovak pride in a distinct identity has been reinforced by the leading role Slovak partisans took in the liberation of 1944. The most visible pressures toward de-Stalinization have also come largely from the Slovak wing of the party, which demanded and secured the rehabilitation of Clementis and other leaders who had been executed or disgraced in the Stalinist period. The example of the Sino-Soviet rift shows how far national passions can mount within a supposedly internationalist communist "commonwealth of nations." It is too early to say whether the common sufferings under nazi and then under Stalinist oppression have basically softened the deep-seated national antagonisms among the peoples of East-Central Europe. In contrast to the supranational spirit that has been moving Western Europe toward genuine integration, East-Central Europe could conceivably react away from the spurious supranationalism of communist hegemony toward an exasperated return to parochial nationalisms.

A positive motivation that has, in part, filled the gap left by the ebbing of ideological fervor and discipline is found in the universal emphasis on better education, on rounding out the national economies and on scientific and technical achievement. Despite all the waste that communist planning has entailed, many new branches of industry have been established; and large numbers of able people now occupy far more important posts than those to which their parents could have aspired.

This upsurge of new skills and career ambitions is not an unmixed blessing for the ruling parties, however, for prestige attaches more to achievement, especially of a scientific nature, than to party rank. Indeed, there are growing signs of a psychological gap between the new intelligentsia and the regime that gave its members many new opportunities for training and advancement. Any sense of gratitude seems to be weakened, at least among those under forty, by several contradictory motives. For one thing, the younger generation is tired of orations about the "sins" of the prewar regimes; it feels no sense of responsibility for them. It is, on the other hand, keenly aware of the "new sins" of the Stalinist and post-Stalinist systems. Having received some advantages from the new regime and its program of industrialization, the younger intelligentsia is impatient to receive still more benefits, including the right to speak its mind freely and to make its rulers listen when it presents concrete proposals for improvement.

The countries of East-Central Europe are caught in a series of creeping crises that add up to an intellectual and moral crisis, not, however, to a political one. A new political crisis, similar to those of 1953 and 1956, is not likely to emerge, except possibly in the Soviet-occupied part of Germany. That possibility is inhibited generally by an almost physical awareness of Russia's strategic hegemony. Any risky political change seems to many less necessary because Russia's interference in the domestic and cultural life of the region is less visible or frequent. Here as elsewhere the realization of what a nuclear war would mean presents another inhibiting factor. Finally, in terms of material calculations, both strategic and economic, Russia's pressure is very strong.

No country, and no combination of countries, within the region could resist a decision by the Kremlin to reestablish its direct control. The armed forces of East-Central Europe are equipped and trained on the Soviet pattern. The economic ties to the Soviet economy are very strong and will remain so. The former satellites depend on the Soviet market to absorb a wide range of goods that they would not be able to sell elsewhere, except at a heavy loss. They depend on Soviet iron ore, aluminum, raw cotton, petroleum and other raw materials to keep their new factories busy. To a considerable though varying extent, they depend on the flow of Soviet heavy equipment and spare parts. Although COMECON limps far behind the European Economic Community in promoting integration and efficiencies of scale, the dependence of each of its smaller members on the Soviet economy is far greater than Soviet dependence on any of them.

Strategic and economic ties, however strong and one-sided, are not necessarily decisive. Yet the political ties that bind East-Central Europe to the Soviet Union, while more complex than in Stalin's day, remain strong despite the decline of ideology. Poland and Czechoslovakia are reminded constantly by communist propaganda that they must rely on the Soviet guarantee to protect them against a possible revival of the German *Drang nach Osten;* unlike Germany's Western allies, Poles and Czechs are inclined to take a thousand-year view of their relations to a powerful Germany. This author believes that they are deeply mistaken in their appraisal of Germany's aspirations, in their opposition to Germany's enhanced role in European and Atlantic organizations and in their resistance to Germany's reunification. But it will take more than rhetoric to correct their judgments and remove their fears. The same argument—fear of a revived Germany —has no similar impact on Hungary and Rumania; there it is to the Kremlin's interest to emphasize Germany's alleged vulnerabilities rather than its growing strength.

A more effective political tie between Moscow and the former satellite regimes derives from their common allegiance to communism, though that allegiance is no longer enforced by Stalinist methods of direct domination. Each of the smaller communist regimes needs Moscow's support, discreetly held in the background, in order to maintain its rule at home. By a word-of-mouth propaganda that is far more effective than the trumpeting of the official press and radio, each regime reminds its subjects frequently that the alternative to the present system of milder, post-Stalinist rule is not Western-style democracy but direct Soviet domination, perhaps in the full panoply of Stalinist oppression. On the other hand, in order to attract the willing support of its own people, each regime takes pride in cautiously displaying various signs of its partial independence from the Muscovite pattern, especially in the cultural and economic spheres. In varying degree each of them endeavors to reaffirm a national continuity and a national sense of pride.

When all is said and done, the new relationship, as it has been evolving, is becoming more a matter of calculation. It is no longer based either on abject fear of Moscow's omnipotence or on absolute faith in Moscow's omniscience. The Kremlin's leadership is quietly criticized and questioned. Its actions are resented when they slight national traditions or humiliate national pride. The present and near future are not a period of active or overt struggle against the hegemonial power. They are a time of rethinking of values, of "small deeds." Ultimate issues, such as that of national and political freedom, cannot be resolved and therefore must be played down. On the other hand, communist "humanism" and communist "internationalism" have a hollow ring, even for many who recently believed in them.

Morally, though not politically, East-Central Europe has been moving into a post-Stalinist and a post-ideological stage of its development, one in which concrete achievements of material and scientific culture outweigh the more universal and overarching ideologies that have so often shaped it in the past. This new stage is characterized by a complexity that challenges Soviet policy to overcome its notoriously simplistic approach of the recent past. The creeping crisis of faith in East-Central Europe presents a no less complex challenge to American and Western policy thinking. The countries of the West need to see this new situation in its undramatic reality and review and reshape their own policies—economic, cultural and political—toward these ancient and proud nations that are neither fully free nor any longer completely bound.

CHAPTER IV

World Communism: Decay or Differentiation?

BORIS MEISSNER

FROM MONOLITHIC GLOBAL COMMUNISM TO POLYCENTRISM[1]

Two EVENTS STAND OUT as of foremost importance in the history of the emergence of world communism. The first of these was the Bolshevik Revolution in the fall of 1917. Seizure of power by the radical wing of Russian social democracy led to establishment of an entirely new form of government, the Soviet state, which set for its goal the achievement of a worldwide communist society. The second key event was the consolidation of all communist and Left-socialist groups seeking the same objectives in the Communist International (COMINTERN), whose first congress met in Moscow in March, 1919.

The first phase in the development of world communism was influenced primarily by the fact that the expected European revolution failed to materialize. An inevitable result was a growing dependence of the world communist movement upon Soviet power, particularly inasmuch as the COMINTERN had its seat in Moscow. The Third or Communist International, originally founded on the principle of the equality of all member parties, was gradually transformed into a centrally controlled global party, modeled after the Communist Party of the Soviet Union. Once the possibility of world revolution through independent local revolutions had been dismissed as illusory, the destiny of world communism became closely linked with that of the Soviet state.

It soon became apparent that the Soviet Union was a universal power with a character marked by two contrasting aspects. The revolutionary state emerged, not only as the base of the world communist movement, but also as a new incarnation of the Russian Imperium, inspired by Soviet patriotism. The Soviet Communist party, which is the nucleus of Soviet power, likewise exhibits two faces. It is a state party, and thus an organ of the state in the broader sense of the word, and at the same time the center of the world communist movement. The Soviet state, over which the party exercises its dictatorship, thus appears as a power that not only asserts its leadership over the system of communist states but also strives to achieve world hegemony through the revolutionary transformation of existing states.[2] A limited historical parallel may be found in the Ottoman Empire of earlier times, which combined the Turkish Sultanate with the Caliphate of Islam.[3] The missionary zeal of Marxism-Leninism is intensified by the demand for a total social upheaval.

The Soviet claim to leadership within a "socialist world system" finds expression in the doctrine of proletarian internationalism among Communist parties, a principle that becomes socialist internationalism when applied to relationships among communist states.[4] The meaning of this principle—from the Soviet point of view—lies in the demand for disciplined leadership from a single center, both of the communist state system and of the world communist movement as a whole. It is, of course, possible to interpret this principle in another way, as a commitment to equality and self-determination of the individual partners rather than as an endorsement of hegemonial and imperial aspirations. The latter interpretation is espoused by all those communist forces that prefer a polycentric—or in the interests of linguistic purity a multicentric—system rather than a monolithic unity. A struggle between the advocates of these two interpretations of proletarian internationalism has persisted ever since the establishment of the COMINTERN.

Under Stalin the COMINTERN was gradually brought under dictatorial control. Lenin's successor made it the obligation of all foreign Communists to defend the Soviet Union, as the "base of world revolution" and the "fatherland of all toilers," from any external attack whatsoever. From 1927 on, he treated loyalty toward the Soviet Union as a test of proletarian internationalism. The individual sections of the COMINTERN were required to obey Moscow's orders without question. Within the COMINTERN itself power was shifted from the elected executive, the Executive Committee of the Communist International (ECCI), to the Central Committee of the CPSU. As Stalinism reached its peak the centralized world party became increasingly dictatorial. Applying the principle of democratic centralism on a world scale, the leadership of the CPSU transmitted its orders, via the foreign section of the Russian party, to the entire apparatus of the Communist International. After Stalin had emerged as victor in the internal conflict within the Soviet Union, which passed through its decisive stage in 1929 and 1930, he was also *de facto* the absolute ruler of the COMINTERN. Castro Delgado, a former delegate of the Spanish Communist party, described conditions in the COMINTERN Executive Committee during the early forties in the following words:

> At the very top is Stalin, the commander-in-chief over all. Those on the middle rungs [of the ladder] obey those who are over them and give orders to those below. And the subordinate always obeys. There are two ways of giving orders: the big chiefs do it in a fatherly but firm tone, while the little functionaries bark in harsh voices like sergeants. But there is only one way to obey. Disobedience is not tolerated.[5]

The Secretary of the COMINTERN at that time, the Bulgarian Dimitrov, remembered for his role in the Reichstag fire trial, was dependent on the Second Secretary, the Ukrainian Manuilsky, who in turn received his orders from the Russian Party Secretary Zhdanov. The latter was one of Stalin's closest co-workers and was generally reputed to be his chosen successor. Zhdanov managed the international operations of the Central Committee of the CPSU from 1934 to 1948; from the vantage point of the party's foreign section he exercised a decisive influence, both over the foreign policy of the Soviet state and over the policies of non-Soviet Communist parties.

The dissolution of the COMINTERN produced little change in this system, since the functions of its executive apparatus were transferred in considerable part to the Moscow headquarters of the CPSU. A whole series of offices continued to exist. Leonhard describes the organizational adjustment in some detail in his well-known book *Child of the Revolution*.[6]

Although Stalin's decision to dissolve the COMINTERN was motivated by purely tactical reasons, it ushered in a new phase in the history of world communism. Under the "national front" policy, a certain degree of autonomy was granted the totalitarian Communist parties in various countries, which were permitted to pursue "different roads to socialism." This development made it easier for Tito in Yugoslavia and Mao Tse-tung in China, both supported by independent national communist forces, to accomplish what Löwenthal calls "emancipation through conspiracy." Tito's rebellion frustrated Stalin's attempt to utilize the Communist Information Bureau (COMINFORM) for the purpose of strengthening Russian control over communism in Europe, while Mao Tse-tung's victory in the Chinese civil war produced a new communist great power in Asia.

The rise of the Soviet Union to world power as a result of World War II and the formation of a system of communist states after that war led inevitably to friction between party and state interests, thus placing the unity of the world communist movement in ever-increasing jeopardy. Development of the communist state system in the shape of an Eastern bloc took place in three stages: (1) through assimilation of the internal structure of the "countries of people's democracy," including the Soviet Occupation Zone of Germany, to the Soviet model—a process usually called Sovietization;[7] (2) through development of a hegemonial-imperial order, disguised in the legal forms of a highly elaborate system of international treaties;[8] (3) through gradual political-military, economic, legal and cultural integration, a process that took place primarily in the European sector of the Eastern bloc.[9] Communist seizure of power in East-Central Europe was made possible by the total collapse of the previous system of governments in this area, which had been formed immediately after World War I. In East Asia, on the other hand, the communist take-over was closely related to the general process of decolonization.

In conducting relations with the ruling Communist parties of the various "countries of people's democracy," Stalin at first undertook to force them into a relation of total subordination such as had developed within the Third International. The old COMINTERN functionaries, trained to render absolute obedience to the central authority in the Kremlin, constituted Stalin's assurance that his orders would be carried out to the letter. Men such as Bierut in Poland, Gottwald in Czechoslovakia, Rákosi in Hungary and Dimitrov and Tschowenkov in Bulgaria toed the Moscow line as expected, even though Dimitrov at times pursued a distinct policy of his own. Stalin made a mistake, however, when it came to Tito, who proved neither obedient nor removable through a Kremlin-inspired palace revolution.

The degree of Stalin's mastery over the Communist parties of East-Central Europe was most impressively demonstrated during the summer of 1947, when Stalin forced the Gottwald government of Czechoslovakia—at that time a "national front" with a non-communist majority and not yet a "people's democracy"—to abandon its intention to send a delegation to the first Marshall Plan conference in Paris. The atmosphere of such disciplinary sessions in Moscow is depicted by Dejider in his well-known biography of Tito.[10] When Dimitrov and Tito broached their project for a Balkan Federation, Stalin summoned delegations from both states to Moscow, where he lectured them in sharp language. He accused the Yugoslavs of having fallen into the habit of never consulting the Soviet Union in matters of foreign policy. On February 10, 1948, he informed the Yugoslav delegation that they were to sign, on behalf of their government, an agreement for joint consultation with the Soviet Union on foreign policy questions. The following day Edward Kardelj, today still Tito's second in command in Yugoslavia, was summoned before Molotov. On reaching the Soviet Foreign Minister's office, he found that all preparations had been made for signature of a treaty that he had never seen before. Kardelj was given no opportunity to consult with his government. As he later reported: "I looked at the two sheets of paper in the blue portfolio. I heard Molotov's strident voice ordering: 'Sign it!' And I boiled with anger." But Kardelj signed.

Since this episode the old guard of COMINTERN functionaries has been eliminated by death or through de-Stalinization. The only exception within the Eastern bloc is Walter Ulbricht. A number of veterans survive in other areas, however, including the South American communist leaders Codoville of Argentina, Prestes of Brazil and Vieira of Colombia. The Cuban Blas Roca has also been a top-level official of his country's Communist party since 1928. The fact that these old COMINTERN functionaries are still active in Latin America serves to hamper Castro's rise to exclusive leadership of the movement, since the other leaders feel that their long service in the COMINTERN apparatus gives them a status of equality.

On closer examination the Stalinist system of Moscow control, developed after World War II in the Eastern bloc, is seen to have possessed many features in common with the centralized COMINTERN apparatus that Delgado had described.[11] This is evident from the following account by Wladyslaw Gomulka, chief of the Polish Communist party since the October revolt of 1956. Gomulka stated:

Within the bloc of socialist states, it was Stalin who stood at the apex of this honorific hierarchy. All those under him bowed their heads to him. Those who made obeisance included not only the other leaders of the CPSU and the chiefs of the Soviet state but also the heads of the Communist and workers' parties of the countries in the socialist camp. . . . The idol of this cult was omniscient, knew exactly what to do about everything, solved every problem, as well as guiding and deciding all matters within his radius of action.[12]

The party was not the only link binding the Eastern bloc into the unity it manifested under the Stalinist-Führer system. There were also the secret police, the omnipresent Soviet Army, the economic dependence of the satellites and the solidarity of the new class of ruling functionaries. The world communist movement was dominated by the heavy hand of the Soviet intelligence and state police services, as well as by the financial dependence of foreign Communists upon Soviet sources.

After Stalin's death in 1953, his successors made efforts to replace compulsion with cooperation to a certain degree. In so doing, they accorded limited recognition to the reform communist intepretation of the "different roads to socialism" theory, and they modified their methods of control. It was necessary to adopt a much more flexible application of the principle of proletarian-socialist internationalism, both in relations among Communist parties and in those of the states constituting the Eastern bloc. The Soviet Union seemed unwilling at first to abandon the COMINFORM, which had been established in 1947, as an instrument of its altered policy. A major shift occurred, however, after the Twentieth Party Congress of the CPSU, in February, 1956, which released the first wave of de-Stalinization. The COMINFORM was dissolved, a reconciliation with Tito achieved and emphasis laid on bilateral interparty relationships. Interstate relations within the bloc have also been placed on a new basis since 1954-55 through a reorganization of COMECON and the establishment of the Warsaw Pact Organization, the Eastern counterpart to NATO.[13] An increasing number of multilateral agreements supplemented the previous system of bilateral pacts.

The Soviet government's policy statement of October 30, 1956— issued immediately before the Red Army's intervention in Hungary— indicated a willingness to base interstate relations within the Eastern bloc, not only on the principle of proletarian internationalism, but also on the "Five Principles of Peaceful Coexistence," with special emphasis on the principle of equal rights. The October revolt in

Poland and the popular uprising in Hungary in October and November, 1956, led the Soviet command to stress once more the hegemonial-imperial aspect of proletarian-socialist internationalism. In order to contain national aspirations toward emancipation within the Eastern bloc, the Soviet government adopted measures in two different areas. In the field of intergovernmental relations, integration of the Eastern bloc in Europe was sought through the conclusion of numerous bilateral and multilateral treaties in the fields of defense, economics, intelligence, culture, science, welfare and law. The activities of the Warsaw Pact Organization and of COMECON were intensified. Additional Eastern bloc organs in areas such as atomic energy, railroads and shipping were established on a multilateral basis.

The Soviet leadership did not, however, content itself with governmental measures to amplify the Eastern pact system and to create an "international division of labor" increasing the economic dependence of the people's democracies upon the Soviet Union. It also took steps to strengthen political-ideological cohesion among the Communist parties, both within and outside the Eastern bloc, and to bind them closer to the Communist Party of the Soviet Union. An additional objective was the establishment of a direct and close relationship between the parties of the Eastern bloc and the major organs of integration on the interstate level, such as the Warsaw Pact Organization and COMECON. These party relationships were activated both bilaterally and multilaterally. One technique used was the participation of party delegations in bilateral negotiations, alone or with government delegations. Another was the staging of international party conferences, either including the world communist movement as a whole or limited to the Eastern bloc or its European sector.

At the communist summit conferences of 1957 and 1960, which have been likened with some justification to papal conclaves, Khrushchev attempted to restore Soviet hegemony within the Eastern bloc and in the world communist movement. Despite all his efforts, the Moscow-Peking conflict frustrated this endeavor. With the cooperation of the Chinese People's Republic, an outward appearance of unity was temporarily restored. This soon proved, however, to be an empty façade, since the renewed avowal of proletarian-socialist internationalism was no longer reinforced by the iron logic of Stalinist terror. The cohesion of the socialist community was threatened, by the unequal stages of development of its members and by the same ideological trends that were also becoming apparent in the communist movement throughout the world: revisionism and nationalism. What this involved became very clear in the confrontations of the Soviet Union with Titoist Yugoslavia and Maoist China. As the situation developed, two centers of leadership and highly variegated shadings of communism emerged in various parts of the world. Like the former centralistic structure of the world communist party, the dogmatic unity of world communism, which Khrushchev had sought to restore at the two Moscow summit conferences, proved incapable of surviving the emergence of a plurality of communist powers.

The Two-Front Struggle of Soviet Hegemonial Power[14]

Under Stalin Soviet hegemony was developing into a system of total rule. Incorporation of the people's democracies of East-Central Europe into the Soviet Union, repeating the procedure used in annexing the Baltic states in 1940, was all that remained necessary to convert the hegemonial league of the Eastern bloc in Europe into a full-fledged empire. Stalin held back from this final step, however, for reasons of both domestic and foreign policy.

In the area of Soviet domestic policy, assimilation of the European satellites would have imposed severe structural strains on the Soviet Union, for none of the nations in question—except for a part of Poland—had ever belonged to the Russian Empire. Their cultural relations with Russia were remote and Pan-Slav tendencies but weakly developed. Their inclusion would have strengthened particularist and separatist forces within the multinational Soviet state, decisively weakening the position of the Great Russian nation as the pillar of state power within the Soviet Imperium. The national and social structure of the Communist Party of the Soviet Union would have been subjected to a radical dislocation whose repercussions could not be predicted. Insofar as foreign policy was concerned, annexation of the satellites without settlement of the German question was unthinkable. Tito's rebellion was, however, the decisive factor that deterred Stalin from crossing the Rubicon.

Tito's historic accomplishment lies in the fact that he strengthened the will of the East-Central European peoples to maintain their identity, thus frustrating Stalin's plan to annex them. The Yugoslav dictator furthermore provided the first concrete expression of a tendency already latent in world communism, that of revisionism. Togliatti's thesis of polycentrism and his testament, which is closer to Djilas than to Tito or Kardelj in its more liberal fundamental attitude, would have been impossible without the Yugoslav Communist party's break with the Soviet-dominated COMINFORM.

Communist revisionism is often referred to as national communism by Western observers. Since the rise of Stalin and Mao Tse-tung, national communism has also existed in the Soviet Union and in China but in totalitarian form and imbued with a sense of universal mission. Revisionism is the liberal form of national communism with domestic and foreign policy goals that justify designation as reform communism. Evolution rather than revolution is the keynote of reform communism.

Reform communism has abandoned the dogma that the party is infallible. It therefore questions the right of the party to exercise total control from above and to inject itself into all phases of social life. It is prepared to accord both society and the individual citizen wider spheres of autonomous action, with a corresponding relaxation of authoritarian rule by the single party. This self-limitation of party autocracy and the consequent attitude of greater tolerance implies a measurable strengthening of the element of freedom and thus a shift away from totalitarianism. The metamorphosis is furthered by acceptance of an economic policy that combines elements of planning with those of the market economy and that concerns itself primarily with the actual needs of society rather than with utopian visions of the future. Although reform communism does not attack the basic philosophical and rational core of communist doctrine, it nevertheless has a pervasive effect in all spheres of life, promoting not only social spontaneity but even personal initiative.

Reform communism appears in variant forms, as developments in the European communist states indicate. Its impact, in terms of constitutional reality, is that of transition from a totalitarian to an authoritarian state, the result still being far from libertarian democracy and the rule of law. This transition nevertheless represents a certain degree of liberalization. This limited liberalization can only be classified as a step toward democratization if and when it results in a significant lessening of the permanent party dictatorship. In spite of its authoritarian character, however, reform communism represents a considerable improvement from the standpoint of freedom when compared with orthodox totalitarian communism, either in its Soviet Russian or Chinese version.

In the field of foreign policy, reform communism advocates a conception of peaceful coexistence that is fully in accord with international law, as well as a realistic appraisal of the capitalist world. This is in contrast to the Soviet point of view, which restricts the concept of coexistence to relations between divergent blocs or countries belonging to them. As a phase of political history coexistence is limited in time, even though it may be of considerable duration. It does not extend to the sphere of intellectual or ideological concepts and beliefs. Within the socialist world as the Soviet Russians conceive it, the principles of peaceful coexistence are subordinated to those of proletarian internationalism. This is another expression for the hegemony of Moscow. Reform communism, however, demands unlimited application of peaceful coexistence within the communist-governed area as well as elsewhere. The coexistence principle, it contends, should be harmonized with that of national self-determination and satisfy the demand for equal rights within a framework of "different roads to socialism." This unambiguous rejection of hegemony exercised by a ruling center, be it Moscow or Peking, results from the manifestly dissenting foreign policy theory of reform communism, which rejects both Zhdanov's two-camp thesis as well as the idea of capitalist encirclement; the latter was also abandoned by Khrushchev shortly before his fall.

Mao Tse-tung's "Hundred Flowers" speech made in 1957 indicates that tendencies toward reform communism were also present in China for a while. With the launching of the people's communes in 1958, however, the pendulum swung in the other direction.[15] The Soviet Russians, who took a reserved attitude toward Mao's elaboration of the theory of contradictions, felt impelled to regard this sudden change of course as a Left-wing Trotskyist deviation.

During the course of his dispute with Mao, Khrushchev at first came appreciably closer to Tito. He did not, however, carry his reform policy beyond certain first steps toward reform communism. Although he had, for instance, accorded special praise to the Yugoslav system of workers' self-administration during his Belgrade visit of August, 1963, he never revised the organization of Russian industrial plants to correspond. The fact that Tito was permitted to address the Supreme Soviet in December, 1963, and that communist

Yugoslavia enjoys a place in the circle of fourteen socialist states from which China is excluded is no indication that the ideological argument with Titoism has been settled. Quite to the contrary, the new 1961 program of the CPSU, for which Khrushchev delivered a detailed explanation and which his successors have adopted, designates reform communism, especially in its Yugoslav version, as the principal ideological danger. According to this document:

> The Communist movement grows and becomes steeled as it fights against various opportunist trends. Revisionism, Right opportunism, which is a reflection of bourgeois influence, is the chief danger within the Communist movement today. The revisionists, who mask their renunciation of Marxism with talk about the necessity of taking account of the latest developments in society and the class struggle, in effect play the role of pedlars of bourgeois-reformist ideology within the Communist movement. They seek to rob Marxism-Leninism of its revolutionary spirit, to undermine the faith the working class and all working people have in socialism, to disarm and disorganize them in their struggle against imperialism. The revisionists deny the historical necessity of the socialist revolution and of the dictatorship of the proletariat. They deny the leading role of the Marxist-Leninist party, undermine the foundations of proletarian internationalism and drift to nationalism. The ideology of revisionism is most fully embodied in the programme of the League of Communists of Yugoslavia.[16]

Reform communism, of which Titoism is only one of the possible manifestations, enjoys two advantages in its conflict with the Soviet Russian version of orthodox communism. In the first place, it opens a prospect of satisfying the aspirations of the social forces liberated by de-Stalinization within the Soviet Union and in East-Central Europe. It offers solutions for problems that cannot be mastered by organizational measures alone. In the second place, Moscow needs to avail itself of reform communist ideas in order to withstand the ideological onslaught from Peking. Reform communism thus not only aids in clarifying philosophical and ideological positions within the communist world, it also strengthens the awareness of intellectual linkage with the West.

The ideological conflict between the western and eastern metropoles of orthodox communist doctrine has, at the same time, become further intensified.[17] The Chinese, whom the Soviet Russians have accused of dogmatism and sectarianism, draw their strength from the fact that they are in harmony with the classicists of Marxism, both in letter and in spirit. In contrast to the Soviet Russians, the Chinese still consider Stalin a classicist. They are, therefore, able to appeal to die-hard revolutionaries within the world communist movement as well as to conservatives of the Stalinist type. Concerning the second deviation, the 1961 program of the CPSU has this to say:

> Another danger is dogmatism and sectarianism, which cannot be reconciled with a creative development of revolutionary theory, which lead to the dissociation and isolation of Communists from the masses, doom them to passive expectation or incite them to Leftist adventurist actions in the revolutionary struggle and hinder a correct appraisal of the changing situation and the use of new opportunities for the benefit of the working class and all democratic forces. Dogmatism and sectarianism, unless steadfastly combated, can also become the chief danger at particular stages in the development of individual parties.[18]

The course of the dispute so far, involving intellectual and ideological factors as well as those of power politics, indicates that it is extremely difficult for the CPSU to defend itself with equal force against both heresies at once. Intensified attacks by foreign "dogmatic" forces have necessarily led to a defensive war of position against revisionist elements within the Soviet Union. This two-front struggle demands an ideological flexibility that the ideologists of the Soviet party, mostly holdovers from the Stalin era, find it difficult to attain. It gnaws at the substance of the CPSU and motivates the party leadership to seek relief in the field of foreign policy.

Basic Characteristics of Hegemony in East and West[19]

Since the advent of Khrushchev the Soviet Union has regarded itself as one of the two pillars, and at the same time the beneficiary, of a bipolar world resting upon an atomic balance of terror. The static notion of the bipolar world, which proceeds from the premise of the coexistence of two ideologically determined systems of alliances taking the form of hegemonial leagues, is qualified by the dynamic aspect of the revolutionary two-world concept derived primarily from Stalin and Zhdanov. It is the hope of Soviet strategists that, with the aid of this dynamic and with observance of certain rules of the game resulting from the Atomic Test Ban Treaty, they will succeed in gradually wearing down their enemy and finally overwhelming him. The bipolar world, however, in which Khrushchev had hoped to establish for himself a revolutionary war of position, turned out to be much less stable than was first assumed in the East or the West. It became evident that hegemony in an atomic age is subject to the same processes of change that took place in earlier epochs of history.[20]

Hegemony has always exhibited two developmental tendencies. One leads to a dispersion of power, to a strengthening of centrifugal forces, and thus to the gradual disintegration of a particular hegemonial league. The other, however, involves further integration of power, the formation of a monolithic bloc and finally the transformation of the hegemonial system into a supergovernment, that is, an empire. These two conflicting tendencies and potentialities for development can remain in balance over long periods of time.

Both tendencies can be observed today in the Western as well as in the Eastern world. Furthermore, each of the two sides is endeavoring to extend its sphere of influence over those states that belong to neither system of alliances, the uncommitted developing countries in particular. A centralized system such as the Soviet communist bloc naturally finds it extremely difficult to adjust itself to the first tendency: that of the dispersion of power and of polycentrism. The United States, because of its own internal structure, finds this adjustment far easier. What is apparent here is the reciprocal dependence of internal power structure and foreign policy, a phenomenon of particular importance in the case of a totalitarian power such as the Soviet Union. The events of 1956 in Poland and Hungary showed how difficult it is for the Soviet leadership to permit a limited domestic relaxation coupled with a certain modernization of its totalitarian system of government, while at the same time modifying its traditional methods of rule in its external sphere of power and influence. When such adjustments are attempted, control can easily slip out of the hands of the hegemonial power altogether. Such control is furthermore measurably weakened whenever another power belonging to the same hegemonial league asserts its own claim to leadership. So long as the struggle of the two rival centers for leadership has not been decided, the individual members of the hegemonial league enjoy a greater mobility, which they use to reduce their dependence on the previous hegemonial power. In a development of this type, the policy of relaxation forced upon the Soviet rulers by the general situation contributed measurably to accelerating internal change and to strengthening centrifugal forces within the Eastern bloc. After the Cuba affair this situation led to the rebellion of Rumania against certain decisions of COMECON and to a limited liberalization in Czechoslovakia, Hungary and Bulgaria. Developments have been conditioned by aggravation of the conflict between Moscow and Peking and by the fact that no official break has yet occurred between these two centers of leadership in the Eastern bloc and in the world communist movement. The problem was further complicated by increasing economic difficulties, which not only beset the Soviet Union and the People's Republic of China but were also evident in highly developed areas, such as Czechoslovakia and the Soviet Zone of Germany. This situation induced Khrushchev to support the Ulbricht regime with all available means and simultaneously, with Gomulka's help, to block any further loosening of controls in Poland.

To carry out this policy, a treaty of alliance between the German Democratic Republic and the Soviet Union was concluded on June 12, 1964.[21] In view of the strong emphasis placed on the territorial integrity of the Soviet Zone in Article 4, this treaty may also be regarded as a guarantee pact. The Soviet-Sovzone treaty was preceded by a renewal of the mutual assistance pact of December 12, 1943, between the Soviet Union and Czechoslovakia. An extension of the mutual assistance pact of April 20, 1945, between the Soviet Union and Poland is expected shortly. All these conclusions of treaties reflect Soviet efforts to reactivate the system of bilateral pacts within the Eastern bloc and to multiply the ties between the East-Central European people's democracies and the Soviet Union. They also indicate that the Soviet attempt to forge the European part of the Eastern bloc into a firm union by means of multilateral treaties did not produce the desired results.

The other tendency mentioned above, that of the integration of power, can be manifested in two possible ways: the integration may either encompass the entire hegemonial system or be limited to a part of it. An initial attempt to weld the entire area of the West into an Atlantic union was undertaken by President Kennedy. Even though little has been said about his "grand design" since his death, the Atlantic conception contained therein remains vital. It is based on the idea of unifying the NATO community on the basis of a partnership between the United States and a Europe "speaking with one voice." The level of economic development and the social homogeneity of the Western states would permit such Atlantic integration without difficulty. If no serious effort in this direction has taken place, the reason must be sought in the slow pace of European integration and in the diversity of views concerning the kind of partnership that the United States and Europe should seek—a diversity amply demonstrated by General de Gaulle. A certain fulcrum of political and military power is, however, gradually developing in Western Europe. Supported economically by the accomplishments of the European Economic Community, this center offers an improved balance within the Atlantic alliance, which continues to depend upon predominant American power.

In contrast to the situation in the Western world, the Soviet leadership has never made an effort to weld the entire system of alliances that we call the Eastern bloc into a true political union, for the simple reason that the Asian people's democracies, the People's Republic of China in particular, are far too underdeveloped. Had an attempt been made to equalize the economic level of the European and Asian sectors of the Eastern bloc, the result would have been a catastrophic dilution of the economic potential today available to the Soviet hegemonial power. It is thus understandable that Khrushchev gave first priority to achieving accelerated integration of the European part of the Eastern bloc, since with few exceptions the East-Central European people's democracies possess important industries, while some of them are more advanced in their development than the Soviet Union. The European area alone offered the opportunity to expand the existing hegemony into an empire of continental proportions. What Stalin had vainly attempted, Khrushchev sought to achieve with different methods.

The goals laid down by Khrushchev are clearly evident in the new party program of the CPSU adopted in 1961. It is the manifest Soviet aspiration to achieve a federal structure, after passing through certain intermediate stages of a confederative character. This federation would comprise an integrated economic area with a unified production plan. A continental economy of this type, committed to plans emanating from a single center, could only be achieved within the appropriate political framework, that is, after the conclusion of political integration. Such a development would necessarily mean the end of the sovereign independence of the European people's democracies and would mark the definitive partition of the German nation. To frustrate a Soviet annexation policy of this kind is therefore in the direct common interest of the peoples of East-Central Europe, the German people and the Western community as a whole. Even though the contemporary situation does not appear to offer these ambitious Soviet plans any appreciable chance of early success, this projection of goals should be taken seriously. By pledging their unqualified support to the party program, the new leaders in the Kremlin have made Khrushchev's objective their own.

The difficulties with which the Soviet Union has been forced to contend in its efforts to achieve a higher degree of integration are in large part a consequence of the internal structure of the individual members of COMECON. Experience has shown that it is much harder to integrate countries with centrally administered economies than it is to merge a number of market economies into a unified area or "common market." The foreign trade monopoly alone, designed primarily to shield the planned economy from outside influences, functions as a system of watertight bulkheads that seal off the national economies from one another. The characteristics of totally planned economies also make it difficult to realize a multilateral payment system with the prerequisite convertibility of the ruble. Such an arrangement would require a uniform price system as well as revalorization of the currencies of the people's democracies, which are currently tied to the ruble at arbitrarily low exchange rates. All this could not be achieved without far-reaching institutional effects. Because of these differences in internal structure, the organization of the European Economic Community has proved to be much more effective than that of COMECON. The Soviet hegemonial power does, however, possess a special instrument in the shape of the governing Communist parties, which under normal circumstances are able to coordinate all forces within their respective countries more easily than is possible in the West.

The actual decisions within the Eastern bloc are normally made in conferences of the first party secretaries or of the heads of parties and governments, who are accustomed to meeting before the formal sessions of the Warsaw Pact Organization and of COMECON. While the Eastern bloc as a whole has dissolved into an extremely loose association, these party conferences constitute an extraordinary organ of the special alliance that has developed within the Eastern bloc, consisting of its European members under Soviet leadership plus the People's Republic of Mongolia. If this important organ of the Soviet Russian hegemonial league has not completely fulfilled the Kremlin's expectations, the reason lies mainly in the fact that some of the former satellite parties have become highly self-confident vassals. This shift in relationships has been measurably stimulated by the rebellion of the Chinese Communist party against the predominance of the CPSU and the policy of integration pursued by that party. The Chinese demand that the economic development of each individual country be based primarily on its own domestic potential. They regard the creation of self-sufficient national economies, although hardly prudent as an economic policy, as the concrete expression of proletarian internationalism. Efforts by the Soviet Union to forestall autarkic development, as in the case of Rumania, are condemned by the Chinese as symptoms of national egoism. Like Yugoslavia, the Chinese People's Republic advocates a kind of commonwealth of communist states. This support of polycentrism reveals a paradoxical area of agreement, not only between the dogmatic and revisionist schools of Marxism-Leninism but also between the Europeans and the Chinese.

The principal explanation for the behavior of the Chinese lies in their disappointment that the Soviet Russian overlords failed to satisfy the hopes they had aroused. The Kremlin assumed all the rights of hegemony but made very little effort to fulfill the corresponding obligations. Initially the Chinese had supported the integration of the entire Eastern bloc to form a coordinated hegemonial league under the leadership of the Soviet Union. In so doing, they were motivated by the expectation that the Soviet hegemonial power would be prepared to make greater sacrifices for the economic progress of the underdeveloped Eastern bloc countries. That Chinese disappointment was one of the principal reasons for their dispute with the Soviet hegemonial power is evident from the following explanation by the Italian communist leader Longo, given after the communist summit conference of 1960:

The conflict between the CPSU and the CPCh has its roots in a much more fundamental question than those concerning peaceful coexistence, the possibilities of avoiding an atomic war or the argument about the Stalin cult. The true reason is a difference in their views concerning the correct road to socialism and communism. The Chinese believe that the development of communism in the various countries should constitute an indivisible whole. Those countries that are economically more developed should therefore show greater interest in the difficulties and sufferings of the more backward socialist countries and should give them their entire material support. Those who support this point of view cannot declare themselves in agreement with the competition between the Soviet Union and the United States and other capitalist countries. Nor can they approve peaceful coexistence or Soviet aid to the underdeveloped countries [meaning India, Indonesia, Egypt, etc.]. Such aid should be given to economically backward countries within the socialist camp.

The Russo-Chinese Struggle for Control of the Eastern Bloc[22]

Chinese resistance to Soviet Russian hegemony has become intensified since the aggravation of the conflict resulting from the twin crises in the fall of 1962—the Soviet operation in Cuba and the Sino-Indian border war in the Himalayas. The Chinese are anxious to win the "brother parties" over to their point of view; where this is not possible they hope at least to form factions of their followers within the individual Communist parties and front organizations. Their efforts to this end have been most successful in East and Southeast Asia. A strong Chinese influence is also noticeable in Latin America and in Africa. In Europe there are small splinter groups that have adopted the Chinese point of view.

The scope of this paper does not permit a recital of the history of the Sino-Soviet conflict, which was first exposed to public view in April, 1960. The following documents make clear, however, that the breach between the two leading communist powers is beyond repair: (1) the two philippics of 1963: the "Twenty-five Theses of Mao Tse-tung" of June 14 and the "Open Letter of the CPSU," dated July 14; (2) the six governmental declarations that were exchanged following the basic statements of position; these were followed by an exchange of correspondence encompassing seven letters, which dealt with, among other things, the possibility of settling the conflict in a general conference; (3) nine commentaries by the Chinese on the Soviet

Russian "Open Letter" and the energetic Soviet reply in the form of Suslov's speech of February 14, 1964, and various commentaries in *Pravda*.

These documents show how closely the ideological dispute interlocks with practical politics. Richard Löwenthal has quite correctly pointed out that an ideologically determined alliance exists between the Soviet Union and the People's Republic of China.[23] Wherever an alliance is rooted exclusively in the common ideology of the ruling totalitarian parties, differences of opinion arising from the divergent situations of the two partners naturally assume the form of different interpretations of this ideology. As soon as an ideological dispute of this kind has become apparent, a pragmatic solution of the basic political differences becomes much more difficult. From the moment of the open collision, the common ideology—which formed the basis of the alliance in the first place—necessarily becomes a major bone of contention between the allies. National interests, which even before the dispute had competed with the demands of the ideology, now move to the foreground of the conflict. Since the concrete issues have made their appearance in ideological disguise, this development necessarily leads to the emergence of two sects and thus inevitably to ideological schism. The course of the conflict between Peking and Moscow up to now has indicated that the ideological circumlocutions cover not only concrete points of political dispute but also different political conceptions. The ultra-orthodox and therefore aggressive ideological line preached by Peking does not mean, however, that the foreign policy of Communist China is actually much more aggressive than that of the current Soviet leadership. The policy of coexistence, which makes such a pacific impression, in no way deterred Khrushchev from building the Berlin wall and establishing rocket bases in Cuba. Khrushchev had no convincing reply to the Chinese charge that the Cuba operation represented a type of reckless politics that could have easily plunged the world into the abyss of atomic war. The same charge was repeated by Suslov on the occasion of Khrushchev's removal.

As Moscow sees things, the principal contradiction in the field of international relations is that between the socialist and capitalist countries, that is, the contradiction between the two blocs: the East-West conflict. For Mao Tse-tung, however, the most important contradiction lies in the conflicts of interest within the Western world and between rich and poor nations. He has propounded the thesis of "two middle zones"[24] and has called for the cooperation of these zones against the two world powers. One of them comprises the developing countries under the leadership of China, while the other is made up of capitalist powers, such as Great Britain, France, the German Federal Republic, Italy and Japan.

Moscow's point of view on this issue differs markedly from Peking's, since the Soviet Union has accommodated itself to a bipolar world and is seeking only a step-by-step alteration of the existing balance of power. The Soviet opinion of the "two middle zones" theory is that it would turn Lenin's theory of imperialism upside down. Mao's theory is suspected as an attempt to encircle the Soviet Union; what is most feared is the future collaboration of a united Europe with a Far Eastern power combination consisting of the Chinese People's Republic plus Japan. In his speech of February 14, 1964, Suslov gave voice to the suspicion that Red China would not even object to an improvement in its relations with the United States.

Peking demands from Moscow the right of codetermination in all questions of the Eastern bloc and the world communist movement or else a clear demarcation of the two hegemonial areas and their appurtenant spheres of interest. Fulfillment of the first demand would require establishment of a duumvirate as the ruling organ of a hegemonial system with joint overlordship.[25] Fulfillment of the second would involve acceptance of the schism as an accomplished fact. Neither is acceptable to the new leadership in the Kremlin, which has, on the whole, given Khrushchev's China policy its seal of approval.[26] The principal charges raised against Khrushchev by the school of thought for which Suslov is the spokesman concern his tactics and personal blunders. A report on the conversations held by a French communist delegation led by Marchais, which visited Moscow immediately after the change of command in the Kremlin, contains the following statement:

> The French bring up the subject of China. This time Suslov replies: "Comrade Khrushchev showed no great skill in managing relations with the communist brother parties, but so far as China is concerned he was too soft in our opinion."[27]

Accounts of Suslov's impeachment of Khrushchev indicate that the former leader was charged with having pushed the conflict with China to the breaking point in a situation that was unfavorable for the Soviet Union, even though this policy had not been approved by the other brother parties. After the breakdown of the bilateral talks in July, 1963, Khrushchev had quite unnecessarily heaped abuse upon his Chinese guests. After calling Mao Tse-tung the "Golden Buddha" and "Genghis Khan," he then likened him to Hitler. The action most strongly held against Khrushchev, however, was his furnishing of technical and military aid to India during its border dispute with the Chinese People's Republic. Although this policy had been in accord with the friendly relations existing between the Soviet Union and India, it had had a highly unfavorable effect on Soviet-Chinese negotiations.

The new Soviet leadership is clearly anxious to place the conflict with China on more of a matter-of-fact basis, eliminating all explosions of feeling but not yielding in questions of fundamental importance. As long as the Soviet Russians maintain their position, the Chinese will continue to oppose decisively all measures of accommodation with the West, as well as any partial integration of the Eastern bloc under Soviet auspices. They will furthermore attempt with all means at their disposal to continue their expansion of power in Southeast Asia. In carrying out this policy designed to produce a change in the status quo, Peking is deliberately accepting open conflict with the saturated Soviet Union. It has adopted this policy because it better reflects the national interests of China and because China itself is imbued with a consciousness of world revolutionary mission equal in every way to that of Moscow.

Russo-Chinese differences of opinion in questions of world revolution and world politics, which will not be discussed here in detail, are in every case acerbated by national components. Russian and Chinese communism are both mixtures of communist and nationalist elements; however, they came into being under entirely different conditions. In Russia it was Marxism that emerged from the Western cultural community, that became amalgamated with the Russian tradition and that found its totalitarian expression in Stalinism. De-Stalinization thus involves not only the relaxation and modernization of totalitarian government but also a strengthening of ties with the West. In China, on the other hand, where Russian Marxism was received in its Stalinist form, the development of an ideology of Mao Tse-tung signifies a progressive return to the distinctive Chinese national tradition. One feature of this development is the aspiration to restore the Chinese Empire in its original territorial dimensions.

This Chinese Empire originally included not only the People's Republic of Mongolia and the small People's Republic of Tannu Tuva, which the Soviet Union annexed in 1944, but also areas that were ceded to Czarist Russia under the so-called Unequal Treaties of 1858, 1860 and 1881 and that today constitute parts of the Soviet Far Eastern Province with its major cities of Vladivostok and Khabarovsk and of the Central Asian Union Republic of Kazakhstan, the capital of which is Alma Ata. It is now public information that in 1954 Mao Tse-tung demanded the return of Outer Mongolia to China and that Khrushchev refused to comply. In a conversation with Japanese Socialists in July, 1964, Mao Tse-tung accused the Soviet Union of annexing territory that did not belong to it, in Asia as well as in Europe. In making this charge, he renewed his demand for the return of former Chinese imperial territory. The Chinese party Chairman stated:

They seized possession of a part of Rumania. They sliced off a part of Eastern Germany and drove the inhabitants into the western part. They amputated a part of Poland, annexed it to Russia and gave Poland a part of East Germany as compensation. The same thing happened to Finland: they cut off all that could be cut. Some people have declared that the Sinkiang territory and the land north of the Amur River must be added to the Soviet Union. The U.S.S.R. is concentrating troops along its borders.[28]

These concentrations of troops were confirmed by Khrushchev, who replied to Mao Tse-tung's territorial demands with undisguised threats. The latter created a tense situation, particularly along the Sinkiang border. During Chou En-lai's conversations with Khrushchev's successors, Radio Peking warned against "any foreign attempt" to detach portions of the province of Sinkiang or to incite separatist conspiracies there. The mutual recriminations alleging border violations, particularly in the Central Asian sector, indicate that the longest land boundary in the world has become fluid. This means that the Soviet Union can no longer feel so safe about its rear as it could a few years ago.

The violence of the collision between Russian and Chinese nationalism is partly a result of racial components, which lend the struggle of the two powers certain atavistic features. The Russians fear that the Chinese might succeed in playing off the various races within the communist camp against one another, thus splitting world communism into white and colored wings, with the latter having numerical predominance. Peking makes use of communist front organizations, such as the World Peace Council and the World Federation of Trade Unions, as well as Chinese-oriented bodies, such as the Afro-Asian Solidarity Conference, as forums for attacking the policies of the Soviet hegemonial power and playing off the colored peoples against the whites. This tactic was much in evidence at the 1964 Afro-Asian Solidarity Conference in Algiers, where tumultuous scenes took place. On his way back from the conference, the leader of the Soviet delegation, the Asian expert Gafurov, said in Paris:

> Don't you French see that the Chinese are trying to unify the yellow and black races against the whites? Don't you see that the National-Socialist propaganda of the Chinese is dangerous, not only for the Soviet Union but for the nations of Europe as well?[29]

This identification of the Chinese version of orthodox communism with Hitler's national socialism, which has already been noted elsewhere, illustrates the degree of tension that the conflict between Moscow and Peking has now reached.

That a new communist summit conference, which the Soviet Russians are still seeking to convene since Khrushchev's removal, will succeed in achieving an amicable settlement of the controversy is hardly to be expected. Even the prerequisite of a full rehabilitation of Stalin, a demand made by the pro-Chinese Albanian Communist party, would probably be totally unacceptable to the new Soviet leadership. Closely interwoven are the differences of opinion in questions of international security and atomic armament. The Chinese accuse the Soviet Russians of having joined Washington, New Delhi and Belgrade in an "unholy alliance" against Peking, thus openly breaching the Chinese-Soviet alliance treaty of 1950. Khrushchev's efforts to reach a worldwide accommodation with the United States on the basis of the status quo are regarded by the Chinese as an attempt to prevent them from achieving their national-imperial goals, the conquest of Taiwan in particular. In order to realize its designs for expansion, China is making every effort to become an atomic power as rapidly as possible. Having its own atomic weapons, it would be able to take advantage of its numerically superior man-power in a conflict limited to conventional forces. With these objectives in mind, Mao Tse-tung has always categorically rejected the universal disarmament advocated by Khrushchev, even though the Russian leader's "pacifism" was clearly for propaganda purposes.

The Soviet policy of keeping the Chinese out of the Atomic Club as long as possible has not changed since Khrushchev's fall. The Soviet leaders fear that support of Chinese efforts to acquire atomic weapons would lead to the atomic armament of Germany and Japan. In 1957 Moscow promised Peking assistance in developing its nuclear weapons; it did not keep its promise. Even though the Chinese People's Republic finally succeeded in exploding its first atom bomb shortly before the removal of Khrushchev, it still has a long way to go before it becomes an atomic power comparable to Great Britain or France. The psychological effects of Chinese experiments with atomic weapons should not, however, be underestimated, particularly where the colored races are concerned.

THE EFFECTS OF THE COMMUNIST SCHISM

The conflict between Moscow and Peking has had a more far-reaching effect on the destiny of world communism than that produced by the disagreement between Belgrade and Moscow. In both cases, the struggle for power has been closely linked with disputes over matters of intellectual and ideological principle. In one instance, the CPSU was attacked as the Soviet state party; in the other case, its authority as oracle of the communist "world church" was challenged. The most evident result of the entire contretemps is the fact that a unified world communist movement and a monolithic Eastern bloc no longer exist. World communism has been split into two camps, grouped around two centers of leadership and speaking what in many respects are two different languages. At the same time reform communism, which has been advancing in all sectors of the communist world, appears with enhanced attractiveness. The communist "world church" has disintegrated into three sects, which have nothing left in common but their commitment to a certain "basic creed."

Within the Eastern bloc and the world communist movement, two hegemonial leagues have formed around the two metropolitan centers of orthodoxy since the Moscow conference of 1960. However, a final organizational split has not yet taken place. The situation may be compared to that of the disintegrating Russian Social Democratic party after the conflict between the *Bolsheviki* and the *Mensheviki* at the party Congress of 1903. As is well known, the final organizational separation of the two groups and the founding of separate parties did not occur until 1912. The Communist Party of China is fond of recalling the example of Lenin's struggle to establish the Bolshevik party. It cites this precedent in disputing the right of the CPSU to presume, in the name of a "majority," to force its views upon the "minority" spokesman, the CPCh. The present situation differs from the historical controversy of 1903 in that the new communist schism affects not only a worldwide movement to which numerous parties belong but also an entire system of states. One billion people who live under communist rule have been split into two camps, with almost three-quarters of them under the hegemony of Peking and only one-quarter under that of Moscow.

The struggle between Peking and Moscow for overriding power has greatly stimulated the process of differentiation within the world communist movement. All organizations within the movement have been touched by it. World communism today presents a highly differentiated appearance; it is necessary to distinguish between the East European, the Eastern and Southeast Asian, the West European and the Latin American groups. Those Communists in the Orient and in Africa who are supporters of Moscow have been instructed to operate within the existing one-party regimes, following the tactic of "licensed infiltration" (Löwenthal) introduced during the fall of 1963.

The schism analyzed in this essay has resulted in a weakening of world communism but not in a lessening of its fundamental aggressiveness. The tendency toward a dispersion of power has been intensified, not only in the Eastern zone, but also in the world generally. As a result, the satellites, especially those of East-Central Europe, have been encouraged to defend themselves against Moscow's plans for integration and annexation. The two-front struggle forced upon the CPSU by the frontal attack of the Communist Party of China redounds to the particular advantage of the progressive forces within Soviet Russia. The conflict between Peking and Moscow thus serves as a catalyst that accelerates measurably the processes of change within the Soviet Union itself and in its relations with the outside world. It likewise affords the European vassals of the Soviet Union the possibility of further consolidating their autonomous position in relation to the Soviet hegemonial power. This in turn opens to the Western world an opportunity to establish closer contact with these countries, which constitute an integral part of Europe.

Even the two great communist powers have not escaped the effects of the schism. Their bitter struggle for the position of superior power has made them conscious that they belong to two worlds that differ fundamentally in their natural characteristics, including racial as well as other components, their national traditions and their habits of thought. This increased awareness of national personality strengthens China's ties with Asia and causes Russia to move once again in the direction of Europe.

NOTES TO CHAPTER FOUR

1. See R. Löwenthal, *Chrushtschow und der Weltkommunismus* (Stuttgart: 1963); B. Meissner, "Das Verhältnis von Partei und Staat im Ostblock," *Die Sowjetunion in Europa* (Wiesbaden: 1962), pp. 33-85; and G. Nollau, *Die Internationale* (Cologne: 1959) and *Zerfall des Weltkommunismus* (Cologne: 1963).

2. B. Meissner, "Soviet Russia's Foreign Policy: Ideology and Power Politics," in *Western Integration and the Future of Eastern Europe,* ed. David S. Collier and Kurt Glaser (Chicago: Henry Regnery Co., 1964), pp. 77-101.

3. See E. Kordt, "Koexistenz als politisches Phänomen," *Moderne Welt,* I (1959), 32 ff. and H. Fiedler, *Der sowjetische Neutralitätsbegriff in Theorie und Praxis* (Cologne: 1959), p. 24.

4. B. Meissner, "Die interparteilichen Beziehungen im Ostblock und das Prinzip des 'proletarisch-sozialistischen Internationalismus,' " *Internationales Recht und Diplomatie* VI (1961), 1947-64.

5. Nollau, *op. cit.,* p. 106.

6. Wolfgang Leonhard, *Die Revolution entlässt ihre Kinder* (Cologne: 1955; American translation *Child of the Revolution* [Chicago: Henry Regnery Co., 1958]).

7. E. Birke and R. Neumann, *Die Sowjetisierung Ost-Mitteleuropas* (Frankfurt am Main: 1959) and Stephen D. Kertesz, *The Fate of East-Central Europe* (South Bend, Indiana: University of Notre Dame, 1956), pp. 103-320.

8. B. Meissner, *Das Ostpakt-System* (Frankfurt am Main: 1955).

9. Z. K. Brzezinski, *Der Ostblock* (Cologne: 1962) and G. Rhode, "Politische und soziale Probleme einer Integration in den Ostblockländern Ostmitteleuropas," in *Ostblock, EWG und Entwicklungsländer,* ed. E. Boettcher (Stuttgart: 1963), pp. 22-50.

10. See Vladimir Dejider, *Tito* (Berlin: 1953), pp. 342 ff.

11. See Meissner, "Das Verhältnis von Partei und Staat im Ostblock," *op. cit.,* pp. 64 ff.

12. *Ibid.,* p. 67.

13. A. Uschakow, *Der Rat für gegenseitige Wirtschaftshilfe (COMECON)* (Cologne: 1962) and *Die Warschauer Paktorganisation,* ed. B. Meissner (Cologne: 1962).

14. *Communism in Europe,* ed. W. E. Griffith (Cambridge, Mass.: The M. I. T. Press, 1964), Vol. I and B. Meissner, "Die Auseinandersetzung zwischen dem Sowjet- und Reformkommunismus," in *Festschrift für Hermann Gross* (Kiel: 1963), pp. 75-100.

15. J. Domes, *Von der Volkskommune zur Krise in China* (Duisdorf bei Bonn: 1964).

16. *Program of the Communist Party of the Soviet Union* (English translation) (Moscow: Foreign Languages Publishing House, 1961), p. 41.

17. B. Meissner, "Der Konflikt zwischen Peking und Moskau," *Europa-Archiv,* XIX (1964), 111-24.

18. *Program of the Communist Party of the Soviet Union, op. cit.,* pp. 41-42.

19. This section is based on thoughts developed by the author in his contribution to the discussion following a lecture by Richard Löwenthal on "Alliance Systems and National Interests" at a conference of the German Political Science Association at Heidelberg in April, 1963. See *Politische Vierteljahresschrift,* V (1964), 95-131.

20. Concerning the concept and problems of hegemony, *see* H. Triepel, *Die Hegemonie* (reprint; Aalen: 1961).

21. H. H. Mahnke, "Der Beistandspakt zwischen der Sowjetunion und der 'DDR' vom 12. Juni 1964," *Europa-Archiv,* XIX (1964), 503-12.

22. W. E. Griffith, *The Sino-Soviet Rift* (London: 1964); and *Moskau-Peking,* ed. H. Reither (Freiburg im Breisgau: 1965).

23. R. Löwenthal, "Staatsräson und Ideologie in den sowjetisch-chinesischen Beziehungen," *Festschrift Fraenkel* (Berlin: 1963), pp. 160 ff.

24. *See* the TASS report on Mao Tse-tung's interview with Japanese Socialists, *Pravda,* September 2, 1964.

25. Concerning the concept of "collective symmachy" relevant in this connection, *see* Triepel, *op. cit.,* pp. 390-91.

26. B. Meissner, "Chruschtschowismus ohne Chruschtschow," *Osteuropa,* Nos. 1-2, 1965.

27. *L'Express* (Paris), No. 699, November 9-15, 1964, p. 14.

28. TASS report, *Pravda,* September 2, 1964.

29. *Frankfurt Allgemeine Zeitung,* April 6, 1964.

Part Two

THE GERMAN PROBLEM
and
EASTERN EUROPE

CHAPTER V

The Image of Germany in Eastern Europe

GOTTHOLD RHODE

W HENEVER THE GERMAN question is under considera-
tion, first attention is usually given to questions of world politics,
long-range strategy and economic opportunities and achievements.
Second priority is accorded to issues of ideology and power politics on
both sides of the Iron Curtain. These aspects are doubtless necessary
and important, but preoccupation with them results in neglect of
an important factor that can be as profound in its effects as economics
or strategy: the climate of trust or distrust, the sympathies and antipathies—in short, the images the nations entertain of one another.

These problems deserve careful attention, since they are of the
foremost importance for the future coexistence of the nations of
Europe, as well as for solving the problem of Germany. It is quite
certain that the present close military and economic cooperation
among the member states of NATO and the Common Market would
never have been possible had France, Italy and Germany remained
under the spell of the old stereotyped images of mortal enmity between France and Germany, of the immorality of the French, the lazi-
ness of the Italians and of German brutality and thirst for power.
Remnants of these primitive derogatory images persist, no doubt,
but they have yielded to more rational and objective judgments.

One of the great accomplishments of West European nations
since World War II has been the formation of objective and correct
images of neighbor countries. In achieving these images Europeans
have had to overcome a quite understandable habituation to moss-
grown attitudes of enmity, hatred and aversion—attitudes that are far

more comfortable, since they demand little knowledge and flatter the ego. The most important development in this area has been Franco-German reconciliation, the historical importance of which was impressively demonstrated by Louis-Henri Parias at the Wiesbaden Conference in September, 1963.[1] However frequently relapses into the derogatory and distorted international attitudes of the past may still occur in Western Europe, the fact remains that significant progress has been realized as compared to forty years ago. While the images with which West European peoples today interpret their neighbors and partners are seldom entirely accurate, they are at least differentiated, based more on personal experience and understanding than on emotions, and more informational than legendary in content.

We have, however, learned through sad experience that ill-considered films and television "documentaries" can easily destroy objective images and revive traditional hostile emotions, which seem to have been lightly anesthetized rather than eradicated. This is why the work of educational organizations such as the International School Book Institute in Brunswick is particularly important. The Institute has already achieved notable success in its task of eliminating derogatory and unfair descriptions of other peoples from school texts in Germany and other countries.[2]

No one in Western Europe would contend that an ideal state of affairs has already been achieved and that nothing more needs to be done to improve popular knowledge of neighbors and partners. The active exchange of secondary school and university students and teachers, the international conferences and the partnerships maintained between English and German or French and German cities (e.g., Mainz and Dijon) illustrate the continued efforts being made for wider understanding and closer reconciliation and rapprochement.

Compared with these developments in the West, the image the peoples of East-Central Europe entertain of Western Europe in general and of Germany in particular seems of secondary importance. Since the peoples of this region cannot express their opinion—or if they can express it, lack any opportunity to translate it into action— the argument that it does not matter what these peoples think of their neighbors and what images of them they construct is plausible. Politics within the Eastern bloc are managed by a very small group of party leaders, whose images are ideologically determined. The sympathies and antipathies of the peoples themselves are consequently of little effect.

While the foregoing evaluation is still to a certain extent correct, it is far less so than was the case in Stalin's day. While the heads of parties and governments in Eastern bloc countries continue to ride roughshod over the desires and feelings of the peoples, they are beginning to avoid frontal collisions with public opinion. They are making efforts to justify and explain their actions and are indeed endeavoring to bring about a certain congruity of leadership and popular sentiment.

Stalin and Bierut, Gottwald and Rákosi gave explanations for their actions, but in their cynical disdain for their subjects they never worried about the plausibility of such explanations. Gomulka, Kádár and Novotný no longer exhibit this sovereign cynicism. They are at least seeking agreement as well as obedience from the people—if not in the realm of domestic programs, then at least in the field of foreign policy. The popular image of Western Europe and of Germany in particular is therefore important, although not decisive, for these leaders.

What is more important for the long-range future of Europe is whether the peoples of East-Central Europe will experience a feeling of trust for the German people and its partners or whether they will, quite apart from communist tutelage, continue to regard the Germans with distrust or even fear. Attention was drawn to this central problem at the Wiesbaden Conference.[3] The decisive factor determining the issue will not be the example set by West European peoples but rather the complex of conceptions and images that East European peoples form of Germany and its relations with its neighbors.

It is thus evident that there are two reasons—one pertaining to the present, the other to the future—the formation of the East European peoples' image of Germany is not only interesting but of the highest political importance. An exhaustive examination of this phenomenon is, of course, impossible within the limits of this brief survey; nor can we delve into more than a portion of the rich literature on the subject. A number of similar investigations—concerned in every case with a single people during a limited period of time—have already resulted in major scholarly articles.[4] The Polish image of the German—not of Germany as such—forms the subject of a lengthy book.[5]

Our present considerations must be limited to the observation of certain principal characteristics evident from a study of the literature and the press, as well as from personal impressions gathered by the author in Czechoslovakia in May, 1964, and in Rumania during the fall of 1960 and the summer of 1964.

SIMILARITIES AND DIFFERENCES IN HISTORICAL BACKGROUND

The images of Germany current among almost all East European peoples, including the Russians, in the past exhibited a significant dichotomy. Each consisted of two sub-images: that of the distant country and its inhabitants and that of Germans who lived among these peoples as immediate neighbors. Except in the case of the Albanians and the Bulgarians, this divided image was to be found among all the peoples of Eastern Europe, albeit in varying degree. Among the Serbs and Rumanians, for instance, only those who lived in the Danubian Monarchy until 1918 had close contact with Germans. The Lithuanians, among whom there were but few German settlements, had far less experience with the Germans as immediate neighbors than the Czechs, who were surrounded by German territory on three sides.

For France and the French, on the other hand, the majority of Poles and Hungarians lived at a great distance, while at least some Germans were close at hand. While the knowledge the French had of England and the British was limited to that gathered from newspapers and books, they had for the most part a personal acquaintance with a number of Germans whom they had met face-to-face. As a result of this personal contact with German neighbors, the French image of Germany was complicated by personal experiences and feelings. For the French the days of widespread personal contacts with the Germans lie twenty to twenty-five years in the past, but the positive and negative aftereffects of these contacts continue. This is in contrast to the situation in parts of Hungary and Rumania, where there are still substantial German elements.

Furthermore, all the nations of Eastern Europe have been confronted with German military power on two occasions during this century. During the military operations from 1915 to 1919, the Germans conducted themselves in a correct manner; their troops even appeared at times in the role of liberators: in Transylvania, for instance, after the invasion of the Rumanian army in 1916 and in Lat-

via and Estonia in 1918. Even then, Germany constituted an occupying power, which is seldom popular even when it makes efforts to
please. During the German occupations from 1939 to 1944 in World
War II the troops behaved correctly with few exceptions; but they
were followed by the civilian administration, which not only failed to
observe international law but conducted itself in a brutal and atro-
cious manner. This civilian administration was not, however, experienced by those peoples whose governments were allied with the
Third Reich: the Bulgarians, Rumanians, Hungarians, Slovaks and
part of the Croats. For these peoples, therefore, the memory of the
German occupation during World War II is associated with discom-
fort but not with lawlessness, violence, genocidal measures and reprisals, as in the case of the Czechs, Poles, Serbs and Slovenes. The experiences of the three Baltic peoples were midway between the two
extremes; in general, they experienced the German invasion of 1941,
which enabled them to reestablish their own administrations, as a
welcome event. These very different experiences with German power
during World War II were bound to result in highly differentiated
images of Germany.

Finally, many East European peoples associate their images of
Germany with memories of the German Reich and the Habsburg
Monarchy; this association is far more intensive than in Western
Europe. The Czechs, Slovaks, Croats and Slovenes, as well as many of
the Rumanians and Poles, had themselves been citizens of the Habsburg Monarchy, which in spite of all its liberality in matters of language usage and in spite of Magyar rule in the Hungarian part of the
Empire nevertheless appeared as an essentially German state. Only a
small portion of the Poles had lived within Germany proper, but the
alliance between the German Reich and the Habsburg Monarchy
was so effective that the cooperation of the two empires seemed to be
a German overlordship over Central Europe—quite apart from experiences during the two world wars. Although almost five decades
have elapsed since the overthrow of the two monarchies, the concept "German" still seems to be associated with ideas such as "suzerainty" (Herrschaft), "Kaiser" and "monarchy," even in the minds of
the generation that no longer experienced the era ending in 1914.

These three elements—immediate contact with German neighbors,
wartime occupation on two occasions and the ostentatiously mon-
archical rule of the two German states—have all played their part in
shaping the image of Germany entertained by East European peo-

ples. The specific effect is different in each case and coupled with distinctive reminiscences.

In addition to these historically determined similarities there are also major differences that are of historical origin. Among the three Baltic peoples, the Estonians and Letts experienced the Germans as a domestic ruling class until 1918 or 1919—a relationship that left behind the normal residue of prejudices. They were, however, linked with this German upper class by their common Protestant faith and their knowledge of each others' languages—even the uneducated Letts and Estonians had some command of German.

The Lithuanians, on the other hand, had experienced the Poles rather than the Germans as a ruling elite. The Germans in Lithuania differed little from their Lithuanian neighbors in social status; the separating factor in this case was the confessional difference between the Lutheran Germans and the Roman Catholic Lithuanians.

Polish-German relations cannot be classified under any common denominator insofar as social and religious differences are concerned. While it is true that the Germans were most numerous among the landowners and wealthy bourgeoisie in those parts of Poland that belonged to Prussia until 1918 or 1920, the Polish nobility exhibited no feelings of inferiority whatever. Those Germans who lived in Russian Poland constituted at best the middle class, rather than the aristocracy. While the familiar saying that the Poles were Catholics and the Germans Lutherans had a general validity, it did not apply in Upper Silesia.

Insofar as the Czechs and Slovaks were concerned, national differences from the Germans were not reinforced by class differentiation. While the nobility in Bohemia was largely German or Germanized, the Czechs and Germans otherwise confronted each other as peoples with roughly similar social structures and with no difference in religious allegiance. In Slovakia, which belonged to the Hungarian rather than the Austrian part of the Dual Monarchy, the Magyars constituted the aristocracy, while most of the Germans belonged to the middle class. There was no sharp contrast in social status, however, between Germans and Slovaks. The relation between Germans and Magyars was quite different, since the Magyars appeared as the property owning, educated and powerful elite, whereas the Germans who lived in Hungary represented the simple peasantry and lower middle class.

Were this fragmentary comparison of local conditions to be completed, it would become apparent that direct propinquity with Germans did not exercise any uniform influence on the respective East European images of Germany. Despite the common factors, there are substantial social, religious and political differentiating factors of historical origin.

As a final factor that has influenced East European images of Germany, mention should be made of the divergent cultural orientation of various countries. Three large and partially overlapping spheres of influence can be distinguished in general terms: the French, the German and the Russian. An Anglo-Saxon cultural influence did not exist for practical purposes until World War II; only since then has English been widely taught and have American films and jazz achieved their current popularity among the younger generation. The cultural influences predominant until 1939 were the French among the Poles, the Serbs and most particularly the Rumanians; the German among Estonians, Letts, Magyars and Croats; and the Russian among the Bulgarians.[6] Among the other peoples, the Czechs in particular, the clear predominance of a single cultural influence and a single foreign language could not be observed.

It is understandably a fact that images of Germany are more detailed and accurate in those areas where it has long been a tradition to acquire mastery of the German language—even outside the educated classes—and where it was customary to rely mainly on German sources in acquiring knowledge of the arts and sciences. Such an association can indeed change, and it can be changed by force, as took place when the Russian cultural influence and Russian language instruction were forcibly propagated during the Stalin era. But the traditional cultural ties have, in general, recovered from the Stalinist *Kulturkampf*. Greater freedom in the choice of languages was introduced in 1956, and (as the author observed in Prague in the spring of 1964) young people who learned no German in school are now making up the deficiency as adults. The highly differentiated relationships with German culture have, however, frequently exerted an ambivalent influence on images of Germany in the countries concerned, simultaneously lending them attractive and repulsive qualities. Members of peoples whose literary language and national awakening have their principal roots in German romanticism and German scholarship (such as the Slovaks and to various degrees the Serbs, Croats and Slovenes) are only willing to evaluate this fact positively at particular stages of their development. Sentiments of gratitude and intellectual dependence can easily be transformed into feelings of antipathy and wounded pride.[7]

In drawing conclusions from these observations and in seeking the correct evaluation of historical factors that have shaped images of Germany, it is apparent that the peoples of Southeast Europe, the Slovaks included, have less difficulty in forming a nonemotional and factual image of Germany than do the Poles or the Czechs, while the three Baltic peoples encounter the least difficulty. One of the obvious reasons for this difference in basic proclivities is the fact that although Southeast Europe no longer needs to fear the reestablishment of the Habsburg Empire, Benes kept this bogey alive in Czechoslovakia for a number of years. So far as the Baltic peoples are concerned, a restoration of the dominant social position occupied by the Baltic Germans before their resettlement in 1939 and 1941 is entirely unthinkable. There are indeed cases in which the years before 1914 are looked upon, not as the age of the Habsburg "prison of nations" or of social injustice, but as the "good old times"—especially by older Magyars or Croats.

THE GERMAN IMAGE IN PARTY PROPAGANDA

In sharp contrast to the multiplicity of attitudes toward Germany and the Germans attributable to differences in historical conditioning, the image of Germany propagated by the ruling parties is almost entirely standardized. This uniform image was crystallized in its present form about 1949 or 1950; it has been modified only in details, not in fundamentals, as a result of the events of 1956 and 1957. The communist image of Germany is little concerned with discussions of such "typical" German virtues as diligence, discipline, sense of order, organizational ability and the like or such corresponding "typical" German vices as thirst for power, ostentation, philistinism and subservience. It is, rather, a skillful composition of historical and political ingredients, in which individual experience counts for naught.

The principal features of this portrait of Germany painted by the Communist party are as follows: The Kaiser's Germany, the Weimar Republic and the Third Reich had the common misfortune of being ruled by sinister forces of monopoly capitalism, militarism and Junkerdom, which were bent on expansion, hegemony over Europe and the concealed exploitation or open subjugation of the peoples of East-Central Europe. Hitler was not an isolated phenomenon but a particularly capable tool of these forces, who bought him for their own purposes only to be partially disappointed by him later. Fundamentally, however, there was no difference between the Kaiser, Friedrich Ebert, Stresemann and Hitler. Confronting these forces of reaction, power-grabbing and brutality, Germany also had its stalwart champions of peace and democracy, personified by such Left Social Democrats as Karl Liebknecht, by the Independent Socialists and the Communists, by a few writers and by the "working masses." These, however, could only protest, since they lacked the power to act effectively. When the Third Reich came, the Communists and the working masses alone resisted national socialism—the resistance of the conservatives, the churches and the Socialists is either passed over in silence or denigrated as dishonest. Upon the founding of the German Federal Republic and the German Democratic Republic, a fundamental ideological separation of the two Germanys took place under Soviet auspices. The G.D.R. has become the place of assembly for all progressive, freedom-loving and democratic forces, which are now building the "first workers' and peasants' state in German history." This state is pacific and cooperative and a friend of all states within the Eastern bloc. The Federal Republic, on the other hand, is the tool of American dollar imperialism and Vatican anti-communism.[8] It plays host to all the forces of reaction, monopoly capitalism, high finance and national socialism, which have reunited for a new attempt to subjugate Europe. Their designs are skillfully camouflaged by noble declamations about European cooperation, the common tradition of the West and peaceful reconstruction. In reality, however, the secret forces within the Federal Republic are only waiting for their opportunity to wreak vengeance, to find an excuse for a new war, to threaten their neighbors and to plunge Europe into misery. This somber picture is, however, immediately tempered by the assurance that the Soviet Union, the G.D.R. and the "friends of peace" within the Federal Republic are so strong that any attempt of this sort would be doomed to failure at its inception.

Official propaganda amplifies this hostile and malicious image of political leadership in the Federal Republic with assorted details that are varied according to circumstances. Until 1960, for instance, the material situation of West German workers was pictured as unfavorable or even wretched, and every minor strike was blown up into a major conflict. This propaganda line has recently been toned down, partly because it is incredible and partly because it has been recognized that the Marxist theory of progressive pauperization of the masses under capitalism can no longer be seriously maintained. Attention has been shifted to the large profits of the entrepreneurs and to individual cases of social injustice, which are mostly factual but represent exceptions to the general situation.

Since the economic prosperity of the Federal Republic cannot be denied, social arguments have been pushed into the background altogether; West Germany is now pictured as the land of philistine militarism, reaction and warmongering. Great emphasis is placed on the costs of arming the *Bundeswehr;* the highways are depicted as clogged with soldiers and tanks; and the heavy expenses for the armed forces are compared with the modest appropriations for scholarships and for students. The smallest Rightist organization is magnified into a mass movement.

Since the Soviet draft peace treaty of January 10, 1959,[9] special emphasis has been given to the accusation that the Federal Republic contains numerous "revanchist and revisionist organizations" that endanger the peace. This line utilizes a particularly dangerous propaganda twist, treating revanche, that is, vengeance and retribution, as the same thing as revision; in reality they are contrary concepts. The word revision correctly used signifies an effort to change and improve a condition with peaceful methods, on the basis of negotiation and rational argument. Lenin's hateful attacks against the revisionists among the Socialists are transferred—through choice of the identical term—to all persons who consider the present state of affairs in Europe and especially in Germany unjust and would like to change it. With this verbal trick they are branded as criminals.[10]

The fact that the expellees and refugees expressly renounced vengeance and retribution in their Charter of 1950 is never mentioned in this official party image of Germany. Instead, there is a constant barrage of accusations that the spokesmen of the "revisionists and revanchists" are primarily Junkers and capitalists whose only desire is to regain their expropriated property; they are never credited with motives of ethics or legality. Special attention is always paid to trials of former National Socialists and to reports that former Nazi party members occupy influential positions in Bonn or in the *Länder.* The trials are consistently reported as though the West German public took no interest in them and as though each trial occurred only under pressure from the Eastern bloc, which had furnished the evidence.

A man such as former State Secretary Globke is pictured by communist propaganda not only as holding a position close to the pinnacle of importance in the Federal government but as having convictions resembling those of the anti-Semitic *Studienrat* Zind, who recently fled to Egypt. The situation as a whole is presented as though all public offices were filled, not only with former members of the NSDAP, but with outright war criminals, who are brought to court only in exceptional cases.

The details thus confirm the general scheme of things:[11] while large sectors of the West German population enjoy economic prosperity, they are being narcotized and possibly seduced into a new war by militarists, capitalists, revanchists, revisionists and returned Fascists.[12]

Compared with the great attention paid to the Federal Republic and West Berlin, the interest that East European propaganda takes in the "democratic part of Germany," the "first workers' and peasants' state in German history," is remarkably slight. Newspapers and magazines print the official reports concerning visits of state and major sporting events such as the Warsaw-Prague-Berlin bicycle race or the so-called Friendship Meet; but beyond this the subject of the German Democratic Republic is evidently devoid of interest. Since praise for the G.D.R. is required, but evidently accorded with reluctance, it is mentioned as little as possible.[13]

In general, the party image of Germany has very little to do with reality and is in no way adjusted to the differences mentioned in the first part of this discussion. The tendency is clear: the German Federal Republic is to be progressively denigrated and defamed as the focus of unrest in Europe, as the potential arsonist and the perpetuator of imperialist traditions. In the communist picture of German-American relations, the Federal Republic no longer appears as the misguided accomplice of "American-dollar imperialism" but rather as the dangerous ally, recklessly aspiring to seduce the United States into perilous adventures. Before Kennedy, Communists warned the Federal Republic against partnership with the United States; today the situation is reversed. By concentrating attention on the Federal Republic and on West Berlin, which is constantly attacked as a headquarters for subversive agents, a nest of espionage and a center of sabotage, communist propaganda hopes to generalize the image of a Germany that is still dangerous and of undiminished aggressiveness.

EXPERIENCE AND PROPAGANDA: CONFIRMATION OR CONTRADICTION?

The question that now occupies our attention is the degree of success such propaganda, with its overall negative tendency, can achieve among the various nations of East-Central Europe. Apart from differences in historical background, resolution of this main question poses two subsidiary questions: what propaganda-free sources of information are available to the population, and what reception is accorded party propaganda in general? We shall first attempt to answer the subsidiary questions.

In all countries of the Eastern bloc, the possibilities of obtaining printed matter and books from the West are severely limited. While certain newsstands and certain libraries in the larger cities of Poland carry English and German papers, only a small portion of the population can avail itself of these opportunities. Other communist countries do not even enjoy this very narrow opening to the West. Even in a hotel largely frequented by Western visitors in Prague during the spring of 1964, the only Western newspapers available were the *Daily Worker* and *L'Humanité,* communist publications. The situation was the same in Kronstadt (Brasov) and Hermannstadt (Sibiu) in Rumania. Even in the state-operated spa of Mamaia, which caters almost exclusively to Western guests, copies of the *Times* or *Le Monde* could be obtained only from other guests who happened to bring them. In Yugoslavia, that is, in Belgrade and Ljubljana, cities frequented by foreigners, Western newspapers are sold from time to time; but it is not simple to obtain them.

Retail trade in books has not fully died out. In practice, however, only scholarly institutes and libraries in the Eastern bloc countries can obtain books from the West, and even they must often depend upon exchanges, since foreign currencies are in too short supply.[14] A private purchaser finds substantial quantities of German, English and French literature in the large, well-stocked bookstores of the *Cizozemska Kniha* (The Foreign Book) in Prague, but most of the German books come from the Soviet Zone, while the English and French offerings are mainly reprints of such old novels as those of

Zola or Jack London, and textbooks. There are a few picture books but no current political or historical literature. Readers in the smaller cities do not even have these opportunities; they are entirely dependent on what their friends send them from abroad. Whether books mailed to Eastern bloc countries are actually delivered is always questionable.[15]

Access to impartial information through newspapers and books is thus limited to a very small stratum of the intelligentsia in Poland; the masses have no such opportunity. In Rumania hardly anybody has access to such information. The radio, which has been subjected to little interference in recent years, thus remains the most important channel for outside news. The Czech-language broadcasts of Radio Free Europe as well as the Polish broadcasts of the *Deutschlandfunk* or the *Deutsche Welle* enjoy a wide popularity, as indicated by correspondence they receive and as the author himself learned through inquiry.

Of at least equal importance is information gathered through personal observation, either during visits to Germany or through travel of Germans in the Eastern bloc states. Travel by East Europeans in Germany is of course much more valuable. Such trips were practically impossible until 1956; since then they have not been entirely out of the question, though they are very difficult to arrange. The shortage of foreign currencies constitutes a major obstacle; but even when relatives or institutions in the Federal Republic underwrite the expense, the would-be traveler often receives no permission, that is, no passport, or his passport is limited to a particular country. It is, for instance, much easier for a Pole to obtain a passport for Great Britain or Italy than for the Federal Republic. Passports in all Eastern bloc countries are not issued with general validity for all countries but are limited to one or two countries. Since travelers are required to surrender their passports upon return, the risks attendant upon violation of the regulations are very great.

Even in 1964 and 1965 there have been practically no travelers from the Eastern bloc in the Federal Republic. The number of exchange professors and students remains very small, even though it is larger than five years ago. While the author regularly welcomes one or two professors from Poland or Czechoslovakia each semester as guests of the University of Mainz, the number of students from Eastern bloc countries at German universities remains insignificant. At Mainz in 1962, the 921 foreigners included 106 Greeks and 196 Iranians; the 84 Americans constituted the third largest group. But there were only 43 students from the Eastern bloc, of whom exactly two, one Pole and one Russian, returned to their home countries. The other 41 were refugees, mostly from Hungary, who intended to stay in Germany and therefore could not influence the image of that country entertained by their compatriots.

Travel by Germans in the Eastern bloc has been possible since 1956 or 1957 but has not always been simple, because of numerous restrictions. Czechoslovakia, Hungary and Rumania relaxed their regulations considerably in 1964; the immediate result was a heavy flow of German visitors to these countries. The German travelers are generally bombarded with inquiries about conditions in the Federal Republic of Germany; they and their automobiles are continually surrounded by local citizens seeking information. The Germans on their part are astonished to learn that many Czechs and Rumanians do not consider the Federal Republic a land of unrest or aggression but rather a kind of paradise. The fact that a worker can undertake a vacation trip abroad in his own car, with his camera and good clothing, has an almost sensational effect, leading to the belief that German travelers can buy anything they want. The German has thus almost usurped the role of the American, who for the average Pole remains the apotheosis of wealth and affluence.

The transmittal of information by Germans or other West Europeans who travel in the states of the Eastern bloc can without doubt be very potent in its effect. However, many travelers neglect to take advantage of this opportunity, since their contacts are limited to official personages, hotel personnel and party functionaries, and they make no effort to converse with the man in the street. That the party leadership considers informative discussions by travelers to be potentially dangerous is indicated by the fact that for a long time a number of countries permitted travel only with a guide or official interpreter, whose function was to keep contacts between the tourist and the local population to the minimum. In recent years, however, this political concern has had to give way to the effort to attract more tourists and foreign exchange. The communist governments have to decide which takes priority: Western currency brought by tourists or protecting the public against objective information.

All things considered, the availability of information to citizens of the Eastern bloc countries is by no means as severely limited as it was in Stalin's time; it is certainly better than in the Soviet Union, where it is not even possible to receive Western broadcasts. Compared with free countries, however, the information situation in this region is still highly unsatisfactory, and only the most gradual improvement is expected in the near future. The ordinary citizen of the Eastern bloc therefore remains dependent upon the official press for much of his information.

But how much is the official press believed? This question demands different answers according to time, place and circumstances. In the so-called bygone era, that is, the Stalinist period, the mass of the population in Poland or Hungary was fundamentally inclined to consider everything that was published officially a lie; they were inclined to believe nothing or the exact opposite of the official report. Through the well-known "trickery of dialectic," communist propaganda frequently accomplished the exact opposite of what was intended—a fact made obvious by the backfiring of the massive attacks against Pope Pius XII and Chancellor Adenauer. Both enjoy the highest public esteem, especially among the Catholic population in the Eastern bloc, as a result of the propaganda directed against them. The man in the street reasons as follows: "A man attacked so violently by the Communists must indeed be their dangerous enemy and worthy of highest admiration." This absolute distrust in official statements went so far that some school children were not even willing to believe that the earth revolved around the sun, since "the teachers were forced to say this."

After the Twentieth Congress of the CPSU, open criticism and objective reports began to appear in the party press, especially in Poland and Hungary. The attitudes of readers have consequently become ambivalent; many are inclined to believe not all but *some* of the material they read, perhaps 20 or 25 per cent. Constant repetition of a statement whose truth cannot be verified has its effect after a while. Knowledge of this principle and its limitations is the reason the Communists have abandoned the practice of describing social conditions in the German Federal Republic as catastrophic. Since about 1960 there have been too many citizens of Eastern bloc states who know from personal experience that allegation of hardship and misery in the Federal Republic is not true. It is, on the other hand, practically impossible to verify whether numerous leaders of national socialism actually occupy influential positions. The individual citizen may therefore be skeptical, but he is not ready to dismiss all statements on this subject as lies.

The most effective propaganda relating to the Federal Republic is, however, the adaptation of bourgeois nationalism, which has assumed a definite function alongside communism—a fact pointed out by Eugen Lemberg at the Chicago Conference in 1962.[16] In a most interesting study applying this insight to Poland, Witold Jedlicki has gone so far as to advance the thesis "that until 1956 the Western territories [taken from Germany] were treated as an extended expression of Stalin's will, as a totally autonomous development over which no influence could be exercised. These territories were viewed with general indifference, and they evoked no passions. Not until 1956 did they acquire an emotional value. The skillfully promoted revival of anti-German attitudes that followed was a secondary phenomenon."[17]

Jedlicki has drawn attention to a highly important development: until about 1956, the communist government appeared to the individual citizen as a foreign incubus. Whatever was said about the Western nations was held to be of little importance, since hardly any distinctions were made—Poland's traditional ally France was depicted in the same somber colors as the Federal Republic. Since the adaptation of nationalism, however, the government is experienced as "communist but nevertheless our government"—a government that the public is prepared to support in foreign policy.

Insofar as images of Germany are concerned, the significance of this development is that there is a receptivity for negative propaganda among those peoples that passed through a series of unfortunate experiences with the Germans in recent times and that also feel widespread anxiety lest the German expellees assert their rights to the land and property from which they were expelled. Both conditions are exemplified by the Poles and the Czechs, apply far less to the Serbs and Hungarians and hardly at all to the Slovaks, Rumanians and Baltic peoples. In order to intensify this negative image, Polish and Czech propagandists make every effort to keep alive memories of the war and the occupation, which are frequently recalled without communist overtones.

As a further propaganda device in connection with the millenial anniversary of the Polish state being celebrated from 1960 to 1966, attention is called to all dates associated with German-Polish enmity. Nationalist sentiments were rampant when the five-hundred-fiftieth anniversary of the Battle of Tannenberg (known as Grundwald in Poland) was celebrated during the summer of 1960.[18] The elaborate and artistically excellent film *The Crusaders,* with its heavily nationalist and openly anti-German accents, was shown at the celebration and had more effect than a thousand newspaper articles. Its message is that the Germans always were and still are the brutal enemies of Poland. It is no longer the capitalists in the Federal Republic but rather the "revisionists" and "nationalists" who are attacked nowadays as particularly dangerous and reprehensible. There is a certain grotesqueness in the fact that none other than the Krupp Company —which symbolized the evil power of monopoly capital in earlier communist propaganda—now enjoys great prestige in Poland, while German Social Democrats are being denigrated as chauvinists and revanchists.[19]

The consolidation of this image of Germany as the eternal enemy, by now practically divorced from communist ideology and placed in a purely nationalist historical setting, is receiving effective assistance from outside the Eastern bloc, particularly insofar as Poland and Czechoslovakia are concerned. During the Polish emigration, propaganda along this line was spread by the magazine *Pologne-Allemagne*, published in Paris by the well-known former National Democrat Zdziechowski. Although this publication was obviously well financed, it was discontinued in 1964. A smaller publication in London, the *Oblicze Tygodnia ("Picture of the Week")*, is often easily recognizable as crypto-communistic. These magazines are, of course, imported into Poland, where they are regarded as "free" voices and make a much greater impression than the party press.

The Italian films of pronounced anti-German tendency exhibited within the Eastern bloc are even more effective, since they are accepted as representing "neutral" opinions. A similar result is achieved when the party newspapers are able to print regular quotations from the *Daily Express* or the *Daily Mirror* containing dire warnings against the Federal Republic and negative characterizations of German political forces. The somewhat primitive veneration of everything "foreign" in many Eastern bloc countries—provided it doesn't come from Russia or Germany—does not fail in its effect.

At this point, however, the success of this communist version of nationalism is jeopardized by a renewed "trickery of dialectic," and the partition of Germany becomes a blind alley for national-communist propaganda. Even before 1956 it was very difficult to explain to the simple but logically thinking citizen of Poland or Hungary that one Germany was "good" and progressive, the other "bad," reactionary and hostile. This *tour de force* was possible as long as the world was neatly divided into the "socialist camp" and the "capitalist camp"; everything negative was associated with capitalism, Wall Street and allies of the Americans and everything positive with socialism, the Kremlin and the allies of the Soviet Union. This may have been primitive, but it was at least logical. However, now that the Federal Republic has become the central target for attack—not because it is capitalistic but because it represents the continuation of the German Reich and because German history is supposed to reveal a perpetual imperialist drive, a *Drang nach Osten*[20]—it is not easy to explain to the man in the street that only the Germans on the Rhine and the Isar, but not those on the Elbe or the Baltic, are dangerous. The sword of historical nationalism that has been raised against the Federal Republic thus proves to be a two-edged weapon. It must logically hit the G.D.R. as well, especially since the latter has for many years taken a positive view of numerous events in German history, e.g., the wars against Napoleon, and is in many respects, for instance in the uniform and discipline of the "People's Army," far more Prussian than the Federal Republic and the *Bundeswehr*.

This difficulty is compounded by a second dialectical problem. When the negative image of the Federal Republic is composed essentially of national elements, when "revanchism and revisionism" are pictured as the principal dangers of our age and when the Federal Republic is labeled "Public Enemy No. 1" because of its efforts toward peaceful reunification and its non-recognition of the Oder-Neisse line, the result is necessarily a magnification of the already mentioned historical differences among the East-Central European peoples. Poles and Czechs are naturally sensitive to the specter of German revisionism made more vivid by renewed recollection of the war and occupation. But what have the Letts, Magyars or the Rumanians to fear from German revisionism? Their reaction can at most be one of indifference, and the films shown in Prague that cleverly associate the memory of the invasion of March 15, 1939, with a motorized column of the postwar *Bundeswehr* meet with no understanding whatever in Budapest or Bucharest. It is no secret that the Rumanian Communists have refused to permit the showing of Czech films that include highly negative representations of German soldiers designed to create an immediate association with the *Bundeswehr*. They have justified their refusal by pointing out that the Rumanian peasant retains a positive memory of the German soldier and that the effect of the film would be the reverse of that intended: it would merely demonstrate the mendacity of communist propaganda.

In undertaking to use national emotions rather than the ideology of class warfare as a matrix for forming attitudes toward the German Federal Republic, communist propaganda has fallen into an obvious dilemma. In Poland at least moderate success can be achieved with mass reprints of highly nationalist nineteenth century novels, which serve to provide a historic basis for the contemporary negative image of Germany and to keep alive the legend of eternal enmity.[21] In other countries of East-Central Europe, such as the Czech lands or Latvia, an association of this kind is possible but more difficult. Among many of the other peoples it is entirely impossible, since their nationalism has involved little or no conflict with the Germans.

CONCLUDING SUMMARY

The foregoing observations may be summed up in a general way as follows:

Despite all the efforts of party propagandists, the contemporary image of Germany in East-Central Europe is not uniform but is very strongly influenced by variant historical backgrounds. The fact of the division of Germany (which is considered in subsequent parts of this book) is a matter of universal knowledge, although ideas about the Berlin wall tend to be confused. The Federal Republic is recognized as the authoritative representative of Germany, the object of sympathy and the only government of importance—often to such an extent that officials of the G.D.R. are given unfriendly treatment. The economic recovery of West Germany evokes general respect and admiration, occasionally mixed with envy or apprehension. In many cases, the economic potency of the Federal Republic is actually exaggerated.

The totally negative image of the Federal Republic spread by party propaganda, compared with which the positive image of the G.D.R. seems lifeless, meets with only limited credence. Its effects in certain countries, however, should not be underestimated. In many places the shadows of the past are still very dark. Their effect is often intensified through, among other things, the Germans' condescending ignorance of affairs within the Eastern bloc and the Allies' thoughtless approach, illustrated by the London tabloid press and the Italian film industry. In general, however, the citizens of East-Central Europe are fascinated by what they have heard about the Federal Republic. Reports that seek to present an objective picture, such as that of the Catholic journalist Kisielewski during the summer of 1962,[22] are greeted with the warmest interest and are violently attacked by the party functionaries.[23]

There is no doubt that numerous members of the East-Central European peoples manifest great confidence in the economic and political abilities and prospects of the Germans. This confidence is combined, however, with a certain uneasiness and in many cases with outright fear. It is up to the Germans to improve the confidence and assuage the worries; their success in doing so depends in part upon the actions of their West European allies and the United States.

NOTES TO CHAPTER FIVE

1. Louis-Henri Parias, "Franco-German Reconciliation and European Unity," in *Western Integration and the Future of Eastern Europe,* ed. David S. Collier and Kurt Glaser (Chicago: Henry Regnery Company, 1964), pp. 162-74.

2. *See* the regular reports in the *Internationales Jahrbuch für Geschichtsunterricht* (Brunswick), as well as the publications of the International School Book Institute of Brunswick.

3. *Westintegration und Osteuropa,* ed. Alfred Domes (Cologne: 1965), pp. 236-37.

4. For literature of this kind, *see* S. W. Kozlowski, "Das Bild vom Deutschen im polnischen Schrifttum," in *Schuld und Verheissung deutsch-polnischer Nachbarschaft* (Ulm: 1958), pp. 27-47; G. Rhode, "Das Bild vom Deutschen im polnischen Roman des 19. und beginnenden 20, Jahrhunderts," in *Ostdeutsche Wissenschaft,* VIII (1961), 327-66; and F. Durčanský, "Das Deutschland- und Russlandbild in der Tschechoslowakei," S. Kudlicki, "Das Deutschlandbild der Polen," and J. Bracz, "Das Deutschlandbild und das Russlandbild der baltischen Nationen," in *Die Barsinghausener Gespräche,* Nos. 11-14 (Leer/Friesland: 1963), 308-71.

5. K. Lück, *Der Mythos vom Deutschen in der polnischen Volksüberlieferung und Literatur* (Poznan: 1938; 2nd ed. Leipzig: 1943).

6. On the French cultural influence during the nineteenth century, *see* E. Birke, *Frankreich und Ostmitteleuropa im 19. Jahrhundert* (Cologne/Graz: 1960).

7. On this point, *see* F. Valjavec, "Die Völker Südosteuropas und die Deutschen," in *Ausgewählte Aufsätze* (Munich: 1963), pp. 116-28, and also in *Ostdeutsche Wissenschaft,* V (1958), 35-49.

8. These attacks against the United States and the Vatican were very much played down after 1956, but a cautious revival of them has recently been noted.

9. Article 20 of this treaty demands the prohibition of "every form of revanchist manifestation calling for revision of the boundaries of Germany."

10. *See* M. H. Boehm, "Revisionismus—Ein Verbrechen?" in *Ostbrief,* V (1959), No. 6 (42), pp. 247-50. Concerning the varied meanings of the term, see *Revisionism: Essays on the History of Marxist Ideas,* ed. L. Labedz (London: 1962).

11. This image is drawn very skillfully by the Bonn correspondent of the Warsaw party organ, *Trybuna Ludu* ("People's Tribune"), Marian Podkowinski, in his pamphlet *Czy zegary NRF-chodza Szybciej?* ("Do Clocks Run Faster in the German Federal Republic?") (Warsaw: 1959).

12. The expression "National Socialists" is, significantly, never used. Instead, the term "Fascist" is employed, often as a collective epithet for non-communist political movements.

13. A telling account of the difficulties encountered in setting off a bright image of the German Democratic Republic from a somber picture of the Federal Republic is given by Joachim G. Goerlich, "Kommunistische Freundschaft an der Oder und Neisse," in *Osteuropa*, XIV (1964), 724-28.

14. E. Turczynski, "Die deutsch-rumänischen Kulturbeziehungen," in *Sudosteuropa-Jahrbuch*, IV (1960), 124-38.

15. The Polish magazine *Kultura*, published in Paris, regularly sends several hundred copies to addresses in Poland. Only a part of these reach the addressees, since the magazines are often stolen in the mails and sold on the "black market."

16. Eugen Lemberg, "Eastern Europe: a Battleground of Contemporary Ideologies," in *Berlin and the Future of Eastern Europe, op. cit.*

17. "Narodowy liberalizm" ("National Liberalism"), in *Kultura* (Paris), 1963, No. 5, (187), 1963, pp. 9-33. Quotation is from p. 23.

18. G. Rhode, "Gomulka und die Geschichte Polens," in *Aussenpolitik*, XI (1960), 506-15.

19. For a comprehensive study of the phenomenon of an alliance between communism and nationalism in Poland and its influence on the emigration, *see* Jozef Mackiewicz, "The Victorious Provocation." To be published.

20. The Czechoslovak-Soviet treaty of alliance of December 12, 1943, explicitly provides that the alliance is directed against this *Drang nach Osten*, the words appearing in German in both texts. The contemporary revival of much of the terminology of war propaganda is significant.

21. *See* G. Rhode, "Das Bild des Deutschen im polnischen Roman des 19. und 20. Jahrhunderts und das polnische Nationalgefühl," in *Ostdeutsche Wissenschaft*, VIII (1960), 327-66. It is unfortunate that a Polish novelist presenting a highly negative image of Germany, J. I. Kraszewski (d. 1887), whose books are permanent best-sellers in Poland, is also a favorite of the Polish emigration. *See* K. Mochenska and Z. Wilczynska, "O czytelnictwie na emigracji" ("What the Emigration Reads") in *Kultura*. Nos. 201-202, 1964, pp. 216-25. Library circulation of Kraszewski is three times that of the most successful modern Polish writers!

22. This report appeared under the title "West European Fortress" in *Tygodni Powszechny*, Nos. 23-25, 1962. This weekly newspaper is considered close to Cardinal Wyszynski.

23. A whole year later, in his speech at the thirteenth plenum of the party Central Committee, on July 6, 1963, Party Chairman Gomulka attacked this report, since it did not correspond to the image approved by the party.

CHAPTER VI

The German Image of East European Peoples

EUGENE LEMBERG

Conceptions peoples form of each other are, whether true or false, of critical importance in the mutual relations between these peoples, especially with respect to their friendship or enmity. These conceptions may even be the decisive factor for war or peace. Such images can be influenced by propaganda to a certain degree. There are well-known cases in which a nation's disliking for another has been aggravated to such an intensity by deliberate propaganda that war could no longer be avoided. The opposite is also possible: there are instances in which favorable propaganda has converted traditional enemies into allies and friends.

But the historical record contains as many or even more episodes that indicate that the field of action for propaganda of this type is narrowly limited. We know that individual behavior is governed by definite laws that are often inscrutable in their operation and are subjects of investigation for psychology and psychoanalysis. In similar fashion, the behavior of peoples in their mutual relations is determined by specific laws that are almost beyond the reach of rational measures. Despite all the accomplishments of cultural anthropology, which has studied the working of these laws among primitive peoples, our knowledge of image-formation and interethnic behavior among the nations of high cultures is by no means as complete as our understanding of individual psychology and behavior. An analysis of the image Germans have formed of their East-Central European neighbors may serve to identify those factors that—often without the knowledge of the peoples concerned—determine this image and the behavior resulting from it. An awareness of these factors will inhibit the common tendency to pass rapid-fire moral judgments. It will make clear all the ramifications of the problem that must be considered if the image one people entertains of another is to be corrected and freed of antagonism.

The image the Germans have of their eastern neighbors—the Poles, Czechs, Slovaks, Magyars, Serbs, Croats and others—is based in the first instance on geographical and historical circumstances that none of these peoples can change. These have nothing to do with what is commonly called national character. National idiosyncrasies lend themselves easily to journalistic exploitation, but they are hard to demonstrate in an objective manner. There is no exact science of national character. The areas of settlement of the various peoples in East-Central Europe are, furthermore, so interlocked, and the ethnic and linguistic boundaries have shifted so frequently, that it is impossible to draw a clear line of demarcation between one national character and another. The Sudeten Germans and the Czechs, for instance, have much more in common than do two dissimilar German tribes, such as the Bavarians and the Lower Saxons. There are, however, other factors more susceptible of exact determination and definition.

THE EASTWARD MOVEMENT OF THE INDUSTRIAL REVOLUTION

A fact of primary importance is the west-to-east movement apparent in the history of the Industrial Revolution and of the development of modern urbanized societies in Europe. Since the Renaissance, that is, since the beginnings of modern natural science and technology, the West European nations have always moved ahead of those in Central and Eastern Europe. It is hard to imagine that the Spaniards were once accepted as masters and preceptors for all Europe—not only in architecture and court etiquette but also in poetry, philosophy and the teaching of constitutional and international law. By the eighteenth century the French had assumed the center of the stage—not only in styles of clothing but also in language and literature, military technology and social philosophy. The Germans played an analogous role with regard to Eastern Europe during the nineteenth century.

This differential timing of phases in the development of modern

European nations gave the westernmost nation in each case a feeling of superiority over those to the east. Thus, seventeenth-century Europe was unanimous in resenting the haughtiness of the Spaniards. During the eighteenth and nineteenth centuries not only the Napoleonic overlordship but also the self-confident behavior of the French contributed significant impulses to the awakening of German national consciousness. The Germans had the same effect on their eastern neighbors: they were regarded as arrogant and presumptuous, as masters and oppressors.

But in the process of awakening, each individual nation saw only its own situation. Each resented what it felt to be the arrogance of its western neighbor, and each sought to convince that neighbor of its own worth and cultural accomplishments. Had these countries turned from their passionate concern with themselves to international comparisons, they would have seen that what was involved was not a distinctive characteristic of the neighboring people—as the apparent arrogance of Germans toward their eastern neighbors seemed to indicate—but rather a reflex of the aforementioned differentiation of phases in the development of European nations. This succession of phases in the Industrial Revolution and in the development of peoples into modern nations imposed on the westerly people in each encounter a specific role in its dealings with the people to its east. In every case, the more westerly of the two peoples concerned found itself looking down upon its eastern neighbor with feelings of superiority and disdain, often mixed with an attitude of indulgence and benevolence. Both attitudes, disdain and benevolence, naturally evoked the same bitter reaction against the western neighbors, the same inferiority complex and, as an inevitable consequence, the same compensation and overcompensation.

Much would be gained if the peoples involved could learn through this kind of international comparison that the low esteem in which western peoples hold their easterly neighbors in no way indicates depravity of character on the part of the western people but is, rather, the natural result of a process that has extended throughout Europe. They would then see that they themselves are as much subject to this process as the supposedly evil neighbor on their western borders. It is common knowledge that the Czechs, the Poles and the Yugoslavs today show a contempt for the Russians similar to that they believe the Germans feel for them. This phenomenon may be observed despite, or perhaps because of, the political suzerainty the Russians today exercise over these East-Central European peoples.

Another characteristic of this succession of phases is the fact that of any two neighboring European peoples the more westerly shows little interest for the people to its east, knows little about it and hence shows little understanding for its problems. It is true that German philosophy set the tone throughout Europe during the early nineteenth century, in Western Europe as well as elsewhere. But at the same time, the West European peoples, the English and French, knew little of the Germans. Even today they entertain what Germans consider a belittling and false opinion of Germany. The same is true of the Germans' relations to their eastern neighbors. In German politics and society, these peoples of Eastern Europe were regarded as a *quantité negligeable*. Even German scholarship let itself be guided by the maxim *slavica non leguntur* (Slavic is not worth reading). Educated persons in Germany have always been and still are expected to be proficient in at least one Western language—English or French. But a person is never considered uneducated because of his lack of knowledge of a Slavic language. Since the Germans, in contrast to other peoples, think it very important to speak foreign languages, if not without accent at least according to their phonetic rules, it is all the more obvious when they mispronounce East European names and expressions without feeling embarrassed about it.

Such behavior naturally strikes the peoples affected as offensive German arrogance. They forget that the Germans in turn suffer from the certainty that they are practically unknown to and grossly misunderstood by Frenchmen, Britons and Americans. If the Germans still persist in showing a deficient interest in their eastern neighbors and if their knowledge of East-Central Europe—even more than of Russia—is somewhat faulty, these conditions should be recognized as phenomena common to Europe as a whole. Their causes must be seen in the movement from west to east that characterized the Industrial Revolution and the awakening of peoples throughout modern history.

An additional relevant fact is that the image one people forms of another is largely determined by the personal experiences of its major population groups in their contacts with the other people. It is immaterial that the East European peoples have achieved a superlative level in culture and art, poetry and music, as represented by Mickiewicz, Chopin, Smetana and Dvorak, and that they possess such magnificent interpreters of national personality as Tchaikovsky, Tolstoy and Dostoyevsky. The broad masses of the Germans, who determine national consciousness, came to know the East Europeans during the nineteenth century as cheap labor, as workers who played the same essential role that today falls to the so-called guest workers from Italy, Spain and Greece. The experience of West European peoples was to a certain extent the same.

The East Europeans came to Eastern Germany as seasonal farm workers; in the Ruhr, in Belgium and in northern France they appeared as industrial laborers. As a consequence, the German middle classes gained the impression that the Poles, Czechs and Slovaks as a whole were primitive peoples, capable of achieving higher learning in exceptional cases only. They assumed that the national characteristics of these peoples destined them to fill subordinate roles in society. In those areas where these peoples constituted national minorities or lower-class groups—as in Austria, Upper Silesia, in parts of Prussia and in the Baltic countries—this role of a subordinate stratum, that of the servant, of the skillful and obliging but servile artisan, seemed dictated for them by providence. Polish and Hungarian magnates were exceptions; these noblemen used the German language, however, in their intercourse with Germans and seemed to many to belong to a German cultural community. The prevailing attitude was by no means anti-Slavic: it was fashionable to admire the so-called gypsy music, which was considered a Hungarian specialty; and Polish mazurkas and Slovak peasant costumes were a source of delight. All these, however, were appreciated as the folklore of simple, unspoiled peoples—just as the nobility of the Rococo age took pleasure in bucolic peasant scenes. Admiration and respect for Chopin and Smetana were mixed with amazement at the high artistic accomplishment of international caliber of which such charmingly primitive peoples were capable.

This attitude is likewise no reflection of specific German national characteristics—even though Europeans generally have that impression—but rather a result of the experience of those strata of the population that determine public opinion. It is the reaction to a casting of roles that was valid for a particular era, and only for that era. This assignment of roles is long since obsolete, but it has echoed for generations in the clichés and stereotypes imagined by the peoples concerned. In the United States analogous notions concerning immigrants from Eastern and Southeast Europe—those of the so-called second immigration, after 1890—were long current and are still observable here and there. The stereotyped image of the beer-drinking and sauerkraut-eating German shows a similar persistence among

West European nations. Today, however, the Germans and the Swiss are in danger of judging the Italians, Spanish, Greeks and Turks according to the images suggested by "guest workers" from these countries.

THE FEAR OF PRIMITIVE VITALITY

The image of simpler, more natural peoples in the East also has its darker side. Ever since Rousseau this image has been accompanied by fear of the greater vitality of these peoples and of the danger their higher birth rates, their purposeful behavior and their solidarity represent for the established nations. Just as the ancient Romans feared the Teutons, so did their descendants of the nineteenth and twentieth centuries fear the Slavs. Beginning with the awakening of the East-Central European peoples during the nineteenth century, a process that is the reverse of the eastward settlement of Germans in the Middle Ages and the Baroque era has taken place: where German peasants had cleared the forests and laid out villages in earlier centuries, and German townsmen had developed handicrafts and founded mines and cities, German cities and villages were now infiltrated by Slavic agricultural and industrial workers. Czechs and Poles in these areas rose to better positions in society; they achieved majorities in these cities and in the provincial legislatures, and they forced the granting of equal rights for their languages, school systems and cultural institutions. The time was in sight when they would also assume political power, outmaneuvering the positions of the Germans in politics, business and society in the process—a development that actually took place at the end of World War I.

As this population development became clearly discernible after about 1850, the German reaction was one of panic and fright, especially in the eastern territories. Most of the nationalist and imperialist utterances heard from Germans during the latter half of the nineteenth century had their source in this anxiety. The Prussian-Polish policy of this time was fundamentally a counterattack against the Polish population element, which, after proving surprisingly able to hold its own, began pushing forward in almost all sectors. The radical nationalism of Georg von Schönerer in Austria sprang from fear that the Slavs in the Habsburg Monarchy, which had been defeated by Prussia in 1866 and which no longer had the backing of the German Federation, would achieve a majority and transform the monarchy into a Slavic state. In propagating this attitude, Schönerer became one of Adolph Hitler's teachers.

The psychological explanation for Hitler's passionate hatred of the Slavs and his plan for military subjugation of these peoples is at bottom one of anxiety provoked by the menace of Slavic vitality, a reaction that might be described as a "Schönerer complex." It must be frankly admitted that an element of this German trauma has been perpetuated in present-day German fear of the communist power behind the Iron Curtain. A circumstance mitigating general misfortune is, therefore, to be recognized in the fact that important groups from among the East-Central European peoples were expelled westward with the East Germans across the Iron Curtain or else forced to emigrate. As a result, the friction of languages and nationalities has been replaced by a conflict of ideologies: by the struggle between totalitarianism and democracy. This development opens the possibility that the tensions that persist in East-Central Europe will no longer be experienced as antagonism among languages, peoples and races, but rather as a conflict of ideologies and systems of government. The enmity between peoples that dates from the Risorgimento may, therefore, give way to a normalization of relations or even to friendly association.

The Influence of German Historiography

The German image of East European peoples includes additional features derived from the history of European culture and of the European mind. The conception of the world and of its history, taken for granted by educated people in Germany and taught in its schools until today, was originated during the nineteenth century in the epoch of classical German historiography. In those days important historians such as Ranke, Niebuhr, Mommsen and Treitschke formed this conception, utilizing ideas of Goethe's day and of the Romantic era, but also drawing inspiration from the spirit of German nationalism, from German aspiration to the state that Bismarck finally realized in 1871. Many features of the German conception of history are thus to be explained as reflections of the situation that existed during a past epoch, an epoch decisive in the formation of modern German political thought. These features correspond to the image of the world then perceived by Germans but also to a large extent by Europeans generally. The Germans are not much more backward in this respect than other European nations.

Only men of unusual foresight, such as Herder and De Tocqueville, had at that time already recognized the indications that Russia would one day achieve a position of world power. This was a time when most of the East-Central European peoples, such as the Poles, the Baltic nations, the Czechs, the Slovaks and the Croats, possessed no states of their own. The United States was also but part way in its national development. The conception of history embraced at that time by Germans, as well as by West Europeans generally, was thus essentially limited to the Germanic-Romanic family of peoples. Thus circumscribed, world history began with the ancient Babylonians and Egyptians, reached a climax in ancient Greece and described the development of the Roman universal empire, the medieval successor of which was Catholic Christianity in Western and Central Europe. For Western Christendom, what is today East-Central Europe constituted an area for missions and colonization analogous to the western frontier for nineteenth-century Americans. For the Germans, this history reached its culmination with the establishment of the German national state in 1871, an event many regarded as the final goal of history. Those Germans who accepted this interpretation could only regard the awakening of the peoples in East-Central Europe, their achievement of their own national states and the emergence of Russian world power following the bolshevist revolution as steps downward from this pinnacle, as dangers and defeats. German historical consciousness has not yet learned to live with these facts.

Events in Central and Eastern Europe since the end of the nineteenth century provoked emotional disturbances among the Germans; such events would have affected the psychology of any people. The peoples of East-Central Europe, who only extricated themselves from German overlordship with considerable difficulties and who saw the Germans only as powerful, haughty and condescending masters, have no conception whatever of the way the Germans experienced the situation. Only recently a Czech historian from Prague explained to this author the tremendous advantages enjoyed by the Sudeten Germans as compared with the Czechs during the nineteenth century. With Bismarck's mighty Reich to secure their rear and with the protection of the Habsburg Dynasty in their own country, these Germans, according to this historian, occupied a position vastly superior to that of the Czechs, who had been frustrated by the Hungarian equalization of 1867 and were forced to depend on their own resources. He was greatly surprised when informed of the frustrations that the Sudeten Germans also had to suffer: Bismarck had sacrificed them and found their German nationalism a nuisance; Vienna, they felt, had written them off and abandoned them to the other nationalities. They saw the disintegration of Austria looming in the distance and with it the loss of their own freedom moving inexorably toward them. This conversation illustrates how much still has to be done before the peoples of Central and East-Central Europe learn to look occasionally at the world around them from the point of view and in terms of the experience of their neighbor peoples.

A second difficulty that hampers the Germans in achieving a realistic understanding of their eastern neighbors lies in the widespread habit of treating history as a history of states rather than of peoples. This is what can be called a statist conception of history. Influenced by the struggle to create a German national state as well as by the philosophy of Hegel, classical nineteenth-century German historiography concerned itself with the history of states, not of peoples. As Hegel defined things, a people did not really have a history until it had founded a national state. It was, however, precisely the peoples of East-Central Europe—those who lived partly in Germany and in Austria-Hungary during the nineteenth century and who are today neighbors of the Germans—who had no national states of their own during this decisive epoch. A mere history of states cannot do justice to these peoples, their problems, their character and their Risorgimento.

The nations of Eastern Europe thus enter the purview of German historical consciousness at the moment when Russia, molded by Peter the Great into a state of West European type, enters the concert of European powers. Nothing is said about the long-drawn-out development of the distinctive forces of Russian national life during centuries of East European history. No attention is paid to the effects of a thousand-year-long destiny that was entirely different from that of the Western world, with no scholastic philosophy, with neither a Renaissance nor a Reformation and lacking the universal experience of the Enlightenment—which touched only the thinnest upper crust in Russia. No consideration is given the fact that Eastern Europe failed to experience the dualism of the Emperor and the Pope, of state and church—a fact of transcendent importance in the development of Western concepts of citizenship and the state.

In contrast to the peoples of orthodox Russia, the peoples of East-Central Europe had experienced the same Western history as the Germans, from the Roman Church through the Reformation and Counterreformation to the Enlightenment and Romanticism. Their relevance to German historical consciousness with its statist premise does not begin, however, until they enter upon the stage of politics and proceed to cause what supporters of the status quo of the nineteenth-century state system necessarily considered disturbances. Pupils in German schools would, consequently, have heard nothing of the Poles had it not been for the partitions of their country. During the nineteenth century the Poles appear briefly as the revolutionaries of 1830 and 1863. They then resume invisibility until 1918, the year in which the Polish state was reestablished. The fact that the Poles survived as a nation during the intervening period, that they experienced their national awakening during this time, that they managed to remain conscious of their national unity throughout 120 years without a state of their own and that this awareness of unity was transmitted by a small elite to the broad masses of the people— all matters that must be of the highest interest to Germans today— are subjects investigated and described by individual historical specialists, but in no way do they form part of the common stock of knowledge, even of a limited group of intellectual leaders.

The Magyars, including the other nationalities of Hungary they were able to assimilate, constituted a *Staatsvolk** when they first confronted the Habsburgs and remained so throughout their subsequent history. German historiography was favorably disposed toward the Magyars as the allies of Prussia in 1866, a sympathy that continued long after World War I. However, this German enthusiasm for the *Staatsvolk* of St. Stephen's Crown served as an obstacle to proper comprehension of the nationalities problem, which proved to be the downfall of prewar Hungary and which is basic to understanding the peoples of the Carpathian region.

As a further result of this remarkable statism that distorts the Ger-

---

*Literally "state people." The term *Staatsvolk*, for which there is significantly no English translation, designates a nationality or coalition of nationalities that founds and reserves for itself a preferred position in a national state, other ethnic groups being relegated to inferior "minority" status.—*Eds.*

man conception of history, the Czechs are encountered for the first time in connection with the peace negotiations of Versailles and the establishment of the Czechoslovak state in 1918 and 1919. The process of national awakening, the renaissance of the Czech language during the nineteenth century and the roots of this renaissance in the German Enlightenment and German Romanticism—which together laid the essential foundations for the establishment of Czechoslovakia—remain subjects of specialized scholarship. Insofar as popular knowledge of these matters exists, it is limited to the Sudeten Germans, who were forced to bear the brunt of the resulting historical events.

THE GERMAN EXPELLEES AS BRIDGE BUILDERS

The image the Germans have formed of their eastern neighbors is thus prejudiced by a number of geographical and historical factors that still have their aftereffects today, even though the emancipation and political organization of these peoples and their demarcation in national states have been completed and the Risorgimento nationalism that characterizes such processes has become obsolete. This bias was, however, aggravated by the disastrous policies of the national socialist regime and the genocidal role it played in this region, as well as by the expulsion of Germans at the end of World War II.

It would be no cause for astonishment had these events and the national hatreds they aroused destroyed the nations' images of one another beyond repair. The older generations of East Germans—those who bore the direct impact of the expulsions—have indeed been left with a bitterness that prevents them from visualizing the peoples that expelled them except as a ferocious and rapacious horde of barbarians—the same way in which these peoples themselves learned to view the National Socialists and, in their image, the Germans as a whole.

But a remarkable thing has happened: the expelled East Germans have today become interpreters of the East-Central European peoples among the West Germans. This assertion is to be understood *cum grano salis,* and there are many facts that seem to contradict it. The foreigner traveling through the Federal Republic who judges the Germans according to the newspapers receives another impression at first. He reads of protests by the expellees' associations against the establishment of trade delegations and diplomatic missions of the

Federal Republic in East European capitals. Having in mind the rights to homeland and to self-determination proclaimed at expellee congresses, he interprets such protests as a cry for vengeance. He may thus possibly reach the conclusion that the West Germans themselves would be only too glad to establish good relations with the Poles and the Czechs, to maintain close contact with them and to revel in the art and literature of the Poles, Czechs and Magyars and that it is only the expellees and their associations that hamper and obstruct these good relations.

The actual situation, however, is almost the opposite. In the first place, the expellees—including some from the Reich German areas east of the Oder-Neisse line but more particularly those from the areas beyond the former boundaries of the Reich, from the Baltic countries, from Poland and from former Austria-Hungary—have, despite the nationality struggles of the past, a far more intimate knowledge of the languages, national character, history and problems of their neighbor peoples. Among the Germans it is precisely they who have occupied themselves as scholars with the problems and cultures of these peoples. The areas from which they were expelled possessed the only professorial chairs and research institutes (except for those in Berlin, Leipzig and Munich) in the fields of Slavic languages and East European history, economics and humanities. During the fifties, most of these institutions were reestablished with great effort and sacrifice at West German universities—in almost all cases at the initiative and with the guidance and collaboration of expellee scholars. That the schools have also introduced East European studies— though with great hesitation and with major reservations—is also a result of the enthusiasm and specialized knowledge of expelled East Germans. The inflexibility of the school system, which is decentralized among the eleven states in the Federal Republic, has unfortunately prevented mobilization of the language skills of many East German teachers for the training of young Germans in the Polish and Czech languages and, initially, the Russian language as well. Those in Germany today with a command of these languages are most likely to be eastern expellees or their children. Germans expelled from the East frequently undertake translations of East-Central European literature. Whenever Czech or Polish artists or scholars come to West Germany to lecture or to study, they find immediate and intimate contact with precisely those Germans who come from their own homeland. These Germans enjoy a conversation in Czech or Polish or an exchange of views on the situation in East-Central Europe with a touch of sentimental nostalgia. Contacts of this kind are most successful when the discussion does not begin with the Oder-Neisse line or the details of the expulsion.

It is therefore a biased judgment when Germans of the Federal Republic who have grown up in the West accuse the expellees from the East of blocking a normalization of relations between the Germans and their eastern neighbor peoples. The complaints of these expellees against the East are—except in the case of the incorrigibles, which every society contains—directed, not against the peoples of East-Central Europe, but against the power that rules them much against their will: the communist system. The experiences of the expellees from the East at the end of World War II have left them with a far better sense of discrimination than that of those West Germans who, having developed their tradition within their own national state, are unable to distinguish between a state and a people. Persons of such limited experience are likely to assume, incorrectly, that by uncritically accepting the propaganda theses of the communist regime in question, they are overcoming national antagonisms.

NATIONALISM AND THE IDEOLOGICAL STRUGGLE

Despite all the differences among various groups in the Federal Republic, it may be stated without exaggeration that the desire of the Germans to bury their national conflicts with their East-Central European neighbor peoples and to familiarize themselves with the life and problems, art and literature of these peoples was never so strong as it is today, particularly among the younger generation. This fact is demonstrated, not only by the unusual interest taken in discussion with members of these peoples, whether living as emigrés or behind the Iron Curtain, but also in theatrical performances and concerts and in radio and television broadcasts concerning these countries and their peoples. It is also confirmed by such a commonplace phenomenon as the stream of German tourists that pours into these countries upon the slightest relaxation of the restrictions on border traffic. Travel to Yugoslavia has been taking place for some years; Germans are now visiting Czechoslovakia and Hungary. One almost gains the impression that the Germans are afflicted with a tragic love for their eastern neighbor peoples; for these peoples find it hardest to overcome the trauma that the Hitler regime inflicted on them. Nor have they moved as far away from the nationalism of the Risorgimento as the Germans. Finally, the communist regime takes care to preserve the old nationalism so that the peoples of East-Central Europe will remain steadfast in the belief that they need Soviet protection against German revanchism. It is all the more important for the Germans not to overlook the transformation taking place underneath the surface in the life of the East European peoples: emancipation from the ideological tutelage of the Soviet Union and intense desire to overcome the provincialism in which communist cultural policy holds them prisoner, as well as the desire to enter into contact with the West and with the Germans in particular.

However desirable and necessary this transformation of the relationship between Germans and East-Central Europeans may be, the following *caveat* must be registered: with the shifting of the conflict from the national to the ideological field, the problem has assumed a new perspective but has not been solved. Now, as heretofore, the danger exists that the Germans will form a falsified image of the East European peoples, if no longer from antipathy toward their language and culture then from revulsion against communism. Just as the earlier period of the Risorgimento witnessed a widespread tendency to picture the other people as a single entity, as a kind of individual with a uniform national character and a common opinion, so do West Germans today show a propensity to visualize communism in East-Central Europe as a monolithic bloc. Many believe that by so picturing it, they are making a particularly valuable contribution to the struggle against communism. To recognize various shadings and nuances among one's enemies, many people feel, amounts to extending them the hand of fellowship.

It is precisely in this respect that the image Germans form of their eastern neighbors again becomes problematical and conducive to errors analogous to those provoked by the national stereotypes and clichés formerly current. For communism in East-Central Europe today is no longer a monolithic bloc. It is passing through a stage of rapid change and differentiation into various camps and sects. It would be a mistake not to recognize that this process of change is taking place and is susceptible to Western influence.

The factors contributing to this change in East-Central European communism are scrutinized more closely in other chapters of this volume. Our present subject is not communism as such but rather the German image of the peoples of East-Central Europe. However, our very concern with this image makes it necessary to point out the dangers of distortion and oversimplification.

The Marxism-Leninism implanted in East-Central Europe was of the Stalinist type. Since the peoples in this region had been educated for a thousand years in the spirit of Western humanism, it was only to be expected that this revolutionary doctrine would be subjected to distinctive interpretations and modifications. Developments in this direction were indicated by the efforts to find special "national roads to socialism" that began as early as 1948. A particularly clear example of this trend was Titoism, against which Stalin promptly hurled his anathema. The Germans know—one of their sources being a book by Wolfgang Leonhard[1]—what an electrifying effect this idea of a special national road to socialism produced on Marxists throughout East-Central Europe. Soon after Stalin's death, in the midst of a process of Sovietization that is still continuing in many respects, a counter-movement made its appearance: an answer by the East-Central European intellectuals to the challenge of communism. Khrushchev, as is well known, gave the starting signal for this movement in his famous speech at the Twentieth Party Congress. Not until subsequent events in East-Central Europe, however, did he learn that he had opened Pandora's box. These events included the Polish spring, the Hungarian revolt of 1956 and some years later a fermentation among the intellectuals of Czechoslovakia. Even in the Soviet Zone of Germany, which is kept under rigorous controls, affairs such as those involving Professors Harich and Havemann have taken place. Although both were disciplined by the regime, they enjoy a growing circle of supporters among the younger generation.†

A remarkable phenomenon is the unanimity with which the peoples of East-Central Europe, hitherto of highly diversified temperament and character, have reacted to Stalinism and to the persistent conservative official interpretation of Marxism-Leninism in their efforts to achieve emancipation. This unanimity is evident in the treatment of two themes with which the younger philosophers of all these peoples are passionately concerned. First of all, they deny the

†Dr. Wolfgang Harich, a graduate of the SED Party School and instructor of philosophy at the Humboldt University in East Berlin, was editor-in-chief of the *Deutsche Zeitschrift für Philosophie*. In March, 1957, he was sentenced to ten years in prison for "forming a conspiratorial group hostile to the state." Harich and his followers had urged that socialist policy concentrate on achieving reunification of Germany, and that the Soviet Zone undertake the reforms necessary to make reunification feasible. Harich was released from prison in 1965. Professor Robert Havemann was professor of physical chemistry and director of the institute in that field at the Humboldt University until his expulsion from the factulty and from the SED in 1964. It appears that he has been at least partially rehabilitated, since he is scheduled to appear in Salzburg, Austria, in a dialogue of Marxists and Catholics.—*Eds.*

scientific character of Marxism and define it as an ideology. Secondly, they are endeavoring to develop a modern anthropology on Marxist premises. Orthodox Communists regard both trends as heretical revisionism that shakes the foundations of Marxism by treating it as an incomplete system dependent in part on Western ideas. This development is, however, in no way limited to the cogitations of abstract philosophers; it has its exact parallels in literature and art, which are escaping from the straitjacket of "socialist realism" more rapidly than in the Soviet Union. Even in the economic field new techniques that smack of capitalism have suddenly become acceptable.

In summarizing the intellectual condition of Marxism in East-Central Europe it can be stated, to begin with, that the overcoming of the personality cult and of dogmatism has operated as a return to normal existence. The intellectuals of this region, including those who have no intention whatever of abandoning Marxism, recognize and enthusiastically welcome this development as a renaissance, as a kind of reformation and as a return to an earlier and more broad-minded phase of Marxism. There are, of course, many different degrees and forms of this metamorphosis. Some Communists are cautious, adhering punctiliously to the directives of the regime and fearing the liberalization, falsification and embourgeoisement of Marxism-Leninism. Exponents of this school already find themselves openly attacked as conservatives. Others suffer from the intellectual isolation into which the so-called personality cult led East-Central European Marxism. Thinkers of this latter type are trying to find their way back into worldwide discussion, which means coming to grips intellectually with systems of thought from the nonsocialist world, such as existentialism and what East Europeans call Left Catholicism. Those moving in this direction consider themselves the pioneers of a new epoch of Marxism. They are beginning to see socialist society in realistic perspective, recognizing that, like every other, it contains problems, grievances and errors that cannot be disposed of summarily by ascribing them to foreign influences as Stalinism was wont to do. Such representatives of the new trend are not prepared to reject important developments in the Western world, including those in literature and art, as decadent and dangerous, even when narrow-minded functionaries command them to do so.

Current developments in East-Central Europe constitute the answer of its peoples to Sovietization—a modification and re-Europeanization of the Marxism that penetrated this region in the form of Leninism and Stalinism.

There are two possible evaluations of this unmistakable transformation taking place within East-Central European communism: It is, in the first place, possible to write off this development as illusory. Communism is communism, whatever its variety, maintain adherents of this point of view; even the revisionists would regard the West as their basic enemy in the last analysis and would seek to indoctrinate and conquer it, perhaps with different methods. Those who judge things in this light can only wait for a collapse of communism in East-Central Europe and hope for the restoration of a bourgeois society. The peoples of East-Central Europe would then have to renounce communism, just as the Germans renounced national socialism after it collapsed in 1945.

But it is not very realistic to expect a restoration of pre-communist liberalism in East-Central Europe. Such a restoration is probably not even desirable. An alternate perspective, therefore, seems to have greater merit. However the life and thought of the East-Central European peoples may develop in the future, the epoch of communism will have left deep-seated changes. The social and economic system will with little doubt retain significant socialist characteristics and structures. For this reason alone—quite apart from their human interest in the spiritual destiny of these peoples—the nations of the West, the neighboring Germans in particular, would do well to pay serious attention to the development within East-Central European Marxism indicated here and to study this development carefully. So long as dogmatic Stalinism persisted, it may well have been pointless to hold discussions with Communists who were nothing but mouthpieces for a rigid dogmatism, without opinions of their own. Today, however, the internal arguments within Polish, Czech, Slovak and Hungarian Marxism—not to mention those of Yugoslavia—offer openings for fruitful exchanges of views. It would be missing an opportunity not to engage in such conversations—not only (to speak in military parlance) to remain in contact with the enemy, but also for the sake of the young, revisionist Marxists, who are seeking contacts and are prepared to play their part in a far-reaching transformation of communism.

NOTES TO CHAPTER SIX

1. Wolfgang Leonhard, *Die Revolution entlässt ihre Kinder* (Cologne: 1955; American translation *Child of the Revolution* [Chicago: Henry Regnery Company, 1958]).

CHAPTER VII

German Reunification and Slavic Attitudes

WLADYSLAW W. KULSKI

Before a discussion of Slavic attitudes toward the problems of German reunification can be meaningful, it is necessary to define the term Slav. The peoples called Slavs form neither a political nor a cultural community. Like the Latins, they represent a linguistic family and nothing more. The English aphorism that Englishmen are racial mongrels could be applied with equal force to the Slavs and all other Europeans. There is no Slavic race, any more than there is a German or a Latin race. A casual glance at the crowds in the largest Slavic cities should provide ample evidence of this truth. To talk about a Slavic race is as much nonsense as it is to write about a Slavic soul, mentality or character. A comparison of Czech patterns of behavior with those of the Poles is sufficient to make it clear that national mentalities, which are extremely difficult to define and are often described in shallow or tendentious generalities, have been molded by history rather than by alleged racial or linguistic affinity.

Culturally, all of us who are Europeans or descendants of Europeans belong to the same great civilization, which this author prefers to call European rather than Western. The latter term is too exclusive and may easily be manipulated for political purposes. For a great many people, the Germans did not belong to the Western civilization during the nazi period. Yet it was foolish to forget temporarily the great contribution of the Germans to the common heritage of our civilization. We might nowadays be tempted to make the same mistake with regard to the Russians, because we are estranged from them by ideological-political strife, as we were a few decades ago from national socialist Germany.

Fundamentally, all European or European-derived national cultures stem from the same Greek-Roman-Jewish source. It is true that the medieval period exhibited two interpretations of the ancient heritage: the Roman or Western and the Byzantine or Eastern. But the two regions met again during the eighteenth century, at a time when the Russians and, in their wake, other Greek-Orthodox Europeans engaged in a cultural dialogue with the Western Europeans. In the twentieth century, after a continuous and intense exchange of ideas over a span of two hundred-fifty years, only a political propagandist would claim that there are two distinct civilizations in Europe. This aspect of the question has been clearly formulated by the contemporary German scholar Klaus Mehnert in his book on Soviet-Chinese relations.[1] It is ridiculous to exclude the Russians or the other East European peoples from our civilization merely because they live under communist regimes, just as it is ridiculous for General de Gaulle to restrict the realm of the European cultural community to the area between the Atlantic and the Urals, thus excluding the Americans by implication.

It is true that each nation has evolved its own original interpretation of our common heritage. The fact is not to be denied that Russian national culture differs from the German or the Polish, but the same can be said about English national culture in comparison with that of France or Italy. An Asian is best able to visualize the overall cultural community, which includes all the national cultures of the Europeans and the peoples descended from them. The vitality and wealth of the European civilization are illustrated by the fact that it thrives on diversity and is rent, from time to time, by contradictory and militant ideologies.

Taking a comparative point of view, one may say that there is a common cultural denominator among the Slavic nations but that this denominator is also shared by the other European peoples. Each Slavic nation has developed its own national culture reflecting its peculiar genius and its unique history. The Latin influence, for example, may be detected in Polish culture, and the German influence in Czech culture. It would strain human credulity to hold that Tchaikovsky, Chopin and Smetana are uniquely related to one another and that all three reflect in their music the so-called Slavic soul —that myth that stubbornly survives among popular stereotypes. In no way do the Slavs form a single cultural unit, not even where they are close neighbors and live within the same state; this fact is immediately apparent when the Serbs are compared with the Croats.

Politically, the Slav peoples have had divergent interests arising from their distinctive geographical situations and historical experiences. They have had quarrels among themselves, quarrels no less bitter than their disputes with the non-Slavic nations. Slavic images of the Germans have varied in response to the relations of Slavic nations among themselves and their relations with non-Slavic neighbors. To take one example among many, at the beginning of recorded Polish history the Germans were at times looked upon as welcome allies against the western Slavs who lived between Poland and the Empire. There is nothing in the prewar history of Russia, Serbia or Bulgaria to indicate any particular dislike of the Germans such as forms a recurrent theme in the history of Poland and Czech Bohemia.

Official Views and Popular Feelings

This diversity among the Slavs having been established, attention may now be turned to the contemporary situation. Two different factors must be clearly distinguished at the outset: the official policies of the various communist governments and the feelings of the peoples themselves. It is impossible to assess the extent to which the Soviet government is considered legitimate by the Russians or the extent to which its foreign policy reflects popular aspirations. There is no way of ascertaining these facts in the absence of free elections and a free press. The Soviet regime took root in Russian soil, not because of foreign intervention, but in spite of it. This regime is now forty-seven years old and has had time to inculcate habits of national loyalty. By contrast, the communist regimes of Eastern Europe were imported on the points of Soviet bayonets, and their hold over the populations is uncertain, as the Hungarian and Polish revolts of 1956 dramatically disclosed.

It is easy to reconstruct the official views of the various East European governments from their statements and documents, but there are no reliable standards for measuring popular feelings. The difficulty is the same as in the case of the Soviet Union: the lack of freedom of expression. One plausible proposition may perhaps be ventured, namely, that all these East European nations, Slavic or non-Slavic, each endowed with a distinct national consciousness, resent the Russian protectorate as they would any alien protectorate. This resentment counterbalances to some extent the bitter memories of nazi occupation.

The official views of East European communist governments are identical with the Soviet stand. There are two existing German states, and the problem of reunification should be left to their negotiations. But a reservation is added, namely, that reunification should not result in the loss of the socialist achievements of the German Democratic Republic. This official communist view amounts to a categorical veto, because a unified German state could not possibly accommodate two such radically opposed political and social regimes under the same roof.

This veto, buttressed as it is by the nuclear power of the Soviet Union, makes any discussion of the reunification of Germany a rather academic debate for the time being. In earlier times deadlocked international issues could be solved by war, although wars often eventuated in solutions the belligerents had neither intended nor expected. As things stand today, neither the United States nor the West Europeans, including the Germans, would be inclined to cut the Gordian knot with the nuclear sword. The net result would probably be not the reunification of living Germans but a vast cemetery covering the territories of all belligerents. This is why the status quo in Europe is frozen by the nuclear stalemate. The situation could be changed by negotiation, but there is no sign that the Soviet Union intends to make a change in the European status quo a subject of serious discussion.

THE SOVIET INTEREST IN THE STATUS QUO

From the Soviet point of view the present status quo in Europe is the best imaginable. The Soviet leaders exercise the dominant influence over the whole of East-Central Europe up to the River Elbe. Their statements concerning the German problem have never varied greatly in substance. Shortly after Adzhubei's visit to West Germany and prior to Khrushchev's dismissal, *Pravda* published the following statement in its lead article of September 27, 1964:

Anyone who thinks that improvement in the relations between the U.S.S.R. and Western Germany may be achieved even in the least degree at the expense of interests of the German Democratic Republic is deeply mistaken. The treaty [of mutual assistance] concluded between the U.S.S.R. and the German Democratic Republic has destroyed the last shreds of these illusions.

Gromyko reaffirmed the same doctrine in his December, 1964, speech before the General Assembly of the United Nations. Not only did he repeat the usual Soviet accusations against so-called revanchist and militarist ruling groups in West Germany, he went further than other Soviet spokesmen in his indictment. He traced the lineage of German militarism from the present-day Federal Republic back through the Nazi Reich, the Imperial Reich, as far back as the medieval First Reich. He seemed to propound the thesis that militarism was an ingrained phenomenon in Germany at all times. This sort of propaganda not only corresponds to the official Soviet opposition to German reunification, it reflects a genuine fear of a reunited and hence powerful Germany. This fear was born in the last war. The Soviet government and, I am afraid, the Russian people remember that the German armies were almost successful in capturing Moscow and perhaps winning the war on the eastern front. They also realize that a reunited Germany would be the most powerful European nation. In the same speech Gromyko proposed the simultaneous admission of both German states to the United Nations. This was, in substance, a demand that the United Nations appose its solemn seal on the permanent division of Germany.

Is this fear of Germany confined to the communist government of the Soviet Union? The nazi atrocities and the enormous human losses among soldiers and civilians suffered during the hostilities and the occupation suggest that it may be shared by the Russian population. For the first time in history an anti-German feeling may be noticed in Russia, which had previously had friendly sentiments toward the Germans and a great respect for the German culture. This was true of the Russian people as well as of the bolshevist leaders. The new attitude is in itself an important political fact that has a direct bearing on the problem of German reunification. Brezhnev, in his new capacity as first secretary, reminded the Soviet peoples in December, 1964, of their suffering during the last war and asked them not to forget that experience.

People inclined to be seduced by historical analogies are apt to fear or hope for a new German-Soviet Rapallo. Politically, this Rapallo might be imagined as a transaction involving Soviet assent to reunification at the price of German withdrawal from the Atlantic alliance. The historical circumstances of today are, however, radically different, not only from those of the twenties, but also from those of any former period of German-Russian cooperation. In earlier days Germany or Prussia was as powerful as if not more powerful than Russia. The intermediate zone in East-Central Europe was open to both influences. The practical policy of collaboration was to strike a bargain in that intermediate zone. This was done many times, beginning in the seventeenth century and for the last time in 1939.

Today Russia is one of the two most powerful world powers, while Germany is divided. Any deal with Germany would primarily involve the Soviet Union in great concessions that West Germany would be unable to repay by corresponding concessions. It is doubtful whether the Russians would sell reunification for a pact of non-aggression and friendship; this century has seen ample demonstration that pacts of this type are hardly likely to survive international tensions. In any event, reunification would be equivalent to a Soviet retreat from the Elbe. If a reunified Germany should uphold the present official stand of the Federal Republic and insist on the recovery of its 1937 frontiers, the Russians, if they wanted to remain on friendly terms, would have to retreat in the second stage from the River Oder, which is just as much the Soviet as the Polish frontier. Eventually, they might be afraid that a powerful and reunited Germany would ask another price for its friendship, namely, a return to the historical pattern of divided influence in East-Central Europe. They would then have to retreat even from the Vistula. All the while, they would not be sure that Germany might not shift toward friendship and closer ties with other Western powers. They would in any case be powerless to control the orientation of German foreign policy. This argument is constructed because there is good reason to suspect that it is present in the minds of the Soviets.

On the other hand, it is doubtful whether West Germany would be prepared to buy Soviet assent to reunification at the price of cutting the security ties that link it to the Atlantic allies. Even a reunified Germany would need this alliance, at least for the period of time during which Germany would not have ready its own effective deterrent to possible Soviet aggression.

It is a singular illusion to believe that Soviet assent to reunification could be purchased at the price of a long-term loan or to think that the quarrel with China may compel the Russians to seek an accommodation with the West at any price, including an agreement on reunification. China is not yet a nuclear peer of Russia and the United States; if one day she becomes a peer, she will have to reckon with the existence of the so-called nuclear deterrent. For the time being at least, China presents to the Russians a troublesome problem but not a serious military threat. They do not need any Western help. It so happens that their main Western adversary, the United States, is also involved in an open and serious conflict with the Chinese Communists. The two major nuclear powers are more than a match for China. If a flight of speculative imagination is permissible, one could toy with the possibility of a mutual understanding between Russia and the United States in the Far East. If Chinese pressure were to bring it about, the community of interests between the two powers would provide a sufficient platform for an understanding in the Far East without either of them demanding any concessions in Europe as a precondition. This author does not foresee any such development in the foreseeable future, because the militant Chinese pressure is directed exclusively against the United States. Washington is preoccupied with the Chinese problem for easily understandable reasons; these reasons may not, however, be fully appreciated by America's European allies, whose main quarrel is with Russia and who have no vital interests to protect in the Far East.

The crux of the German reunification problem is the Soviet veto. The feelings of other Slav nations are immaterial. If all the non-Russian Slavs were to conclude that Germany should be immediately reunited, they could do nothing in the face of the preponderant Soviet might. Should one or another communist government in Eastern Europe decide to oppose the German policy of the Soviet Union, it would no doubt be quickly reminded of the Soviet reaction to the attempt of the Hungarians to proclaim their country's neutrality in 1956. The last word unfortunately belongs to the Soviet Union.

ATTITUDES OF NON-RUSSIAN SLAVS

From the purely ideological point of view, no government would overtly deny the Germans the right of self-determination. Even the Communists pay lip service to that concept and loudly proclaim that they also are in favor of reunification. The ideal of self-determination is too popular throughout the world for anyone to challenge it openly. It would be particularly hard for the Poles and the Czechs, and, as a matter of fact, for all the East European Slavs, to deny this right to the Germans, as they themselves were the great beneficiaries of that principle after World War I. There is no moral issue regarding the reunification, but at the same time there is a wide gap between the verbal homage to the principle of self-determination and the fact of Soviet political expediency.

The non-Russian Slav nations may be divided into two groups. The Bulgarians, Slovaks, Ukrainians, Serbs and Croats as well as the non-Slavic East European nationalities, such as the Hungarians and the Rumanians, have never nourished a lasting animosity against the Germans. Those peoples have no reason to fear the emergence of a reunited Germany, which might appear in their eyes as a desirable counterbalancing force against Russia and possibly as a guarantee of their own independence.

The matter is much more complex in the case of the other Slavic group, composed of Poles and Czechs. These have many unpleasant recollections of their past coexistence with Germany. These recollections do not reflect the total history of their relations with the Germans, but they were brought to the fore by the last war. Poland illustrates the phenomenon in question. It would be misleading to reduce the medieval history of German-Polish relations to the struggle with the Teutonic knights. The Polish-German frontier remained peaceful and stable for long periods of time, while the Poles were waging wars on their eastern frontiers. Apparently there was no general distrust of the Germans in the seventeenth century, when a Polish king did not hesitate to fight shoulder to shoulder with the German Emperor and the German princes in the defense of Vienna. The same must have been true in the eighteenth century, when the Poles twice elected German princes to the Polish throne and when they conferred the hereditary throne on the family of Saxon Electors in their last Constitution, that of 1791. The post-partition period and, in the immediate past, the tragic experience of nazi occupation left bitter memories and the inclination to recall former quarrels with the Germans rather than periods of good-neighborly relations. Even now friendly overtures on the part of Germany might encounter a certain incredulity. Some Poles might ask whether these overtures were not calculated to evoke suspicions in Moscow regarding Polish intentions and thus motivate the Russians to seek an understanding with Germany at Polish expense. Two experiences are not easily forgotten. The Polish-Prussian Alliance of 1790 was only a prelude to the Prussian-Russian understanding and to the last partitions of Poland. The period of friendly relations with nazi Germany, from 1934 to 1938, eventually led to the Soviet-German agreement of 1939 for a new partition of Poland. The Czechs well remember the Munich agreement and might fear its repetition, this time through German agreement with the Soviet Union. Anxieties of this type may be considered unfounded, but such fears, nourished on historical reminiscences and revived by the last war, do exist. It may take a long time to dispel this distrust of Germany.

There is, however, no reason to be discouraged, because time is a great healer. Memories of recent events gradually recede and become history for the rising generations. Eventually, the image of Germany will be molded by the present and future rather than the past attitudes of Germany toward its eastern neighbors; nothing will change the fact that these nations must live in the same part of the world. The Germans, Poles and Czechs might also remember that the last war began with their disputes and ended in variously disastrous ways for all three peoples.

There is no point in glossing over the obstacles that must be confronted along the road toward better mutual understanding. There is the distrust of German ultimate intentions because of historical recollections. The hypothesis of Soviet assent to German reunification immediately brings to Polish and Czech minds the question whether these nations would have to pay the price of more friendly relations between their two mighty neighbors.

This aspect of the question involves territorial disputes. Nothing divides two neighbors more than a quarrel over frontiers. Territory is one of the most vital factors in the concept of any nationality. This is as true of Pakistan and India as it is of Germany, Poland and Czechoslovakia. Czechs may be inclined to fear that a unified Germany would raise the question of the return of Germans expelled from the Sudetenland and thus would re-create the explosive problem of the German minority. The Poles have the same tendency to fear being dislodged from the territories situated between the Oder-Neisse line and the 1937 frontiers.

This territorial problem, although the subject of lively polemics, is academic as long as Germany is divided. It is academic because the frontiers cannot be changed as long as the Soviet Union intends to maintain the status quo. If Russia were to change its point of view, the same frontiers could be modified in any conceivable way, whether the Poles and the Czechs liked it or not.

This factor of Soviet power makes the present polemics rather a waste of time. No amount of historical, ethnic, strategic or economic argument ever changed an inch of any international frontier; frontiers were modified only if one of the parties to a dispute was favored by the international distribution of power. In 1918–19 the distribution of power favored the Allied powers against defeated Germany, and today the distribution of power between the West and Russia favors the post-1945 status quo. It is truly irrelevant whether learned archeologists prove that the contested territories were inhabited in antiquity by Germanic or Slavic tribes. Yet the territorial issues affect the parties emotionally; while the protagonists overheat themselves in their exchange of arguments, the chanceries of third states usually remain cool in the face of such polemics. The third nations become interested in the arguments accumulated by one of the parties to the territorial dispute only on the day when they decide that their own national interests would be served by a change in frontiers. In the meantime, the argument that continues between governments, scholars and publicists of both parties is not of such a nature as to promote friendly relations.

There is no need to sit in judgment on the German territorial claims and the Polish or Czech counterclaims. The important question is the effect of the polemics on the prospect of mutual understanding. The official German stand that Germany should return to the 1937 frontiers and that the German expellees from present-day Poland or from the Sudetenland should be enabled to return to their former homelands and the German terminology that makes distinctions between Western, Middle and Eastern Germany—all these, as it is easy to guess, irritate the Poles and Czechs. It is sometimes forgotten that a return to the 1937 frontiers would also include an amputation of present Soviet territory; northern East Prussia with Koenigsberg has been annexed by the Soviet Union, not by Poland or Czechoslovakia.

The matter does not rest here. An apprehensive Czech might wonder whether the return of the Sudeten Germans would not one day lead to a renewed claim for the union of the Sudetenland with Germany. A no less apprehensive Pole might wonder whether a Germany reunified within its 1937 frontiers would feel happy with the reestablishment of the free city of Danzig, presumably repopulated by the descendants of its former German inhabitants, and with the renewed existence of the Corridor, which was considered an open wound in the German national body during the period between the two world wars. A Poland returning to its 1937 frontiers in the west could not, on the other hand, possibly dream of restoring the 1937 frontiers in the east, as the Polish-Russian borders of today are and presumably will be upheld by superior Soviet power.*

All these problems must be brought out into the open because the purpose of German-Polish-Czech reconciliation will not be served by empty phraseology or by silently passing over these controversial matters. It is a fact that practically all Poles insist on the Oder-Neisse frontier and that Czechs resist the claim for the return of Sudeten Germans, while the Germans officially insist on the 1937 frontiers and on the right of expellees and their descendants to return to their former homes. It seems unlikely for the time being that anything spectacular may be done to bridge this gap. It would be unrealistic to expect the German government to abandon its claims, and it would be equally unrealistic to expect Poland or Czechoslovakia, with or without a communist government, to accept the German claims as long as they cannot be enforced over the Soviet veto. We face here a Gordian knot, and no Alexander is to be perceived on the international horizon.

There are, of course, ways of eluding this reality. One of them is to indulge in glib talk about a future European union that would cause all frontiers between European nations to lose their political significance. Imagine, for the sake of analogy, a German claim to Alsace or an Italian claim to Corsica, and you would be compelled to predict the end of the "Community of Six." A Europe united according to the Gaullist formula from the Atlantic to the Urals could exist only if the participating nations were satisfied with the frontiers dividing them. A German imagining this sort of united Europe would probably feel that the insignificance of intra-European frontiers should persuade the Poles to accept easily a return to the 1937 status quo. A Pole, indulging in a similar flight of imagination,

*Aside from the question of relative political power, it should be observed that the present boundary, which approximates the Curzon Line proposed in 1919, corresponds more closely to ethnic divisions than did the boundary obtained by Poland through the Treaty of Riga in 1921, which included large Ukrainian, Belorussian and Lithuanian populations within the Polish state.—Eds.

would hope that the Germans would then accept the present boundary line. As a matter of fact, the short history of the "Community of Six" indicates that every partner is mindful of its national interests and that these interests do not always coincide, even though the six are not divided by any territorial disputes.

First Steps Toward German-Slav Reconciliation

Is it hopeless to try to work for an improvement in the relations between the Germans, on the one hand, and the Poles and Czechs, on the other? By no means—provided the start is *not* made with an attempt to reach agreement on highly controversial political questions that are for the time being unsolvable. The most fruitful first step is, rather, a search for better knowledge of the other nation. There is a widespread assumption that neighbors who have lived side by side for centuries should be perfectly acquainted. This is far from the truth. Their mutual knowledge is likely to be distorted by the emotions that usually permeate their relations, emotions derived from historical recollections that are often unpleasant.

Truly to know a neighbor means to overcome the barrier formed by inherited prejudices, slogans and prefabricated images. It is all too easy to fall into the habit of visualizing foreign nations as though they were collective living organisms, forgetting that nations are composed of individual human beings who do not necessarily resemble one another. International exchanges of persons make possible the discovery of individuals formerly hidden by the images of their nations. Ties of friendship are thus formed between individuals of two nations, and those individuals may discover that the national images they formerly considered true are either false or not quite exact. These exchanges of professors, students, teachers and representatives of various associations can do more than anything else for the laying down of psychological foundations on which the future friendship between the Germans and the Slavs—notably the Poles and the Czechs— can be built. The Germans will discover that the cliché of *polnische Wirtschaft* may not be quite accurate as a description of Polish mentality, while the Poles and the Czechs will find out that the Germans are not modern incarnations of the Teutonic knights or of the enemy who fought the Battle of the White Mountain. Personal contact is the most effective way of gradually overcoming mutual distrust and ingrained antipathy.

A new look at the respective histories of mutual relations would also be of great value. These histories should be rewritten on the basis of critical comparison of the national versions, which differ greatly from each other. The first steps in this direction have already been taken. This valuable effort should continue. The following example will serve to illustrate the problem. If the medieval German *Drang nach Osten* is interpreted exclusively as a Christianizing and civilizing venture, the distrust of Slavic neighbors is immediately aroused, because they know of the somber implications of that *Drang* for the Slav peoples. To talk about the historical role of Germany as a bastion of Western civilization does not help promote friendship with eastern neighbors. As a matter of fact, the Poles have also enjoyed picturing themselves as the frontiersmen of Western culture. It should not be overlooked that peoples located east of the self-styled bastion feel insulted when they are relegated to the unenviable position of barbarians threatening the civilization. It is far more productive of good feelings to insist on the common cultural heritage rather than to claim unilaterally the privilege of being its guardian.

A more truthful version of history would convince the Czechs and the Poles that the German was not always the "hereditary enemy" and that at times he was helpful and friendly.

The process of reconciliation between France and Germany has been incomparably easier, for various reasons. The last war did not leave any territorial dispute in its wake. The mutual animosity did not go back any further than the Napoleonic invasion for the Germans or than the War of 1870–71 for the French. Those observers old enough to remember the period between the two world wars must, however, be amazed at the speed with which former resentments and suspicions have been forgotten and an atmosphere of friendliness created. Who could have predicted in 1940 that General de Gaulle would become an ardent apostle of reconciliation? This example should encourage the Germans, Poles and Czechs to take the first steps in the same direction. The effort will be long and at times frustrating, but it is necessary, because we all live in the nuclear age, which is not propitious for attempts at solving problems between neighbors by war.

Personal contacts and cultural exchanges are not to be rejected because of the existence of communist regimes in Eastern Europe. These regimes make contacts difficult but not impossible. The American experience in this respect is not discouraging. American scholars and students who visit the Soviet Union or Eastern Europe come back with additional contributions to our storehouse of knowledge of that part of the world. Soviet and East European visitors bring back to their countries an image of the West very different from the clichés disseminated by communist propaganda. The personal contact with the West seldom if ever fails to make a significant imprint on the minds of visitors coming from the communist countries. In short, the experience of the United States and other Western countries indicates that the West derives political benefits from cultural exchanges, which should not be confused with conferences on current political topics between intellectuals selected from both camps. Conferences of this type tend to become dialogues between the deaf or, to put it another way, a fruitless succession of monologues.

Contacts with individuals and institutions in Eastern Europe cannot be replaced by contacts with East European exile organizations. The Germans would deceive themselves if they thought otherwise. The history of all political emigrations proves that political exiles, however patriotic they may be, gradually lose contact with those countries and cannot speak with authority on behalf of their countrymen who have not emigrated and who are the nation.

It may be stated in conclusion that the political problems that divide Germany from Russia, Poland and Czechoslovakia cannot be solved today in any way acceptable to all parties concerned; this is why the polemics related to those problems are rather futile and apt to irritate mutual relations. This fact should not discourage a steady effort to cultivate personal contacts and cultural exchanges, since these contacts and exchanges will eventually help to correct existing distorted images of the neighbor. More exact and unprejudiced knowledge will elicit mutual respect, which is the precondition for any true international friendship. It is to be hoped that the mutual trust that would be built up in this way would eventually pave the road toward a settlement of political disputes that today appear insoluble. The road is long and arduous, but according to a Polish proverb, which has its counterparts in other languages, "Cracow was not built in one day."

NOTES TO CHAPTER SEVEN

1. Klaus Mehnert, *Peking and Moscow* (New York: G. P. Putnam's Sons, 1963).

CHAPTER VIII

Hopes and Fears of German Reunification: A Polish View

JERZY HAUPTMANN

T WENTY YEARS AFTER the end of World War II the German problem is still the center of European and world concern. In the early days of May, 1945, there were many who expressed the opinion that Germany would cease to be a problem, that the world had finally found a way toward a definite solution of the German question, that the Allied powers would see to it that twenty years later the German issue would not become the basis for world conflict again. Twenty years passed between Versailles and 1939; twenty years have passed between the May of 1945 and the days of our conference. The problem of Germany is again alive. The Allied powers did not solve it after World War II; it was, rather, their disunity and conflict that placed Germany again in the center of European and world concern.

Now we know that it was not realistic to expect a solution of the German problem after a war, that such a solution would have been a vindictive one, that it would have carried within itself the seeds of another 1939. In the meantime, during the twenty years since World War II, two separate political organisms have developed in Germany after imposed reduction of her size: the German Federal Republic and the so-called German Democratic Republic. Whereas the Federal Republic maintains close relationships with the Western world and has indeed become a main partner of Western politics, the Democratic Republic has accepted (obviously not voluntarily) the posi-

141

tion of a member of the Soviet bloc. The Federal Republic has insisted on maintaining the position that it is the only legal German government, speaking for Germany as a whole, according to the Hallstein Doctrine, while the Democratic Republic has slowly chipped away at this claim of single representation and has recently achieved some remarkable successes.

In this situation, which can only be sketched in broad outline here, the issue of German reunification still plays a major role. Is reunification really possible? Under what conditions could it happen that the two "German states" would reunite again? This is not an academic question, especially not for the countries of Eastern Europe. The memories of World War II are still vivid, and they are maintained and kept alive by official propaganda. According to the official communist view, reunification of Germany would be nothing more than an extension of the power of the German Federal Republic to the area of the German Democratic Republic, an increase in population and industrial potential, a revival of the old threat.

What reactions to such a possibility can be ascertained? Although it is our main purpose to look at the picture of Germany from the Polish point of view, many of the statements made will be valid, with some modifications, for the other East European countries as well.

ALTERNATIVE POLISH APPROACHES TO GERMANY

The clearest approach to Germany can be gleaned from the pages of the Polish press. What are the themes most commonly stressed? There is obviously the lack of democracy in the Federal Republic, there are the problems of the German army, the statute of limitations concerning war crimes, the war criminal trials, etc. And so *Zachodnia Agencja Prasowa* writes on February 5, 1965, about the German army:

> Today the old traditions of the Prussian and Hitler militarism, symbolized by the Iron Cross, are again revived. The same cross is the common motif of the military flags of the Kaiser, of Hitler and now of Bonn.

The German economy is entirely geared to military production. It is Germany that is interested in the Multilateral Force and that wants to utilize the military alliance with the West for its own purposes. *Nowe Drogi* in January, 1965, expressed this as follows:

Western Germany will try to play off the differences among the NATO members to gain a complete freedom in atomic armaments. These differences will intensify should the MLF ever become a reality. . . . The Bonn government still hopes that it will be able to use the whole Atlantic alliance in the service of its revisionist aspirations.

Then there is the vision of revisionism. Marian Podkowiński, the Bonn correspondent for the Warsaw newspapers, wrote in *Sprawy Miedzynarodowe* in December, 1964: "The plenary sessions of the Bundestag are a general debate in support of the interests of West German revisionism." In accord with this tendency, certain personalities are identified as the "bad people" of German politics. Close to former Chancellor Adenauer and Mr. Strauss looms the figure of the Social Democratic deputy Dr. Wenzel Jaksch. The Polish weekly *Kultura,* on December 20, 1964, described him as "an advocate of a *Lebensraum,* A.D. 1964"; and Podkowiński wrote in his account of the convention of the German Social Democratic party: "Although away from the table of the presiding officers, the shadow of Wenzel Jaksch and of his adherents oppressed the convention hall."[1]

This is the first and major alternative approach to Germany that can easily be ascertained from the Polish press. Quite in agreement with it is a second approach found, not in Poland, but in the Polish emigration. Józef Mackiewicz gave this approach the name "polrealism"—an approach that claims to look at the Polish situation from a realistic angle. This realistic angle simply means that Germany remains the major enemy of Poland, that the threat of German revisionism is very real and present and that only a connection with Russia (the name always used for the Soviet Union by adherents of this view) can defend Poland from the German threat. By accepting these ideas the Polish emigration is forced ultimately into a position of agreeing with the Warsaw regime, and so it can only echo the voices from Warsaw. A central position in this approach is the warning not to talk to the Germans, not to give anything away to them. Awareness of this approach forced this writer to make the following statement while reporting on the Wiesbaden Conference: "It should be stated, to pacify some of the readers, that nothing Polish was sold or given away at this conference. It even was not offered by anybody, nor demanded from anybody."[2]

An interesting new alternative, the third in our series of four, is suggested by Aleksander Bregman in his book *Jak Świat Światem?* (*"As Long as the World Will Remain the World?"*). The book analyzes the implications of the old Polish proverb that contends that Germans and Poles cannot become brothers as long as the world remains the world. Bregman denies the applicability of this proverb and states quite openly: "Regardless of the method by which the problems of Eastern Europe will be solved, a friendly and neighborly cooperation between Poland and Germany will be one of the central conditions of our peace and security." He goes so far as to claim that the hostility between Poland and Germany serves only those who do not want the Poles to be free. Bregman's book created a furor both in Poland and in the Polish emigration. One of the emigré papers, *Wiadomości,* September 20, 1964, carried a review of this book under the title "What did you do, Bregman, to the people?"—reflecting some of the negative approaches to the book. On the same page, however, another reviewer called this book a "courageous book." Similar new approaches are suggested by recent conferences of Germans and Poles, such as the Barsinghauser Conversations and a recent venture of the German sponsor of this conference, a seminar in Lindenfels. Writing about this seminar in the emigration *Kultura* (Paris) of January, 1965, one of its Polish participants stated: "Not one of those present had in mind any kind of a resolution or decision. Just because of the lack of political accents, this meeting may have a substantial political importance."

A fourth very interesting approach should not be forgotten. It is identified with Józef Mackiewicz. In "The Victorious Provocation"[3] he criticizes the present Polish policy toward Germany and makes the reader aware of the fact that something more than the Polish national interest is at stake, something so important that all differences and hostilities should be placed far in the background. He writes:

> In reality . . . the choice is between Germany and international communism. In this case the battle is not over the freedom of the nation but over the freedom of man. It becomes a choice for all those who want to remain free men, and no other choice is possible.

It must be stated clearly that the first two views are accepted by the majority of the Poles both at home and abroad. The third and the fourth view attract attention, nevertheless, because they point to alternatives different from the prevailing ones, because they question the assumptions of the existing situation and because they seek an understanding of problems hidden behind the façade of clichés and stereotypes.

ALTERNATIVE GERMAN APPROACHES TO POLAND

If we reverse our approach and look now at the situation from the German point of view, what do we discover? The central point is probably the great attractiveness of Poland in present-day Western Germany. Even Podkowiński writes that the "fashion for Poland is growing in Western Germany—but obviously not in Bonn."[4] The many books on Poland, translations of Polish literature—among them splendid translations of Polish poetry by Karl Dedecius—the attractiveness of Polish films, the frequent seminars and radio programs on Poland—all these are signs that there is a curiosity about Poland; some may even call it a fascination with Poland. Bregman discovers the same phenomenon in his book, and any observer of the West German scene will find his judgment confirmed by first-hand observation. The meaning of this fascination is, however, not entirely clear. One can be fascinated by a friend as well as by an enemy; one may also be fascinated simply by an element of strangeness in the object observed. Others may even feel this attraction as a result of a guilt feeling and the desire for some kind of penance. Regardless of the motivation, this curiosity has to be registered, especially since it may remain no more than curiosity, with no action of any significance resulting from it.

More dynamic is what we may call the economic approach. Its core is the necessity of establishing trade connections with Poland and the other East European countries. It is hoped that close commercial contacts will lead to closer cooperation in other fields also. This may be an interesting prospect; but when one reads Polish economic papers, e.g., *Zycie Gospodarcze,* one gains the impression that this is not at all the intention of the current Polish regime. It may be argued that such closer cooperation may occur regardless of the intentions of official Polish circles. Still the answer remains that this would be a rather long and arduous road.

Occasionally connected with this economic approach but also appearing independently of it is the West German hope for a liberalization in the communist-occupied countries. These hopes appear in cycles; but their central argument is always that some kind of nationalistic reorientation is taking place in Poland as elsewhere in the Eastern bloc and that in time, if only proper care, attention and caution are maintained, this will lead to a lessening of Soviet controls and perhaps—after a Tito-like stage of national communism—to some kind of "socialism" in the democratic fashion. These are the views currently expressed by various leading German politicians to whom some reference will be made later in more detail.

A new and very interesting alternative may be detected in German circles—a determination to put German-Polish discussions on a new and different base. Meetings of historians and other scholars are attempting to discover new bases for understanding. It is encouraging to note how many of the Germans involved in these discussions come from Poland. It may be mentioned parenthetically that several of the Germans, Poles and Americans discovered at the Lindenfels Seminar that they all had come from Lodz, the great industrial city of Poland. Beyond the economic attractions and the political hopes and fears, there are Germans who want to approach the problem of Poland without preconceptions and prejudices.

This analysis would not be complete without mention of the revisionist circles in Germany. They still play an important role, are still active in politics and still try to determine the direction of future German policies. For them the borders of 1940, 1939 or 1914 are just slogans covering up the desire for an expansion of Germany to the east. For them a discussion with Poland is possible only on the basis of a superior-subordinate relationship; they would perhaps even prefer a kind of German satellite status, not only for a truncated Poland, but for many of the other East European countries as well.

THE PROBLEM OF GERMAN REUNIFICATION

Only after having surveyed the attitudes of the Poles and the Germans is it possible to look in detail at the problem of German reunification. Any approach to reunification will depend on the present attitudes, which must be taken into account.

The first and second Polish views (official Warsaw view and "pol-realism") can hardly be expected to look at German reunification positively. Such a positive attitude may result only from the third and fourth views (Bregman and those sharing his standpoint and Mackie-wicz).

Correspondingly, the assessment of German views by Poles may also determine how German reunification will be approached. Only the first and the fourth of the approaches listed (fascination with Poland and the current discussions) offer some hope for a revision of the picture of Germany that will make a discussion of reunification plausible. The economic and evolutionist approaches (second and third) have some potential. The problematic area of these approaches lies in the fact that they presume the acceptance of the Warsaw re-gime as a political reality, and it is rather doubtful to expect, at least for some time, that this regime will be interested in a reunification of Germany. Needless to say, the last of the approaches mentioned (revisionism) destroys any opportunity for even considering the case for German reunification.

A methodological remark is in order here. When the term "Ger-man reunification" is used in this chapter, it designates a combina-tion of the present two "German states" into one Germany within the Western political tradition. This clearly excludes two other pos-sibilities: (1) a combination of the present two "German states" into one Germany dominated by the Soviet bloc or neutralized on Soviet terms and (2) a confederation of the present two "German states" that would essentially maintain the current ideological division but would make possible some joint actions modeled after, e.g., the joint German Olympic team.

Furthermore, the term "German reunification" is employed here without regard to any border problem. The problem of the Polish-German border can hardly be a subject of discussion at the present time. Western Germany does not border Poland, so Poland has no real interest in discussions, whereas Western Germany could not gain from them either. The problem of the borders has to be bracketed out for the time being as not essential for our purpose. Only a reuni-fied Germany and a genuinely free Poland can discuss this problem, and these two conditions (reunification and genuine freedom) are not yet present. This discussion, therefore, is directed toward the es-tablishment of one of these essential conditions, the reunification of Germany.

FEARS OF GERMAN REUNIFICATION

It should be obvious to any observer of the European political scene that German reunification does not enlist shouts of wild enthusiasm. On the contrary, many politicians and many common people look with fear toward such an eventuality. This fear is evident, not only in Poland, but also in other circles. What are the elements that produce this fear?

The first fear factor is obviously the rejuvenation of the *Drang nach Osten,* a replay of a historical drama. The argument runs as follows. As a result of the reunification, German armies will stand on the Oder and Neisse. Who can guarantee that they will remain there? They will most certainly, in line with their militaristic and revisionist traditions, proceed farther and farther. They may not want to stop. A reenactment of the two world wars in a nuclear version will then be unavoidable. The lesson is simple. It is necessary to make the first step impossible. Only if the first step does not occur will it be possible to prevent the escalation toward a full blown revisionism or worse.

Another fear factor recalls a different aspect of history. A reunited Germany, even originally on the Western side, may want to talk with Russia (the term "Soviet Union" is carefully avoided in this argument) and to bring about a new Rapallo at the cost of the countries situated between Germany and the Soviet Union. The danger of a Rapallo increases with the increasing power position of Germany. Since, so goes the argument, a reunited Germany will obviously be very powerful and since a Germany ending at the Elbe is certainly less attractive as a Rapallo partner, we should prevent a reunification.

The third fear factor emanates from a generalized defense of the status quo. Whether or not we like all the features of the existing situation, it is argued that something can be said in favor of maintaining stability. The alternative to the stability of the status quo is an element of flexibility introduced into international politics. Who knows in whose favor this flexibility will ultimately work out? It may mean a complete reshuffling of boundaries in the east of Europe. Who will gain from this? Perhaps the status quo is preferable to the unknown quality of flexibility.

Finally, some politicians fear a reunification of Germany because this may make it more difficult to maintain the communist domination over Poland. They like their present power positions, achieved through ideological commitment or opportunistic drive; they fear the end of their power at hand and so obviously resist the first step, which would likely lead in this direction.

All four fear positions are quite realistic. They assume certain features of international politics that have been quite common in the past. The changes resulting from the abolition of a status quo certainly could not have been foreseen before they took place. The dynamics of change are certainly unpredictable—but do they mean that history has to repeat itself as the first and the second factor clearly suggest? Perhaps repetition of old alternatives is the simplest way out of difficult situations, but one may wonder whether such a limited capacity of politicians in the field of international affairs should be assumed. In addition, why should the status quo be sanctified? Has it not been built upon the violation of basic rights of nations, groups and individual human beings? It certainly has, But the defenders of the status quo are just those who have gained by its establishment. Do we identify ourselves with those defenders? What does it mean if we join them in their position? It can only mean that we have to approve of the status quo, and this is rather difficult to do.

Thus, while recognizing that the reunification of Germany may upset many cherished positions, as would any change of the status quo, we are obliged to look forward to it, since it is the only way that opens up the opportunity for a return to principles in international politics and in the life of individual human beings.

Hopes of German Reunification

The change of the status quo here projected means a reunification of Germany on terms of political freedom. What are the possibilities and hopes inherent in such a reunification? Can elements be found that would counteract the fears discussed above? It seems that such elements are ascertainable, if one only wants to look for them.

A reunified Germany would mean that the West would come closer to Poland. The contact with the West would henceforth be direct rather than circuitous. This closeness certainly would not remain without results. Poland, which has always been Western in its culture and which has maintained substantial elements of pro-Western sympathies even within the existing communist framework, would face, in such a case, a new and challenging alternative. The closeness to the West would bring more penetration of Western ideas, and a movement for change in the political sense perhaps would be unavoidable.

In the second place, a reunification of Germany would end the difficult strategic and political position of Poland, which has to face the Soviet Union on both the east and the west (in view of the Soviet troops stationed in the German Democratic Republic). These pincers would in such a case have lost one of their arms, so that Poland would immediately enjoy an increased freedom of political movement. One could argue the same point in a reverse fashion, as Bregman does, by saying that a free government of Poland would make the existence of a Soviet-sponsored government in Germany impossible, so that freedom for Poland could be regarded as a precondition for German reunification. The first alternative seems to be more plausible, but the point remains the same—a unified Germany would become the exponent of Western ideas on the borders of Poland.

Thirdly, the nature of the German presence at the borders of Poland requires some closer attention. We called a unified Germany the exponent of Western ideas. Perhaps it should be called, more specifically, the exponent of Europe and of a European federation. The presence of a Western-oriented Germany at the borders of Poland would mean that united Western Europe would be reaching out to the east to claim its rightful possession of areas that have been Western for centuries. Dr. Wenzel Jaksch stated this point quite clearly at the Chicago Conference: "East-Central Europe should be claimed as an integral part of a future united Europe and of the Free World."[5]

Lastly, a reunified Germany offers a hope for political change. The abolition of the Soviet-controlled Ulbricht regime would indicate to the peoples of Eastern Europe that the end of the satellites is near, that the communist domination will indeed pass away and that freedom is about to be resurrected. In this case the reunification of Germany would become a symbol for the oppressed nations of the world, and the significance of such a change would go beyond the borders of Europe. Once Germany is reunited, the political change could not be stopped.

One can easily see why German reunification cannot be welcomed by the defenders of the status quo. Its significance goes beyond Germany. It would destroy the assumptions of the whole system created on the alleged cooperation of the World War II allies; it would de-

stroy the chance for a communist-controlled Europe; it would mean
the reversal of a tide that has threatened to swallow even Western
Europe. And one also can easily see why German reunification can
be and has to be welcomed by the opponents of the status quo. We do
not claim that the opponents of the status quo will overnight become
friends of Germany and will forget the past. We indicate rather that
they would recognize the desirability of a reunification of Germany,
regardless of their historically determined attitudes and objections
toward Germany. The point to be emphasized is that to favor German reunification it is not necessary to be pro-German or in the service of German circles, since cool and objective reasoning may lead an
opponent of the status quo to such a position. To talk with the Germans means at the present time to recognize that German reunification is the first step toward freedom for Poland.

TO TALK WITH THE POLES?

But do Germans want to talk with the Poles? To be meaningful, a
conversation has to have two partners. Those who recognize that
there is a hope for Poland in the reunification of Germany need a
conversation partner, but with whom do the Germans of the West
really want to talk?

There are, as we have indicated, many in Germany who want to
talk with the Warsaw regime. After Fritz Erler, one of the leaders of
the German Social Democratic party, stated the necessity of talks with
Warsaw, the Hamburg weekly *Sonntagsblatt* commented on January 24, 1965, as follows:

> Our disappointment results from the reaction in Poland.
> There was no echo at all to the statements of Erler—nothing
> that could give some courage to those of us who constantly em-
> phasize that Germany has to come to sensible relations with her
> eastern neighbors. The silence compares to the conscious isola-
> tion of our trade mission in Warsaw. Is there in Warsaw no in-
> terest in talks with the Federal Republic, or at least with the
> Germans in the Federal Republic?

The evaluation of the situation by the Hamburg paper is rather dis-
appointing. It does not seem to recognize that the Warsaw Poles do
not have any interest in any kind of talks. For them Germany is the

Germany presented at the beginning of this chapter. Even its trade missions are regarded with a certain skepticism; after all, the story of the Trojan horse and of King Priam's advice *"Timeo Danaos et dona ferentes"* still may have some meaning.

Somewhat more realistic is an editorial in the *Rheinischer Merkur* of January 22, 1965, written by P. W. Wenger. It also suggests a discussion of border problems with Poland and Czechoslovakia, but it proposes that this take place as part of a united European approach, centering around a French-German agreement on policy. It introduces Mao Tse-tung's questioning of the Soviet occupation of Eastern Poland and advises that the problem of border revisions should not stop at the German-Polish border. But the same problem remains. Why should the current Polish regime be interested in such discussions?

What is quite obvious is that for many German circles the desire for early conversations with the Poles means talking to the Soviet-sponsored Warsaw regime. Adherents of this school of thought obviously approach the problem of German reunification indirectly. What is implied in their argument is that once an agreement with Poland is reached, once Poland is liberalized and economically assisted (the *Rheinischer Merkur* even suggested that economic assistance should be focused in this area), the problem of the German Democratic Republic will be solved by itself.

One wonders whether this is the real solution. Perhaps this essentially short-run approach should be used, but not all hope should be centered around it. There is also the necessity of using a long-range approach, of talking to people who are genuinely interested in German reunification and of forgetting. In a paper read at the Chicago Conference this author stated:

> Forgetting means the search for human values, which may make it possible to discuss the value of each single individual, regardless of whether he calls himself a Pole, a German or an American.[6]

THE SEARCH FOR A POLICY

The idea of German reunification, as we have seen, evokes various hopes and fears in different circles. An analysis of the mutual views existing between Poles and Germans had led us to the hypothesis that a reunited Germany offers some hope for Poland. We also had to notice that this is a minority position, that the majority of the Poles distrust Germany and that many leading Germans want to talk with the Poles in Warsaw, although they are not received too well.

Can this problem of German reunification be solved within the narrow confines of Europe? This is rather doubtful. One of the co-authors of this volume, Freiherr zu Guttenberg, concluded his recent challenging book *Wenn der Westen Will* with the following words:

> Everything is at our disposal to bring about a victory of free-dom: ideas, people, knowledge, economic goods and armaments. It is essential to use them at the right time, in the right way and toward the right objective. The scale will tip toward freedom—if the West wants it.[7]

These words contain the real policy problem. The precondition of a successful policy is that it really is wanted. Is a German reunification really wanted?

We do not know whether the West German public really would be willing to take the risks involved in the pursuit of a policy directed toward a reunification of Germany on Western terms. We can hope they do, but ultimately it is their decision to make. As far as Eastern Europe is concerned, we have suggested that a reunification of Germany should be viewed as a ray of hope, not of fear. It is, however, paradoxical to suggest deliverance from oppression through the hands of a former oppressor.

During the Warsaw insurrection of 1944 a poem was circulated exclaiming: "We are waiting for you, Red pestilence"—to deliver Poland from the terrible military situation. Here we waited for one oppressor to end the oppression of the other, although this could have meant no more than a change of oppressor, as history proved later on. The point in this connection is that our approach to German reuni-fication could easily be analogous to the poem just quoted—a choice of an evil that at the moment appears lesser. This is essentially what is hoped will not happen. The argument made at the Chicago Con-ference on the importance of forgetting was really a proposal for a change in our whole approach to Germany, as well as in the whole German approach to Poland.

One could critically remark at this time that this is easily said by one who at the present time is not in Poland, who at any critical time would have the position of looking at the destruction of the status quo from the far removed Middle West of the United States. This is certainly a valid criticism, but at the same time distance gives perspective while leaving the emotional involvement intact.

It would be most undesirable for German policy to take a direction of economic determinism. Germany may want to buy friendship and concessions from the East European countries through trade, economic assistance and gifts. Credits, new machines, and indeed whole industrial plants may take the place of the proverbial colored glass beads by which colonial powers bought the "friendship" of the natives of Africa and Asia. Must it be emphasized here that friendship was not purchased in this way? Must we repeat that national policies frequently disregard economic motivation?

There is a valid case for the reunification of Germany, but this case can be made only if reunification is viewed as an inseparable part of a worldwide struggle for the freedom of man, for the freedom of the individual. The reunification of Germany viewed in this way becomes not the basis of a renewed German nationalism to be feared by everyone, especially in Eastern Europe, but rather the basis of a renewed hope for the individual, which all men of good will, especially in Eastern Europe, should share.

NOTES TO CHAPTER EIGHT

1. Marian Podkowiński in *Polityka*, December 5, 1964.
2. Jerzy Hauptmann in *Quarterly of the Polish Western Association of America*, January, 1965.
3. Józef Mackiewicz, "The Victorious Provocation." To be published.
4. Marian Podkowiński in *Polityka*, January 2, 1965.
5. *Berlin and the Future of Eastern Europe*, ed. David S. Collier and Kurt Glaser (Chicago: Henry Regnery Co., 1963), p. 19.
6. Jerzy Hauptmann, "Overcoming Historical Antagonisms," Collier and Glaser, *op. cit.*, pp. 143-44.
7. Karl Theodor Freiherr zu Guttenberg, *Wenn der Westen will* (Stuttgart: Seewald Verlag, 1964), p. 234.

CHAPTER IX

Hopes and Fears of German Reunification: A German View

AXEL SEEBERG

THIS ESSAY IS NOT offered as a statement of "the" German position on reunification; rather, it summarizes the personal observations and opinions of the author, who, as a German, cannot avoid a feeling of involvement in many respects: an involvement that is necessarily reflected in the description and analysis of specific problems.

As the preceding chapters have shown, the problem of German reunification is closely linked with a number of questions of world politics in general. Only a few of these questions can be considered here. Among those omitted are the reunification question as an aspect of American foreign policy and as it impinges on the policies of East-Central European states. Among the issues considered, a certain overlapping of facts and ideas is unavoidable, a circumstance indicating that these are partial aspects and variations of a total problem requiring a unified solution.

REUNIFICATION AS A MORAL ISSUE

Moral judgments of political issues are frequently misused for propaganda purposes. They do, however, have significance going beyond the propaganda function, since in an age of democracy even so-called *Realpolitik* cannot escape the political force of moral argument.

The following moral arguments pertaining to the German question have made a considerable impression in all parts of the world, particularly in uncommitted countries:

1. The partition of Germany is a crime against humanity, since it seriously obstructs or destroys altogether the personal relationships of individuals and families. Attempts by the Soviet Union or the German Democratic Republic to exact political concessions in return for cooperation in meeting human needs is to be regarded as a particularly reprehensible form of political blackmail and as a violation of the dignity of man.

2. Political conditions in the Soviet Zone of Germany constitute a systematic suppression of basic human rights, particularly man's right of free self-determination of his personal and political destiny.

3. The rulers of the Soviet Zone are engaged in a systematic attempt to transform human consciousness, a practice to which the Chinese have given the familiar and appropriate name brainwashing. Such attempts to manipulate human personality belong among the gravest crimes against humanity and are little better than the physical destruction of human beings, since the distinguishing feature of human personality is spiritual existence.

Not only Eastern propagandists but also certain sectors of Western public opinion sometimes treat the partition of Germany as though it were a punishment for German war guilt in World War II. The fundamental rights stipulated in the Charter of the United Nations cannot, however, be denied permanently to the German people, particularly since more than half of the Germans now living are too young to have had anything to do with political events before 1945.

PARTITION, REUNIFICATION AND WORLD PEACE

The partition of Germany created a political vacuum in the center of Europe. This vacuum has been one of the primary causes of contemporary East-West tension; the disturbance it has caused has been aggravated by ideological differences.

The destruction of the Third Reich led with inexorable logic to the continued presence of Soviet troops in the eastern part of Germany and Western troops in West Germany, the function of each force being to prevent the other from occupying the rest of Germany. Unlike the Korean War of a few years ago and the contemporary war in Vietnam, this situation results in the immediate confrontation of

Americans and Russians, thus increasing the danger of war, since every incident poses the threat of an immediate armed clash between Western and Eastern troops. The special circumstances of the Berlin situation, which permit those who control the Soviet Zone to apply pressure to the access routes to Berlin whenever they please, also increase the danger of incidents that could escalate into armed hostilities or a full-scale war.

Against the foregoing theses, Eastern propagandists maintain that efforts to achieve reunification endanger the status quo, disturb the laboriously maintained world balance of power and thus constitute a menace to peace. Any possible danger inherent in the movement for reunification is, however, eliminated by the other objectives of German foreign policy (*see* below), among which are the maintenance of peace and renunciation of the use of force. The danger of a world crisis is, furthermore, far less in the case of a reunification under the sponsorship of the Four Powers than that which might arise incident to reunification or attempted reunification through a spontaneous German people's movement.

PARTITION OF GERMANY AS A PROBLEM OF GERMAN FOREIGN POLICY

The foreign policy of the German Federal Republic seeks the following objectives: security for the Federal Republic, maintenance of world peace, European unification and German reunification. Because of moral considerations, because of popular desire for a policy of peace and because it recognizes the limitations of the German power potential, the government of the Federal Republic has renounced any aspirations toward world power. In this respect it has set its goals lower than those of the Kaiser's Germany or national socialist Germany. This fact is reflected in the German renunciation of atomic weapons. German abandonment of claims to world power has its effects, both in shaping the specific political goals leading to reunification and in the choice of means to achieve them.

During the first ten years of its existence, the Federal Republic accorded security a certain priority over other goals. After a degree of military balance and the resulting limited security had been achieved through NATO, European and German goals assumed a more prominent position. The overtly nationalist policy of President de Gaulle in matters involving the Common Market has resulted in the strengthening of public support for national political goals within the Federal Republic. Reunification, however, never has been and is not now the only foreign policy objective of the Federal Republic. The goal of reunification and the other goals of German foreign policy exert significant mutual influences on each other.

The following arguments are advanced in Germany to support efforts toward reunification:

1. The sundering of human ties is unbearable; the unity of Germany corresponds to the general national structure of states throughout the world, especially in Europe, and most particularly in Eastern Europe. The will to reunification is therefore a natural, spontaneous and elementary phenomenon.

2. Denial of German unity violates the principle of democratic self-determination.

3. Only German reunification can lead to genuine relaxation of tensions and thus to a durable peace.

4. Reunification will reduce considerably the danger of a bolshevization of Europe.

5. The reunification policy of the German Federal government is expressly recognized by the Western powers in the General Agreement of 1954 and thus accepted as a goal of Western policy.

Various arguments against German reunification are advanced by Eastern bloc governments and Communist parties, as well as by certain political commentators in the West. Among these arguments are the following:

1. A contention commonly heard from governments and official propagandists in the East admits the possibility of German reunification in principle but attempts to eliminate it as a subject of quadripartite negotiation and thus to hamper reunification altogether by focusing attention on the establishment of two German partial states, which are supposed to negotiate with each other.

2. Reunification is impossible in any case because of the different political structure of the two German states. A variation on this argument contends that reunification can take place only when the "socialist achievements" of the German Democratic Republic are extended to all Germany.

3. Every now and then a limited demilitarization of Germany is mentioned as a prerequisite for reunification.

4. One argument that is *not* encountered is that a new popular consciousness, that is, a new nation, has arisen in the Soviet Zone.

Opposition to reunification in the West does not as a rule take the form of frontal objection to the idea of reunification as such. Instead, the impossibility of reunification is suggested by a variety of indirect arguments, such as the following:

1. Reunification cannot be realized because of Russian objection. In the interest of general relaxation of tensions, therefore, the demand must be set aside.

2. The German people does not strongly desire reunification, and a new national consciousness is emerging in the Soviet Zone. The latter argument, as we have noted, is not heard from Eastern propagandists, who, being more familiar with the situation in the Soviet Zone, evidently feel that it is too preposterous to be plausible.

3. A reunited Germany could not be integrated into the Western military system and would therefore destroy the existing system of Western military security.

4. Considerations of security would lead a reunited Germany to follow a policy of military strength that would involve it once more in the quest for world power. Finally, a reunited Germany would, through its size and strength, exercise a natural hegemony within the European Economic Community. Such a development would either make European unification impossible or lead to its abuse by Germany.

Insofar as the attitude of the German people and the alleged new national consciousness in the Soviet Zone are concerned, these objections are without any foundation. In assessing popular movements, it is never to be expected that they will involve all people to the same degree. The test is rather that of mass resonance to goals actively promoted by relatively small elites. Resonance to the movement for German unification is clear and generally positive in both parts of Germany. Only the small minority of convinced Communists reject unification, and they are by no means unanimous about it. There is no difference in the opinions of political parties, religions or sociological groups in West Germany concerning the desirability of German reunification.

It is theoretically possible that a new national consciousness might some day emerge in the Soviet Zone. Such processes tend, however, to last several generations, especially when they have to overcome traditional forms of political awareness. Because the Soviet Zone is closely linked to current happenings in West Germany through television, radio and other media, the process of separatist political development would probably take longer than would have been the case in earlier centuries. At the present time the vast majority of the population in East Germany regard the Communists as tools of Soviet imperialism. A certain identification with the misery of the region may also be observed but does not change this fundamental attitude.

PARTITION OF GERMANY AS AN ASPECT OF SOVIET FOREIGN POLICY

Soviet foreign policy of recent years has been characterized by two different sets of motives, which presumably will continue to guide the Kremlin in its foreign affairs in years to come. These two sets of motives exert a reciprocal influence and are inseparable as a matter of political practice. One set reflects traditional Russian imperialism within regional limits, and the other is an expression of communist world revolutionary politics.

Imperialism as a *Leitmotiv* of Russian foreign policy finds expression in the continuation of specific principles of state policy concerned with the region of which Russia is a part—principles that have persisted (though with occasional interruptions) since Czarist times. Like all imperialisms, the Russian variety has both an offensive and a defensive motivation, which are hard to isolate from each other. The Soviet Communist party has adopted Russian imperialism for the practical reason that—in Europe at least—the state has proved to be the most effective, indeed the single effective, vehicle for spreading communism. In Moscow's East European vassal states, communism rests on the points of Soviet bayonets.

Soviet foreign policy recognized the outcome of World War II as an opportunity to pursue an active Central European policy—an opportunity it was quick to grasp. For a few years after the war, its objectives and methods were limited by the fear that the Western powers might exploit the industrial power of West Germany. For this reason the Kremlin considered for a while the restoration of a reunited German state, which it hoped could be neutralized or perhaps even bolshevized. The Soviet political line at this time manifested two contradictory tendencies: socialization within the Soviet-controlled area and the desire to persuade the western half of Germany to embrace a neutralist policy. The internal contradictions of this

German policy pursued by the Soviets caused it to fail. Since 1955, therefore, Soviet foreign policy has adopted the objective of making the partition of Germany permanent. Western fears that an incident involving Berlin might lead to a military collision have provided the Kremlin with an effective means of exerting pressure on the West.

The idea of a reunification under communist leadership still reappears briefly from time to time. This concept is frequently camouflaged by the slogan of "Rapallo" politics. The possibility that the Kremlin might some day develop and execute a policy along this line should be taken seriously.

From the contemporary Soviet point of view, the following reasons militate against a reunification of Germany: (1) the possible deterioration of Russia's strategic position in Europe; (2) the danger that reunification would raise for Russian or communist hegemony in East-Central Europe; (3) fear that a reunification would be regarded as a defeat for the Soviet Union and for communism in Europe; and (4) the pressure of world revolutionary agitation by China.

There are also, however, a number of factors that might lead Soviet policy to take a more favorable view of German reunification. These include the following: (1) the realization that the German people will never abandon the goal of reunification, so that the Russian position in Eastern Germany is bound to collapse whenever the U.S.S.R. is shaken by a serious crisis, possibly jeopardizing Russian hegemony throughout East-Central Europe (as Stalin put it: "Hitlers come and go, but Germany remains"); (2) the realization that, because of the importance of the German Federal Republic, with its twelve divisions, for Western strategy, any attempt to achieve relaxation of world tensions through a Russian-Western arrangement without a solution of the German problem is certain to founder on the rock of German resistance; (3) the prospect of far more rapid growth of the Soviet economy through the reallocation of wasteful armament expenditures for productive purposes—a reallocation that a genuine solution of the German problem would make possible; the attractiveness of this prospect to the Soviets might well be enhanced through the contingent offer of sizable long-term German credits for the development of the Soviet economy; and (4) the speculative hope that the Western powers might be willing to guarantee the current Soviet position in East-Central Europe in return for concessions in the German question. Such a compromise would dissolve the possibly fatal connection between the Russians' position in Sovzone Germany and their hegemony in East-Central Europe.*

There is no doubt that contemporary Soviet foreign policy is dominated by negative considerations. The Soviets hope to overcome the Western powers, the Federal Republic and the resistance in the Soviet Zone through a policy of attrition. They look forward to symptoms of fatigue in the democracies and to peace initiatives that propose to abandon reunification as the price for relaxing tensions. It is therefore their objective to induce the Western powers to accept the theory of two or three states. From time to time, however, the Soviets modify the two-state theory to suggest a "federation of both German states." This tactic is probably dictated by the hope that establishment of such a federation could have a neutralizing influence on Western Germany.

Should the Western powers ever abandon the goal of German reunification, however, they could expect with certainty to become the targets of communist-inspired charges of treason against the German people analogous to those that followed the partition of Vietnam. The rulers of the German Democratic Republic have never renounced the nationalist symbols of Tauroggen and Rapallo. In the extreme case, were the German Federal Republic itself to abandon the objective of reunification, the German Democratic Republic would proceed without delay to usurp its role as the champion of German unity.

Finally, it is necessary to warn against the false hope that the so-called liberalization in the Soviet Union will have any significant influence on the European policy of that state. Talks on relaxation of tensions are designed to achieve a consolidation of the position of the Soviet Union in Central Europe *combined with* a reduction in armaments. They do not contemplate the liquidation of Soviet imperialism in that area.

POSSIBLE SOLUTIONS OF THE GERMAN QUESTION

In considering the possibilities of finding a solution to the German question it is hardly necessary to observe that neither war nor

*The reader need hardly be reminded that this section deals with strategic speculations of the Russian communist leadership. There is no implication that responsible Western statesmen would or should barter the freedom of certain peoples in return for that of others.—Eds.

the threat of war is an acceptable means. Both are excluded by the realities of atomic warfare and the atomic pact. For this reason the strategy of pressure once contemplated by John Foster Dulles is no longer available. Aside from the possible exploitation of unpredictable events, such as a serious weakening of the Soviet Union, the only way to achieve reunification is through agreement of the Four Powers, all of whom are both formally and in fact responsible for the German question.

The Western powers are definitely determined to achieve the goal of reunification. The Soviet Union has attempted since the mid-fifties to secure the abandonment of this goal. A change in the Soviet attitude is only conceivable if the interest of the Soviet Union in solving the problem can be aroused.

A Soviet interest in solving the German problem might emerge as a consequence of the Soviet desire for disarmament or arms limitation—a desire that is a matter of controversy in Soviet internal politics. It might conceivably be an attractive prospect for the Soviet Union to be able to employ its own economic potential for general development of the country, especially for internal consumption, and as a tool of foreign policy to gain influence in Asia and Africa rather than expending it on the armament of military divisions required to hold its position in Germany. With this thought in mind, the Kremlin might be led to accept the idea that disarmament must be accompanied by appropriate solutions of political problems, without which it remains impossible. Considerations of this kind formed the basis for the Herter Plan, which contemplated the combination of gradual disarmament and a gradual solution of the German question. Pursuance of the plan was blocked by the Soviet hope of achieving disarmament or arms limitation without concessions on political matters, as well as by the change of government in the United States.

A more or less automatic solution through relaxation of tensions (following which German reunification would fall like the proverbial ripe apple from the tree) is highly improbable, because the German question would inevitably arise at a certain stage in the general negotiations intended to produce relaxation. The attempt to exclude it from the agenda would confirm Moscow in its renitent attitude.

Nor would greater independence of Moscow's vassals in East-Central Europe improve the prospects for restoring German unity. For one thing, some of them take a skeptical attitude toward reunification. For another, the Soviet Union would most likely seek to compensate the greater mobility accorded these states by tightening its grip on the Soviet Zone of Germany.

Under these circumstances, the most probable chance of solving the German question would appear to lie in a combination of disarmament and reunification. Recently, in London, Gromyko called renewed attention to the Soviet view that there is a connection between the problem of armaments in Central Europe and the German question. The Soviets, it follows, are naturally unable to agree to German reunification without a simultaneous solution of the security problem in Europe.

From the American point of view, on the other hand, a shift in the military status quo in the heart of Europe can be considered only if it promises not to result in increased danger for Europe. Military security in Central Europe, disarmament and solution of the German question are thus as closely linked in American as in Russian eyes. There is interest in this connection in the remarks of General de Gaulle made at a press conference on February 4, 1965. A guarantee of a new status quo for Central Europe by the participating world powers and interested European powers, the French President indicated, would not necessarily meet with German resistance, provided the solution showed promise of a certain durability.

The Soviet thesis that reunification is a matter for the two German states need not be an insuperable obstacle. As soon as the world powers reach agreement on the basic question of reunification, the matter of procedure would drop to secondary importance. It is, however, urgently important to avoid recognition of Moscow's two-state theory before such agreement of the world powers has been achieved. Such premature recognition would fulfill Moscow's wishes and would cement the partition of Germany.

The idea of supplementing the two-states theory with a German confederation would at first only help the Soviet Union to achieve its goals. The one possible compensating advantage, with long-range rather than immediate value, would be that the thesis of the necessity of special political ties uniting the Germans would have been accepted in principle. This thesis might be utilized to bring about unification, should a suitable opportunity arise. An immediate real political value in the sense of a genuine convergence of internal policies in the two German partial states is not to be expected from this type of arrangement. It would, rather, involve the danger of persistent Eastern interference in the affairs of the Federal Republic.

The "policy of patience" followed by the Soviet Union, which hopes to impose its will in the German question by out-waiting its opponents, must be countered with a "policy of even greater patience" on the part of the West. Only when the Soviets realize that their objectives are unattainable even in the long run is there a possibility that they will change their point of view. The relatively frequent shifts in Western political strategy in the German question are, therefore, acceptable only if an unalterable will to achieve the reunification of Germany is apparent behind them. (President de Gaulle's press conference of February 4, 1965, is to be welcomed from this point of view, as is Harold Wilson's statement during his recent visit to Bonn.)

To maintain the objective of German reunification as an active political factor, it is necessary that the Western powers accept without reservation and undertake to satisfy the German demand for a never-ending series of new Western initiatives concerning Germany, particularly on the part of the United States. As things stand today, the principal purpose of such initiatives is to impress upon Moscow that the Western powers will not yield on the German question. Whether immediate practical results can be expected from new initiatives is a question of secondary importance.

Part Three
EASTERN EUROPE
and
WORLD POLICY

CHAPTER X

Cultural Exchange With Central and Eastern Europe: Problems and Prospects

ROBERT F. BYRNES

O NE OF THE striking features of relations between the United States and its European allies and the Soviet Union and the states ruled by the Communists in Eastern and Central Europe during the last few years has been the role played by various forms of cultural exchange, of which the most widely publicized have been exhibitions of art, tours by various dancing groups, distinguished artists and musical organizations and the scientific and technical exhibits staged in some major cities. In addition, delegations of various kinds have toured briefly while their members have conferred with colleagues in the same disciplines or professional fields. Young and old scholars have given lectures in the other countries and have often stayed for prolonged periods of time for research in laboratories, libraries and archives. In recent years the Soviet Union and the communist states of Central and Eastern Europe have ceased jamming Western broadcasts and have on occasion allowed Western performances to be televised. Finally, Poland and Yugoslavia and to some degree Hungary have allowed the distribution of some Western newspapers and magazines, a form of intellectual exchange not tolerated within the Soviet Union or, as yet, in the other communist states. In short, while exchange of information and relations of an intellectual and cultural character are by no means free and unrestricted, the peoples of Central and Eastern Europe are no longer as isolated as they were; and cultural exchanges now play an important role in our diplomacy, as in that of the states ruled by Communists.

The recent prominence of cultural exchange is a reflection of the more relaxed and civilized policies of the communist governments and of changed policy of the United States and its allies toward East-Central Europe over the past decade. American policy toward the Soviet Union since 1947 has been defined accurately as containment, the policy enunciated first by George F. Kennan and put into effect by Secretary of State Marshall and President Truman. This policy reflected the conviction of the American government that the expansion of Soviet power had to be resisted "with unalterable counterforce at every point where they [the Russians] show signs of encroaching on the interests of a peaceful and stable world." It rested on the assumption that successful containment of communist expansion would "increase enormously the strains under which Soviet policy must operate, to force upon the Kremlin a far greater degree of moderation and circumspection than it has had to observe in recent years and in this way to promote tendencies which must eventually find their outlet in either the breakup or the gradual mellowing of Soviet power." Containment was based on the development of American and Allied military strength, the economic and political recovery of Western Europe and its continued economic growth, progress toward some form of economic and political unification of the West European states and toward the creation of an Atlantic community and, above all, the demonstration by the United States and its allies of their determination to resist communist expansion—by force, when necessary, as in Greece, Korea and South Vietnam.

During the early years in which the United States and its allies followed the containment policy and during the same years, when the Soviet Union and the communist states tightly restricted relations with the rest of the world, few connections of any kind existed between the United States or Western Europe and the states of East-Central Europe. In fact, even tourists were very few; the Western radio was jammed; and the Western states in the early fifties were reduced to sending balloons over Czechoslovakia and Poland, with leaflets being released by mechanical or chemical devices to float down upon peoples completely isolated from the rest of the world.

Containment has been a remarkably successful policy, but there have been periods when large numbers of Americans turned against it. For example, the policy of the American government from early

1953 through the summer of 1954 was labeled liberation, and President Eisenhower, Secretary of State Dulles and their leading colleagues before and after the election of 1952 spoke of liberating East-Central Europe and of rolling back communist power with a "positive foreign policy," which was generally believed to mean increased application of external pressure upon the Soviet system to hasten its collapse and thereby the emancipation of the peoples under Soviet domination. The policy of liberation frightened our friends and allies, enabled Communists throughout the world to portray the United States as an aggressive militaristic power and had no apparent effect upon the power or policy of the Communists.

We therefore returned to containment in 1954, only to find ourselves helpless to aid the embattled Hungarians in the fall of 1956, when Soviet power faced a serious crisis reflecting the successes of the containment policy, the thaw and so-called relaxation of tensions, which the Soviet leaders had gradually introduced after Stalin's death, and the explosive resentments felt by the peoples in East-Central Europe under communist rule. The revolt in Hungary was brutally and effectively crushed; but the events of 1956 were political disasters of the first magnitude for the Soviet Union. Some believed that the disintegration of the communist empire was beginning. Others called it a mark of the military power and spiritual weakness of the Soviet system. Others were impressed by the fact that the darlings of the Communists—the workers, the intellectuals and the students—had turned against the system, thus proving that the power and influence of communism had been exaggerated. The 1956 revolts rendered questionable the value of the disloyal area to the Soviet Union, and the communist movement outside the communist countries suffered a kind of spiritual crisis.

After 1956 the United States and its allies returned to their defensive and reactive containment policy, strengthening the areas of the world most susceptible to communist pressure; persuading the communist rulers that we would resist expansion, by war if necessary, but would not attack the communist states; seeking to direct the energies of the entire world toward a peaceful solution of the problems which threatened peace; and exploring new peaceful, political ways of strengthening contacts and increasing influence among the peoples living in East-Central Europe.

In 1957 and 1958, however, Kennan, several members of the British Labor party, various continental Socialists and a number of European intellectuals flirted with a policy known as disengagement, which suggested creation of a "thinned-out zone" or "a mutual withdrawal from the heart of Europe in order to reduce tension and armament." Thus, Western and Soviet troops were to move away from the line that separated them in East-Central Europe, with the Western forces possibly evacuating all of West Germany and the Soviet troops moving back from East Germany and Czechoslovakia. This proposal was based on a false analysis of the causes of the conflict and of probable Soviet policies. Above all, it reflected the belief that the Western powers could do little to assist the peoples of East-Central Europe, whose lives and philosophies were, presumably, being reshaped under communist rule. Indeed, Mr. Kennan wrote in 1958:

> If things go on as they are today, there will simply have to be some sort of adjustment on the part of the peoples of Eastern Europe, even if it is one that takes the form of general despair, apathy, demoralization and the deepest sort of disillusion with the West. The failure of the recent popular uprisings to shake the Soviet military domination has now produced a bitter and dangerous despondency throughout large parts of Eastern Europe. If the taste or even the hope of independence once dies out in the hearts of these peoples, then there will be no recovering it; then Moscow's victory will be complete. . . .[1]

Fortunately, Western policy was little affected by those who were tempted by disengagement, and the opportunities that have been seized and that are now even more full of promise than before have developed because of the achievements of containment, the errors of the Communists and the faith and resolution of the peoples of East-Central Europe. The economic and political progress of Western Europe, the extraordinary achievements of the Common Market and its impact on East-Central Europe, the disarray and growing disunity within the international communist movement and the determination of the peoples living under communist rule have together provided us an opportunity for promoting peaceful change within the Soviet Union and Eastern Europe, which no one would have thought possible even a few years ago. We have naturally been aided enormously by the growing conflict between the Soviet Union and Communist China, which has contributed to the ideological collapse of the international communist movement and to the development of polycentrism.

American policy in the last decade has begun to take advantage of the considerable opportunities open to it. The actions of the American government in providing economic assistance to Poland and both economic and military assistance to Yugoslavia; the splendid programs launched by the Ford Foundation to bring Polish, Yugoslav, Hungarian and Czechoslovak scholars to Western Europe and the United States; and the exchange programs established by the Inter-University Committee, the National Academy of Science and the International Institute of Education have all contributed to the expansion of freedom in the states of Eastern Europe. The signing on November 9, 1964, of an agreement between the United States and Yugoslavia for the exchange of Fulbright scholars and professors may be the first step toward similar agreements with other communist countries, the kind of cultural exchange from which every country involved can only benefit and that will also help to weaken communist rule.

As opportunities for greater cultural contact with the peoples of East-Central Europe have increased, the American government has relaxed its attitude toward trade and cultural exchange with each country, recognizing, as Secretary Rusk said in February, 1964, that we should establish a system for "treating different communist countries differently." The address of President Johnson at the Virginia Military Institute on May 23, 1964, in which he spoke of building bridges across the gulf between the West and the peoples of Eastern Europe marked another stage in our growing understanding of the need for weakening the communist grip over these people and for encouraging the idea of independence among them. Briefly, American and Western policy has been directed toward increasing the differences among the states of Eastern Europe and toward encouraging each one to strike out on its own to achieve its own goals and to seek gradually to reestablish normal relations with the people of the West.

In order to reach these goals, the United States and its allies must make use of many instruments, of which cultural exchanges are only one and by no means the most important. In fact, one of our problems is to recognize that the base of our position must remain military, economic and political strength, continuing coordination of policy among the Western states and resolution. We must not overestimate what can be achieved through cultural exchanges; but we do need to recognize that splendid opportunities for peaceful development have emerged, that this is an age in which the speed of change is extraordinarily great and that we are a part of an irreversible process that is carrying the entire world to new levels of political development. Moreover, we must recognize that the effectiveness of our policy in cultural exchange will be immensely affected by our domestic and foreign policies. For example, the rapidity and humanity with which we provide equal rights and opportunities to all Americans will exceed in importance any policy we devise for East-Central Europe itself.

The recent expansion of cultural exchanges with the countries of East-Central Europe has naturally been achieved with the advice and consent of the communist rulers of those countries. Indeed, these men, presumably devoted to their philosophy and to their system of government, have aims and ambitions with regard to cultural exchange that persuade them that the increase in contact is to their advantage, and not to ours. In short, our goals are quite different from those of the Communists.

The main purpose for expanding cultural exchange, insofar as the United States and its allies are concerned, is to assist the peoples of East-Central Europe to grow in freedom and to help them create opportunities for developing their own resources and for again achieving normal relations with the rest of Europe in a world framework that can improve the prospects for peace. In other words, our main goal is a political one—that of building a bridge into East-Central Europe over which we can help these people attain their goals. Moreover, we must act in the full knowledge that processes encouraged in East-Central Europe will have profound influence within the Soviet Union and throughout the rest of the communist movement everywhere in the world. Every communist state is a door to another communist state.

We naturally have other goals, particularly those of increasing our knowledge of the culture of these peoples, of whom we are very ignorant, multiplying the number of specialists in this country who will be equipped to educate others about Central and Eastern Europe and, naturally, increasing knowledge of us in these regions. At the same time, although the United States and the West European states in general are superior in science and technology, the Western peoples can surely benefit from closer acquaintance with the art and science of the states of East-Central Europe.

The ambitions of the communist rulers in these exchanges are quite different from ours; they are also different from those of the people they rule. The peoples of East-Central Europe are eager to expand cultural exchanges because they reflect an opportunity to become again a free part of the European community and to attain the economic benefits of the scientific and technical revolutions of this century. For the communist rulers, however, and presumably for the Soviet leaders who stand behind them, the principal goal is without question the acquisition of scientific, technical and military information, which will enable them to stengthen their economy and their military systems. They are no doubt as eager as we are to increase the number of their specialists qualified to make judgments concerning political, scientific and technical developments in Western Europe and the United States. Moreover, they almost certainly see cultural exchange as a fruitful form of political warfare, not only in providing respectability in the eyes of their own people and in the eyes of the world for the communist system, but also in terms of propaganda and prestige. Finally, we must note that cultural exchange can be a financially profitable enterprise for the communist states, just as some forms of cultural exchange can benefit private entrepreneurs in the West.

The great gap or conflict between our goals and those of the Communists constitutes one of the great hazards this exchange faces. Perhaps even more important, particularly for those who are critical of such relations with communist states and who accept either liberation or disengagement as more effective alternatives, is the possible moral demobilization that may result from doing business with communist countries and from accepting the continued existence of communist rule. Some believe that this kind of relationship will not only weaken the resolution of the Western states, it will undermine and perhaps even destroy the faith of those who have been forced to live for so long under communist rule.

Moreover, while many see cultural exchange as a means of weakening and dividing the communist states, others see it as an instrument that may boomerang and divide the West itself. Many in most Western states lack the political sophistication to support a policy of enlightened opportunism, particularly during times of crisis. Moreover, as the Western states scramble with one another for advantages in cultural exchange and for the increase in trade often associated with it, the political divisions that already afflict them may multiply. Finally, as relations become more and more relaxed, local Communist parties and "friendship associations," particularly in Western

Europe, may come to play a prominent role in the exchanges, diverting them from the goals envisaged by Western governments and creating serious political hazards that may threaten the very existence of the programs.

We must assume, in addition, that the scientists and other scholars sent to the West by the communist governments will acquire important knowledge of a scientific, technical and military character, knowledge that may be far more substantial than we appreciate and that may on occasion help produce truly significant increments to communist power. Moreover, we must also assume that some of those who travel in the West on exchange programs may be spies and may engage in subverting the countries in which they are temporarily living. In other words, the communist governments can make use of the cultural exchange program in order to increase their power and to strengthen their systems. Curiously, cultural exchange programs may also be placed in jeopardy and even wrecked should Western intelligence agencies seek to take advantage of this opportunity to insert Western agents into East-Central Europe, thereby poisoning the entire well of the exchange and leading many to think that there are no differences between the two systems.

The relaxation of controls in Eastern Europe and the gradual modification of Soviet control in the last few years may blind some Americans to Soviet sensitivity concerning this region. The progress of change throughout the area must be slow and gradual, or the Soviet rulers may be excited into a violent reaction against ideological coexistence and end the process, as they sought to do in Hungary in 1956.

Another serious problem is that posed by the Soviet Zone or the German Democratic Republic. One of the greatest hazards for the United States and its allies with regard to increasing cultural exchange is the impact such a policy may have upon the strong and proper German interest in the unification of Germany and, consequently, upon West Germany's reliability as an ally. In short, the more relaxed relations are between the other East European states and the West, the more resentment is likely to increase in West Germany as the likelihood of reunification seems to fade away. Greater Western efforts to increase and expand intellectual and cultural relationships with the communist states of East-Central Europe imply the acceptance of the political status quo and suggest in particular that the reunification of Germany may be sacrificed to a general effort to loosen communist control over the other countries of East-Central Europe. Thus, including Sovzone Germany in any American or Western program of academic exchanges, for example, would naturally cause the greatest resentment within West Germany and would split the Western alliance. On the other hand, if the Soviet Zone were ignored in our cultural exchange policy, its isolation and growing dependence would raise most serious problems for the states of East-Central Europe, increase the gap that already separates their development from that of Sovzone Germany and raise such serious problems for the Soviet government that it might choose to intervene in the other states ruled by Communists.

Perhaps the most serious hazard of all in the expansion of cultural exchange is the possibility that the Western peoples will not have the patience, endurance and simple faith in themselves and in others to support a policy whose results may appear to come in a slow and undramatic fashion. We must remember that Mr. Kennan himself, the architect of the containment doctrine, wrote in the spring of 1956 that there was a "finality, for better or worse, about what has happened in Eastern Europe." In addition, in 1958, less than two years after the successful Polish revolt and the unsuccessful Hungarian revolution, Mr. Kennan assumed that such "bitter and dangerous despondency prevailed" in East-Central Europe that the likelihood of a complete victory for Moscow there was very great.

Expanding cultural exchanges is a relatively inexpensive process, compared to research in outer space, but costs do create special problems, even for a wealthy state or for an alliance of rich and powerful countries. Thus, if the costs are to be met for an efficient and expanded program, Western governments must play a very active role in intellectual enterprises in which the government of the United States traditionally has not participated. The powerful intervention of Western governments in programs launched in large part by private organizations, such as the Ford Foundation, in which sensitive and independent intellectuals participate, will inevitably change the character of the exchange programs, introduce government bureaucracies where they had not existed before and create administrative problems inevitable in a situation in which government and private organizations together deal with issues that require consistent, sensitive and skillful direction. Moreover, these issues will also certainly be further complicated as our cultural exchange programs with East-Central Europe are related to new trade and credit policies.

A brief examination of the role of the American universities, organized as they now are in the Inter-University Committee on Travel Grants, might play in expanding cultural relations with East-Central Europe may demonstrate this point. The university cannot be remote from the society in which it functions and which it serves. In order to serve society most effectively, however, the university in any country must remain true to its primary educational goals. It is a curious paradox, borne out by experience, that "political warfare" use of the universities and of the arts is futile and in the long run destructive. When universities, artists and scientists operate independently, on the other hand, doing their own work in their own best way, they can have a very powerful impact. Our recent experiences with the Soviet Union have revealed the direct correlation between quality of independent scholarship and impact on Soviet society. To achieve this goal most effectively, the universities must play a significant role in the exchange of scholars and artists.

Our educational institutions, our art centers and our learned societies are free and independent, suspicious of government and accustomed to their own ways of conducting their affairs. They are sovereign in their own areas of responsibility. They must be allowed to remain sovereign, to conduct their business of research, instruction and creation as they see fit and to have a large share in the direction of educational and cultural relationships, in which they have had long experience, or increased intellectual contact with the communist world simply will not be productive. Indeed, any attempt by our government to manipulate our educational institutions and their relations with other countries would cause incredible harm to our own society.

Moreover, our programs and relationships must be created and organized on the basis of quality, not quantity. In both cultural and political terms, one highly qualified participant will be many times more effective than ten persons who are only "representative Americans." Given the organization of communist societies, we must seek to send our best minds there and to have them send their best minds here.

One of the principal problems is that of coordinating the various institutions—government, academic, private and commercial—of the various countries that are interested in cultural exchanges so that there is no friction or conflict and the most efficient use is made of the relatively scarce resources available. In fact, the Western states ought to form a coordinating body to pool information, to provide for consultation concerning problems and negotiations, to coordinate plans and policies and to carry out combined operations in a very difficult and complicated field. In fact, the need for cooperation and coordination in cultural exchanges is just as important as in military operations. The United States and its allies should recognize that they face an opportunity almost as great as that of 1947 and that the spirit and structure of the organization that should be established is even more important than the amount of money made available.

Of even more significance, the West needs a new concept of Europe and a new structure of Europe, just as it required a new approach to the economic and political problems facing Europe in 1947 to enable that great continent to achieve political and economic progress. We need a new definition of Europe, a new approach to common problems, so that Europe can be reconstituted "within its historic boundaries." If a new concept of Europe that draws the sympathy and understanding of Europeans wherever they may be can be created, a new link may bring Eastern and Western Europe together, just as another new link may tie the new Europe into the larger Atlantic community, which may one day extend from San Francisco to Vladivostok.

Anyone with confidence in the West must assume that we can surmount the hazards these policies raise and that we can continue to take advantage of the opportunities we face. Indeed, rather than fret over the hazards and costs of an expanded program of cultural exchanges, we should rejoice that the sterile barriers of the past have to some degree been lifted and that we now have an opportunity to compete with intellectual weapons on a peaceful field for the minds and souls of the world in circumstances far more favorable to democratic governments than those Stalin devised. We now stand to benefit from the achievements of the containment policy and to enable free men and the passage of free ideas to work as our strengths. It would be tragic if we were not now prepared to collect the dividends from these long, hard years and succumbed instead to the perils of prosperity. The cultural vitality of the West is so great, from Louis Armstrong and *My Fair Lady* to exhibits of Western prints and the work of young scholars in Russian history, that we should regard cultural exchange as a splendid opportunity to work in an area in which silence has been one of the characteristics of cultural life.

The long-term goal or purpose of cultural exchanges under the umbrella of Western military strength and unity should be clear in our minds. If we can create a new concept of Europe, coordinate the policies of the Western states and identify and establish a program that discourages destructive nationalism in Eastern Europe while encouraging improvement of the standards of living and the growth of freedom and independence, we may through these peaceful means achieve a situation in which the countries of Eastern Europe can become independent without constituting a threat to the Soviet Union, achieve a normal relationship with the states of Western Europe in a new European community and begin to cooperate in the common interest of all Europeans in helping to resolve the other, larger problems that now face the world.

NOTES TO CHAPTER TEN

1. George Kennan, *Russia, the Atom, and the West* (New York: Harper & Law, Inc., 1958), p. 35.

CHAPTER XI

East-West Trade Policy and Economic Cooperation

HERMANN GROSS

PROBLEMS OF TRADE POLICY and economic cooperation between the West and Eastern Europe arise from the different stages of development and the fundamental contrasts between the respective economic systems, as well as from different priorities in satisfying the demands of populations in the two groups of countries. The over-populated East European countries, which are passing through a stage of rapid technological and economic development in spite of meager capital resources, form the first group; the highly developed industrial countries of the Western world form the other.

In the Western market economies, where private ownership of capital goods prevails, producers and consumers generally determine the pattern of investment, production and trade. Long-term economic policy in the centrally planned East European economies, however, is decided by the totalitarian state, which also owns and controls the capital resources. Under communist rule economic policy is frequently determined with noneconomic, mainly ideological or technological, objectives in mind. The governments belonging to COMECON believe that their aim of transforming the backward agrarian states into dynamically expanding industrial economies can only be achieved if production is centrally planned, prices are fixed by the authorities and foreign trade is channeled via state trade monopolies.[1]

This forced industrialization was undertaken at the expense of agriculture, which was responsible for the export surpluses before the last war; the result was a decline in the living standard of Eastern bloc populations. The negative effects were enhanced by the fact that production, instead of being planned for maximum efficiency, consisted mainly of uneconomical, costly local experiments in the capital goods sector. This so-called Stalinist economic policy produced very disturbing disproportions between the various branches of industry and productive units as well as serious trade and payments deficits. Though a more realistic industrial and agricultural policy is being sought since the events in Poland and Hungary in 1956, the East European states still suffer considerably from their previous uneconomic, autarkic development. The internal difficulties resulting from this development and from unrelenting central economic planning obstruct rational economic cooperation among the COMECON states as well as intensive economic relations between them and the Western market economies. The principal difficulties in this respect are:

1. Prices in each of the Eastern bloc states are fixed and manipulated by the state authorities on different levels and according to different economic principles, often irrespective of the actual cost of production and the effective demand.

2. There is no convertible currency in any of the Eastern bloc states.

3. There are no uniform criteria by which to compare and evaluate existing investments and investment opportunities.

There is no measure, like the price level in a market economy, by which to determine in which Eastern bloc state it would be most economical and otherwise advantageous to produce certain goods. As a result the COMECON states, even in trade with one another, are still forced to follow capitalist world market prices of 1958.

State price-fixing and manipulation combined with state trade monopolies, on the other hand, enable the state-trading countries, much more effectively than any market economy, to favor or discriminate against their trade partners in import and export transactions. With the exception of Czechoslovakia, the Eastern bloc countries are not full members of the General Agreement on Tariffs and Trade (GATT); thus they are not subject to the GATT provisions concerning the most-favored-nation clause or the obligation to refrain from practices that obstruct free competition. Even Czechoslovakia, though a full member, does not enjoy the liberalization measures taken within GATT or the benefits of the most-favored-nation clause because, as a state-trading country, it is largely unable to fulfill its obligations under these headings. Poland has been an associate member of GATT since 1960 and can participate in the work of the contracting parties by special arrangement. Yugoslavia, an associate member since 1959, and Egypt were admitted in 1962 as provisional members, the step preliminary to full membership. By agreeing to admit two countries with a state-trading system, GATT has created an important precedent. This makes it necessary to reexamine the problems of commercial relations between countries with a market economy and countries with a state-trading system.[2]

For instance, the application of the most-favored-nation clause has quite a different practical importance in the two economic systems. Under the most-favored-nation clause, the Eastern trading enterprises, as representatives of the national state-trading monopolies, enjoy the same rights of establishment and trading as domestic or other foreign private enterprises in the market economies. These opportunities have only a very limited business value and effect for Western firms, even if they are permitted to establish in state-trading countries, for such countries do not import what their consumers or producers demand but what is deemed necessary by the planning authorities.

The most-favored-nation clause has, however, a certain importance in connection with the establishment of export agencies of Western firms and the maintenance of permanent trade missions in the COMECON states, since these permit an intensive and realistic study of markets and demand situations. Besides, direct contact can be established with the competent state import and export agencies or enterprises and the administrative, economic and technical intelligentsia, who are becoming more influential all the time. Finally, the trade missions are valuable, particularly for the Federal Republic of Germany, which does not entertain official diplomatic relations with the countries of Eastern Europe (with the exception of the U.S.S.R.), in reviving and confirming traditional cultural relations, including tourism, which are matters of general interest.

The attitude of the United States toward German efforts to reestablish trade relations with Eastern Europe was recently stated by Ambassador McGhee as follows:

My Government welcomes the imaginative efforts of the Federal Republic to establish the foundation for improved relations between the Federal Republic and the countries of Eastern Europe. By negotiating trade agreements and establishing trade missions on a reciprocal basis with several of these countries— Poland, Rumania, and Hungary—the Federal Republic is improving the ties which Germany has in the area. German trade with the area has been maintained at a healthy volume—well over half a billion dollars a year. This is a field in which Germany can take an important role in the interest of the West as a whole. At the same time Germany can contribute to the security and stability of all Europe. We wish you well in this significant undertaking.[3]

As a rule, the most important concession of the state-trading countries in return for most-favored-nation treatment is the granting of import quotas, the manipulation of which is one of the most effective instruments of their foreign trade strategy. By these import quotas the Eastern states try to stimulate the profit interests of Western exporting firms and benefit from their competition for Eastern sales markets. For this reason most Western states grant most-favored-nation treatment to their Eastern trade partners, though this means conceding a one-sided privilege to the latter.

The granting of most-favored-nation privileges by Western states may assume more far-reaching importance in connection with customs tariff agreements, particularly within the framework of the Kennedy Round. This is so because the significance and effect of customs duties are fundamentally different in the two systems. In the state-trading countries, customs duties are not an instrument of trade policy, they are merely a means of adjusting the low prices of imported goods to the high domestic prices; and imports, as we have seen, do not depend on the rate of duty but on requirements as dictated by economic planning. The state must import essential goods regardless of the price. As a result, customs tariff agreements that comprise tariff cuts and the most-favored-nation clause in trade with Eastern bloc partners do not give Western entrepreneurs and exporters a proportionate advantage, though they are not quite valueless.

Accordingly, an international linear 50 per cent cut in customs duties, which is the objective of the Kennedy Round within the framework of the GATT negotiations, would not fulfill its real purpose insofar as the Eastern bloc states are concerned: a scaling-down of customs duties would not directly promote the export of Western goods to Eastern states. Nevertheless, the improved sales opportunities for state-trading countries, which are opened through Western tariff reductions, may indirectly promote Western exports to the East. Due to the bilateral character of Eastern bloc trade agreements, the volume of their imports generally depends on the volume of their exports. In other words, the volume of East-West trade depends largely on the ability of Eastern states to deliver and compete.

This dependence of imports on exports in the East may induce Eastern states—particularly in case of an urgent demand for Western foreign exchange, either for repaying credits or for paying for essential imports—to force their exports to Western and developing countries at dumping prices.

On the import side, state-trading countries may be compelled to cut their imports drastically in order to save foreign exchange. These restrictions might affect not only countries that extend them credit but also other Western countries, depending on the Eastern regime's intentions. This might produce undesirable disturbances in Western markets and serious balance-of-payments disequilibria between Eastern and Western states. The state-trading countries, by their economic system and foreign trade monopoly with manipulated prices, are technically quite able to adopt all such trade policy measures. Therefore, commercial exchanges and credit relations with Eastern Europe represent special problems and require the elaboration of a specific trading and credit policy on different principles from those customary between democratic countries with more or less free market economies and convertible currencies.

Up to the present, Western states have been able to protect themselves against the dangers the economic and trade systems of state-trading countries represent for their markets with the help of import quotas and price-equalization levies, as well as import and export licenses within the framework of bilateral trade agreements.[4] The advantages of bilateral agreements are:

1. The agreement is a means of limiting imports from the East that could cause damage to domestic producers or to established third-country suppliers. While the Eastern country receives most-favored-nation tariff treatment for its exports, the effective control is the import quota.

2. The agreement has the advantage of enabling each Western country to achieve a certain minimum level of exports to the East.

3. The bilateral agreement permits the individual Western country to exercise some marginal influence on the composition of its exports to the East.

Yet there is no uniform concept of trade policy vis-à-vis Eastern

Europe. The defensive protective measures in Western states are practiced in very different ways and with varying degrees of strictness. As a result, cheap Eastern products may be imported indirectly via third countries.

However, a common Western trade and credit policy could be applied, not only defensively, but also as an offensive instrument in relations with the communist bloc. The present splitting up of the formerly monolithic Eastern bloc makes it possible to differentiate the treatment accorded individual East European countries. The example of Yugoslavia proves that revisionist ideas developing within the communist bloc are much more dangerous for its unity than the systematic enmity of capitalist states. Consequently, nothing should be left undone in promoting national differentiation and independence in world communism. This policy, however, demands a minimum of coordination in the West, if it is to be successful.

At the present time, each Western government is trying to "soften" the Eastern bloc in its own way; each lays stress on different aspects, so that one can hardly speak of a selective promotion of satellite aspirations for independence. The policy of selective treatment of the Eastern bloc states is being defeated, not by an autocratic Stalin, but by a lack of coordination in the West, for Eastern polycentrism has its parallel in Western neonationalism.[5]

The establishment of the EEC has given rise to some new economic and political realities in the West, which offer the opportunity to develop a common foreign trade policy of at least the six member states vis-à-vis Eastern Europe. By establishing a full economic union the EEC will be in a much stronger position than its individual member states have been to influence the general course of East-West economic relations. A coordinated trade and credit policy of the Western countries would decidedly strengthen the bargaining position of the West and enable the Free World to thwart any attempt on the part of communist countries to play the individual Western states against each other.

This assumption seems justified for several reasons. Consequently, an attempt is made here to outline the fundamental problems of East-West relations and those relating to a future coordinated trade and credit policy of the West by analyzing the trade and economic relations of the EEC member states with the East European countries.

One reason for presuming that a uniform trade policy of the EEC may decisively influence East-West economic relations is the fact

that the Common Market is by far the most important Western trade
partner of the Eastern bloc. East-West trade represents about $10,-
500,000,000, that is, 3.5 per cent of total Free World trade, which
runs to an annual value of about $300,000,000,000. The United
States' share in East-West trade is very small. American exports to
Eastern Europe have exceeded $100,000,000 in recent years and
reached $167,000,000 in 1963, while American imports from Eastern
Europe have ranged between $65,000,000 and $85,000,000 annually.
Less than .5 per cent of United States foreign trade is with the Soviet
bloc, as compared with from 3 per cent to 5 per cent for most West
European countries and considerably more for a few, such as Fin-
land (20 per cent) and Iceland (17 per cent).[6]

Trade by the countries of Western Europe with the communist
world, taken by itself, accounts for more than 60 per cent of the
world's entire East-West trade, the EEC being responsible for from
40 to 50 per cent of the West European share. East European trade
with the non-communist world amounted to from 27 per cent to 40
per cent of the total foreign trade of Eastern Europe in 1963. Trade
with the EEC accounted for more than 50 per cent of the Western
trade of Rumania, 45 per cent of that of Bulgaria, 39 per cent in the
case of Hungary, 26 per cent in the case of Poland and 21 per cent
in that of the U.S.S.R.

Over and above this, trade between the EEC and the Eastern bloc
states, apart from trade with the comparatively industrialized state
of Czechoslovakia, is an exchange of commodities between economically underdeveloped and advanced industrial states, a characteristic
reflecting the overall structure of East-West trade altogether. About
75 per cent of the EEC imports from the Eastern bloc consists of primary products—food, mineral fuels and raw materials—which the
West can buy anywhere and ought by preference to procure from the
newly developing countries. The remainder, which consists of finished goods, has diminished since 1958, which is surprising, considering rapid industrialization of the Eastern bloc.[7] This may be
attributable to the poor quality of the products and to the lack of
efficient service, particularly insofar as the delivery of spare parts,
etc. is concerned.

Finished goods clearly predominate in the EEC's exports to the
Eastern bloc. Their share is 75 per cent, or even 90 per cent of the
total, if chemicals are included. Most of the finished goods are valuable modern capital goods the Eastern bloc is unable to produce

either in comparable qualities or early enough to assure the completion of the various economic plans. This qualitative aspect of Eastern purchases in the West makes East-West trade vitally important for the Eastern bloc and forces the Eastern states to export to the West. For lack of a coordinated trade policy vis-à-vis the East, however, the Western countries have not yet drawn proper benefit from the bargaining power they derive from Eastern dependency on Western deliveries.

Though, up to the present, it is impossible to speak of a common trade policy of the EEC generally, and specifically in relations with the Eastern bloc, certain attempts have been made in that direction. The entire matter is extremely delicate and complicated because it not only involves tariffs and import quotas, it also requires consideration of underlying principles in various sectors of economic policy. Foreign policy and defense aspects also play a decisive role, for any common trade policy is part of a common external policy. This is particularly true in relations with the communist Eastern bloc, where, admittedly, foreign trade is looked upon as an important instrument of politics and ideology. This circumstance demands a common external policy of the EEC that goes beyond economic union.

In approaching a common commercial policy, the EEC has, since 1961, been making efforts to arrive at a unification of trade agreements of the various members with foreign states generally and the Eastern bloc states in particular. To this end, a so-called EEC clause, or one-year cancellation clause, is being inserted in all trade agreements the member states conclude with third countries during the transitional period. In addition, the member states are asked to consult with the EEC Commission prior to opening negotiations looking toward bilateral relations with East European countries. So far, however, this consultation procedure has not functioned satisfactorily; it is to be made more effective pursuant to a proposal of the EEC Commission made in 1964.

The EEC Ministerial Council in 1962 adopted a program calling for the step-by-step introduction of trade regulations, which are supposed to lead to the application of common import regulations for all products from state-trading countries by the end of the transitional period. Their effectiveness is hampered, however, by exceptions the member states claim under the pretext of national protective measures pursuant to Article 115 of the Rome Treaty, by which market isolation is continued instead of being removed.

While foreign trade in industrial products thus still underlies separate national regulations, a common regime of foreign trade in agricultural products has existed since 1962, when the common EEC agricultural policy came into force. In addition, common import regulations for a number of farm products, including grain, pork, beef, milk and dairy products and eggs and poultry, from the state-trading countries have become valid in the meantime. National import quotas have been replaced by so-called evaluation amounts based on the average quantities imported in 1960–61 or the quotas of 1962. Their purpose is to register and keep track of actual imports with a view to preventing them from becoming excessive. Each member state is entitled to stop imports as soon as the imports reach the evaluation amounts. If the imports surpass the evaluation amounts by more than 20 per cent, and if the market in a member state is thereby disturbed, the EEC Commission is entitled to interrupt such imports on its own initiative or on application of a member state. Since the imports of certain food products from all countries are also subject to price equalization levies, exports of agricultural goods from the Eastern bloc states have to jump two hurdles.

These EEC regulations concerning imports from state-trading countries do not affect the Soviet Union, whose exports consist largely of raw materials, mainly crude and refined petroleum, so much as the East European countries. The latter export more farm products to the EEC than their total exports to all other countries. Over 50 per cent of the EEC's imports from Poland, Hungary and Bulgaria, for instance, is in argricultural products. The exports of those products, which are now subject to equalization levies, have declined considerably in some cases. Here the poor quality of East European products as compared with Western farm products had unfavorable consequences, since their low prices led to imposition of equalization levies at especially high rates.

The effect of the EEC's new trade policy system on the food-exporting countries of Eastern Europe is illustrated by the example of Polish egg exports to West Germany (Poland is Eastern Europe's largest exporter of agricultural products). In 1961 and in 1962, before the first provisions of the EEC's common agrarian policy became effective on August 1, 1962, the customs and other import charges on a ton of Polish eggs imported to West Germany amounted to some $50. In 1963 the compensatory charges exacted from all non-member countries reached $225 per ton of eggs. In addition, because they were being offered at below the market prices, Polish exports of eggs were subjected to the price equalizers. This put an additional charge of $125 on every ton of Polish eggs. This meant in practice a tariff charge of $340 in 1964 as compared with a mere $50 in 1961: nearly a sevenfold increase. Although Poland does not recognize the EEC officially, it nevertheless negotiates with it. In talks held in Brussels in March, 1965, Poland guaranteed to refrain from offering eggs at prices below the market level, in return for which the EEC, acting pursuant to its Regulation No. 109, Article 4, rescinded the additional charges on Polish eggs.

Because of these huge compensatory charges there was a sharp decline in 1963 and 1964 in Poland's exports of eggs and pork to West Germany and Italy, the two largest food importers of the EEC.

Yet this fact should not be overestimated, because Poland's total exports to the EEC, even in 1963, continued to increase, though at a slower pace than in the preceding years; the decline in certain items was overcompensated by higher increases in others. The same observation applies to the general development of East European trade with the EEC, which is growing at an astonishing pace.

Between 1958 and 1963 the trade turnover of the EEC with Eastern Europe (other than the Soviet Zone of Germany) increased at a rate of 100 per cent for imports and 72 per cent for exports, which is proportionately twice as fast as trade with other nonmember countries. The same phenomenon is observable in the rate of increase in the trade turnover of some countries of Eastern Europe, especially Rumania, with the EEC area, which expanded at twice the rate as that with the majority of their COMECON partners. The imports of the EEC from Bulgaria, Rumania and Hungary almost tripled; those from the Soviet Union almost doubled. Rumania, Hungary and Bulgaria also rank foremost in the EEC's exports to Eastern Europe; deliveries to Rumania increased fourfold.

Trade with the Common Market was much more profitable than intrabloc trade and provided badly needed foreign exchange, with which an Eastern country could shop freely for any goods unobtainable within the Eastern bloc. Expanding consumer demand in the countries of Western Europe provided increasingly lucrative markets for food and semimanufactured goods produced in Eastern Europe. Despite the low quality of East European goods, lower prices enabled them to compete successfully with far superior products of other countries. This advantage of low prices has been wiped out for the few agricultural products subject to levies and sliding price equalizers. The result has been a slight decrease in EEC imports from Eastern Europe in 1964.

Altogether, agricultural and industrial products from Eastern Europe will only have good sales prospects as time goes on if their quality is brought up to international standards and if dumping practices are avoided. To avoid disturbances of the market, the EEC intends to introduce anti-dumping clauses in its trade agreements, as Great Britain, the U.S. and other states have already done.

In view of the continual rise of incomes and purchasing power in Western Europe, the EEC may be expected to constitute an expanding market for East European goods, the sources of which are relatively close to the market. Already the emergence of the Common Market has had an overall beneficial effect on the economies of East European countries, which have acquired almost a vested interest in the prosperity of the EEC countries. East European states have a great interest in expanding their trade with the Common Market as well as with other Western states.

All countries of Eastern Europe, however, must depend on substantial foreign credits if they are to rationalize and modernize their economies and at the same time find jobs for their increasing populations while satisfying their peoples' demand for better living conditions. Since the capital resources of the COMECON states, including the Soviet Union, are by no means sufficient to meet all these requirements, they all make great efforts to obtain credits from the West. These efforts coincide with the wish of Western industrial exporters to secure a rising share of the East European market by concluding long-term delivery contracts, not least because the Eastern bloc states have proved to be relatively safe borrowers and reliable contracting parties as compared with some of the newly developing countries. Besides, the governments that grant long-term export guarantees may give consideration to the above-mentioned political aspects. In doing so, they unfortunately do not always respect the recommendations of the Berne Union of export credit insurance companies, according to which the terms of export credits granted to Eastern bloc states should not be longer than five years. This has made the danger of a creditors' race, by which the East will profit more than the West, acute.

Agreement in this matter was not even arrived at within the EEC. This is the more deplorable, because, as we have seen, an economically and perhaps even politically successful intensive cooperation between the East and the West for the benefit of the peoples on both sides can be arrived at only if Western credit policy is properly coordinated and directed to main points of interest. Dr. Jaksch makes valuable suggestions for such well-aimed, top-priority investments in his study "Western Europe—Eastern Europe—Soviet Union—Perspectives of Economic Cooperation." He lays emphasis on cooperation in the infrastructural sector, for instance in the development of inland waterway shipping and *Autobahnen* (trunk roads) that connect both parts of Europe, coordination and expansion of power production and transmission and mutual promotion of recreational and health-restoring tourism as well as cooperation in vocational training and the exchange of young people.

In this context the employment and training of manual and white-collar workers from Eastern Europe in West European enterprises, in a way similar to that various European countries are already carrying out with workers from Italy, Turkey, Greece, Spain and Yugoslavia, might be considered. The Eastern bloc countries would, of course, have to allow their citizens freedom of movement for changing their places of work and traveling abroad, as Yugoslavia is already doing.

Closer cooperation between East and West could also help to promote the striving for structural economic reform that is evident in all the East European states. This author agrees entirely with Dr. Jaksch that all outside aid through trade and credits would be in vain unless the Eastern bloc states give up their costly, uneconomical and bureaucratic central planning systems. Economic practices would have to be adjusted to the principles of market economies, with cost-prices that are internationally competitive. Finally, the foreign trade regime must be relaxed by abandoning the monopolization of foreign trade by the state.

Should developments in this direction be realized, the negotiations of Polish government agencies with the Federation of Belgian Industries and the Krupp interests on the project of direct economic cooperation between individual private Western firms and Eastern state enterprises would have a certain chance of success. The idea is that a Western capitalist firm will carry out a joint project with an Eastern communist state enterprise, with the former supplying management, machinery and what is generally kown as technology, while the Eastern state itself supplies no more than the site, the plant buildings and the manpower. In practice this would mean a kind of subcontract, largely in the form of having Eastern factories turn out semifinished products. These would be sold by the Western firm on Western markets and by the Eastern enterprise on markets of the communist bloc; sales to markets belonging to neither trade bloc would be effected jointly. Reports on items to be produced mention trucks, agricultural machinery, road-building equipment, technical instruments and other products.

The project of coproducing through joint operation of a plant by a Western firm and a Polish state enterprise is a pilot project meant to become a model for other joint ventures between individual Western firms and Eastern state enterprises on both sides of the Iron Curtain. Such direct economic cooperation seems to offer a real possibility of increasing Eastern foreign-exchange earnings in the West appreciably. There is no doubt but that the manpower shortage in Western Europe and the labor surplus in Eastern Europe provide a good and purely economic reason for establishing this type of cooperation. But this is a complicated issue that requires more detailed analysis than is possible in the present context.

Besides, the matter also has a political aspect. In an angry article of February 21, 1965, Poland's official Communist party organ, *Trybuna Ludu,* reacted very sharply against the extensive coverage of and speculation concerning the negotiations between the Polish government and Krupp in the Western press. It therefore seems premature to expect that the proposed cooperation between capitalist Western firms and communist Eastern enterprises can be handled as a purely economic proposition without being treated as a political and ideological issue by the communist regime.

Worth mentioning in this context is a hopeful sign: Yugoslavia has to a certain degree set an example of promising cooperation between a communist state and its enterprises with Western countries and their capitalist firms. Since having been expelled from the community of communist states in 1948, Yugoslavia has discarded the Stalinist central planning system and assumed some of the aspects of a free-market economy by granting more autonomy to individual cooperative enterprises. Foreign trade regulations have been liberalized, and the licensing system has largely been replaced with a fixed tariff that, incidentally, is based on the same Brussels tariff classification as the common external tariff of the EEC. Foreign trade is gradually being decentralized by allowing factories as well as trading enterprises to deal directly with foreign customers and to make purchases abroad with the foreign currency they earn through exports. For the rest, Yugoslavia has developed and expanded her economy mainly in close economic, financial, technological and scientific cooperation with the West, not least with the aid of the U.S. Though Yugoslavia has also, since her reconciliation with Moscow in 1955, tried to intensify economic relations with the Eastern bloc countries as far as possible, and entered into a limited association with the COMECON in 1964, the share of Eastern bloc states in total Yugoslav foreign trade ran to no more than 25 per cent in recent years but rose to 30 per cent in 1964. By far the larger part of Yugoslav external commerce is with the West, including the U.S. Western Europe by itself accounts for from 50 per cent to 60 per cent of the total foreign trade of Yugoslavia, with the EEC providing 26 per cent and 28 per cent of the total imports and taking 34 per cent and 28 per cent of the total exports in 1963 and 1964, respectively.

The importance of Yugoslav trade with the West is almost surpassed by the role of Western states, particularly those belonging to the EEC, in the granting of licenses designed to develop and improve Yugoslav production and to facilitate cooperation with foreign firms. Of 256 production licenses acquired between 1954 and 1962, only 11 came from Eastern bloc states, while 70 were acquired from West Germany and 54 from Italy. The licenses were distributed as follows: engineering, 28 per cent; electrotechnical products, 21 per cent; automobile production, 13 per cent; chemical industry, 6.2 per cent. In connection with the acquisition of licenses, a certain amount of co-production has developed between Yugoslav enterprises and Western firms. For example, the license acquired from a West German company by an enterprise in Sarajevo for the production of motor bicycles is being paid for by the delivery of semifinished products to the German company.

Yet, the recent difficulties of the Yugoslav economy—particularly the serious shortage of foreign exchange, which often makes it impossible to repay credits received in former years as they fall due—prove that it would have been better to pursue a more sensible Western credit policy, directed toward well-considered essential projects, even vis-à-vis Yugoslavia.

Because of their close links with the Soviet Union and COMECON and their rigid economic system, the other Eastern bloc states were unable to enjoy the above-mentioned advantages made available to Yugoslavia. The consequences of a technical rather than an economic division of labor and cooperation within COMECON are becoming progressively more noticeable in the COMECON member states as economic development proceeds and economic relations with the West expand. Motivated by these reasons, as well as by a desire of the people and the government for greater independence, Rumania in recent years has successfully resisted multilateral planning and the carrying out of common projects within COMECON, thereby preventing COMECON from being developed into a supranational monster planning agency whose member states would have continued to be largely dependent on the Soviet Union and the other members of COMECON. At the same time, Rumania was successful in independently expanding economic and cultural relations with the West. Similar tendencies toward greater national independence and closer relations with the West are observed in other Eastern bloc states.

In summary, the West should welcome and favor a normal growth of commercial and cultural relations with the individual countries of the Eastern bloc, though not with COMECON as a unit. Such a development of East-West relations must not be permitted to produce an improper, one-sided, economic as well as political advantage for the communist regimes, which would, incidentally, enable them to employ their foreign trade monopolies and concerted dumping practices to produce serious disturbances in the Western market economies and in Western economic relations with the developing countries. This danger seems to be inherent in the structure of the totalitarian, centrally planned state economies and their state-trading systems. Since we have to reckon with these facts, it will also be necessary in the near future to develop economic relations with these countries on principles different from those governing the relations customary between countries with more or less free economies, until a profound reform of the economic system of the East European countries has been achieved. Economic relations may be one means of promoting the necessary economic reforms while at the same time encouraging the evolution toward greater national independence and peaceful cooperation of the individual countries of Eastern Europe with the West.

NOTES TO CHAPTER ELEVEN

1. On problems of trade between countries having different economic and social systems, see *Economic Bulletin of Europe* (Geneva), Vol. XVI, No. 2 (November, 1964).

2. *Report on Commercial Relations Between Member States of the Council of Europe*

and the Countries of Central and Eastern Europe (Strasbourg: Council of Europe, Consultative Assembly, September 30, 1963), Doc. 1676.

   3. *Department of State Bulletin* (Washington), LI, No. 1325 (November 16, 1964), 720.

   4. *See* Robert B. Wright, "East-West Trade: The Iron Curtain Eighteen Years Later," *Department of State Bulletin* (Washington), LI, No. 1328 (December 7, 1964), 817.

   5. *See* R. Sannwald, "Die Europäische Wirtschaftsgemeinschaft und der Osthandel," *Europa-Archiv* (Frankfurt/Main) No. 4 (1965), p. 117.

   6. Wright, *op. cit.*, p. 816.

   7. *See* "Some Factors in Economic Growth During the 1950's," *Economic Survey of Europe in 1961* (Geneva: Economic Commission for Europe, 1964), Part 2.

CHAPTER XII

The Concept of a United Europe

WENZEL JAKSCH

In APPRAISING THE prospects for all-European unity from the standpoint of economic and political reality, it is necessary to remember how much has been accomplished within a short span of time. This author recently met the untiring crusader for pan-Europe, Count Coudenhove-Kalergi, and was delighted to find at least one prophet who had lived long enough to see some of his visions come true. As Coudenhove tells the story of his life, he started crusading for European unity shortly after World War I. To begin with, he issued a manifesto for a European movement, which was printed in the leading Vienna and Berlin newspapers. All in all, about fifty people responded—mostly cranks or eccentrics as Coudenhove ruefully admits.[1]

Notwithstanding the lack of popular response, Count Coudenhove decided to tour the capitals and courts of Europe as a modern minstrel and to raise his lonely voice for a united Europe. Along the way he met Briand and Herriot of France, Seipel and Renner of Austria, Masaryk and Benes of Czechoslovakia as well as Stresemann and Löbe of Weimar Germany. Coudenhove also visited the United States for the same purpose, but access to President Coolidge was denied him through some petty intrigue.

It is perhaps appropriate to recall the enormous difficulties under which the idea of a united Europe had to be launched. The Europe of the twenties, as Count Coudenhove reminds us in his memoirs, was already a battleground of such conflicting ideologies as nationalism, communism, pacifism and social democracy. Nevertheless, leading statesmen began to ponder the new concept. By 1925 Aristide Briand had accepted the idea of a united Europe yet felt obliged to move cautiously because of the strong nationalist feelings in his country. At the same time, the liberal Chancellor Gustav Stresemann battled German nationalists for reconciliation with France. The two statesmen, supported by the peaceful intentions of Great Britain then represented by Foreign Minister Austin Chamberlain, crowned their efforts with the Treaty of Locarno in 1926. The Locarno Pact unveiled for the first time the prospect of an ultimate reconciliation of France and Germany. Seen in retrospect, it was a courageous move toward solving the major problem of European integration between the great wars.

On reflection, however, it seems clear that the pioneers of European unity, including Briand and Stresemann, were ahead of their time. On both sides of the Rhine, traditional thinking in terms of rivalry and *Erbfeindschaft* had not disappeared over night. Moreover, the economic depression of the thirties aggravated disunity and extremism on the European continent. The dispute about the merits and demerits of large reparation payments blocked a proper assessment of the common economic interests of victors and vanquished for many years. Both found themselves sitting in the same boat, but they were rowing in different directions. Nor was the economic and financial interdependence of the Old and New Worlds sufficiently understood. Blinded by the make-believes of economic nationalism and isolationism, the countries of Western Europe and the United States plunged headlong into the catastrophe of the world depression.

Looking back over those troubled years, it is necessary to recognize the major roles played by the demons of nationalist passion as well as by economic factors that caused the downfall of parliamentary government, first in Italy, then in Germany and Austria and finally in Spain. Nothing could be more erroneous than to consider these tragic episodes unique accidents of history. The phenomenon of totalitarianism cannot be understood by those who cling to the Victorian faith in automatic progress. In no way has man's lust for power been extinguished by the increasing complexity of civilization. Modern technology provides fearful instruments for the destruction of freedom from within a society. Totalitarianism, in both its fascist and its communist variants, is the offspring as well as the master of modern weapons and modern propaganda. It can only be checked by a kind of democracy that puts freedom above profit and accepts worldwide responsibilities.

As far as Europe is concerned, its progress toward integration has deeper roots than the advantages of lower tariffs or the fear of Russian domination. Here again, it is interesting to note Coudenhove-Kalergi's observation in his memoirs that "one of the most remarkable phenomena of the new Europe is that nationalism, which caused two great wars, became extinct."

Coudenhove takes a highly optimistic view of the state of mind of European peoples. This author's own observations suggest a more cautious estimate. Certainly the old type of negativist nationalism, chauvinism or jingoism, as the British call it, is in retreat. In an age of ideological warfare it is a luxury and an anachronism to divide the nations of the same continent into friends, neutrals and archenemies. We must rather face the complex situation of having friends in hostile countries and foes in allied countries.

It would be unwise, however, to think exclusively in terms of ideological divisions. Soviet communism is still a two-faced affair. It promotes the idea of world revolution on purely ideological lines. But world revolution's twin brother is Soviet patriotism, which supposedly expresses the aspirations of the peoples of the Soviet Union. In facing such a deadly combination of ideological conquest and sheer Soviet power politics, the nations of the West still need a good measure of old-fashioned patriotism and of brotherly feeling toward allies, for the sake of survival if for nothing more.

Notwithstanding these reservations, we can agree with Count Coudenhove insofar as the younger generation is concerned. In general, the young people of Western Europe seem to have outgrown the emotional and intellectual limitations of national sovereignty; many care seriously for Europe, others follow a strong nonpolitical current and care only for blue jeans or hot music or Beatle imitations. There is cause for concern in the extent to which the "American way of life" is copied on the European continent because Europeanism may one day reassert itself in the undesirable form of anti-Americanism. For the time being, however, the outward attractions of Americanism penetrate the Iron Curtain as a kind of Trojan horse, as every visitor to East European countries can observe.

We are told there is a reassertion of nationalism in Eastern Europe, especially in Rumania, Hungary and Poland. This seems on the whole to be a defensive nationalism, reacting against Russian domination and against the subservience of neighbors to Moscow. This factor explains why visitors and tourists from West Germany are accorded favorable receptions in all parts of Eastern Europe, while our unfortunate brethren from *Mitteldeutschland* are treated with less courtesy and even with contempt, since they are suspected of being German Communists of the Ulbricht brand. American visitors to Eastern Europe will find hardly a trace of popular anti-Americanism, despite twenty years' official propaganda and the new anathemas recently hurled in Moscow.

To understand the ups and downs, progress and setbacks of European unity, we need some theory of, or at least a deeper insight into, the working of European history. Since the days of Charlemagne, the interplay of integration and distintegration has been a dominant factor in shaping the destinies of European peoples. The inroads of extra-European forces and influences constitute a second element of major importance. Out of the ruins of the Roman Empire, for instance, arose the Franconian Empire, which met the needs of the innermost regions of Europe for protection against Arabic invasions from the South, Avaric invasions from the Hungarian plains and Nordic raids on the Atlantic coast. By this time the Germanic tribes had already consolidated their positions and established communities and governments west of the Elbe and the Bohemian Forest, after a long retreat from Eastern Europe during the first migration of peoples. The desire for security was beyond a doubt the mother of statecraft during those formative years eleven centuries ago. But religion also played an essential role. Hand in hand with the extension of secular power went the spiritual revolution of Christianization. It is interesting to see on the map how the basic structure of modern Europe, the Franconian Empire, covered (with small exceptions) the territory of the six countries that founded the Common Market in 1958. Had Charlemagne foreseen this development, he could have introduced another law of succession preventing his descendants from dividing his estate—an estate we are now putting together again.

In the past, as now, the structure of Europe has always reflected human foresight as well as human failure. For many centuries acts of integration and disintegration filled the pages of European history, until the centralized nation-state emerged in the West. In the East, pressure from outside helped again and again to form larger states, such as the Romanoff Empire, Jagellonian Poland or the Danubian Monarchy. Intermarriage worked as a factor of integration, culminating in the Austrian-Spanish realm of Charles V, which even embraced vast parts of Central and South America. The struggles of the Reformation had, on the other hand, a divisive effect in Europe. The

Thirty Years' War, in particular, administered a disastrous setback to the cause of European unity. To make matters worse, the fragmentation of Germany through the peace of Westphalia permitted Russia to become the arbiter of Central Europe, a position she held up to the middle of the nineteenth century. The czars, needless to say, were never enthusiastic about European unity.

Among the operative forces of European history, we can list Napoleon's designs—even including his Russian campaign—as a great effort to integrate Europe from the West. The highly individualistic American Declaration of Independence and the more collectivist ideology of the French Revolution carried the Western message far into Eastern Europe and Russia.

After Napoleon's defeat, the Holy Alliance under Metternich's resolute management and Britain's balance-of-power policy kept the peoples of the European continent apart for the remainder of the nineteenth century. The constitutionalist movements of 1848 leapt across artificial borders but failed to overcome them. The next chapter of European history was written by the forces of national unification. As Professor Lemberg has pointed out,[2] modern nationalism made its first appearance as an integrating element. In an age of expanding industry, it produced viable economic units, such as modern Italy or Bismarck's Germany. In the ethnically mixed regions of Central and Eastern Europe, however, the creation of small and medium-sized nation-states in 1918 contradicted the secular trend toward larger economic units and supranational groupings in Europe.

During the period between the two world wars, therefore, the problem of European unity posed itself acutely, particularly inasmuch as the Russian superstate embarked on a long-term policy of ideological and territorial conquest under Lenin's leadership. Pan-Europe still remained the dream of a few. Where democracy failed, Mussolini and Hitler appeared to offer the postwar generation new horizons. It was in large part the provincialism of purely national politics and the ineffectiveness of the League of Nations that enlisted the many recruits gained by satellite Fascist parties in Northern Europe, in Belgium and Holland, in France and Spain and even in Switzerland. Soviet communism and fascism swept over the European continent as two powerful crosscurrents. The most important lesson to be learned from the history of Europe between the two world wars is this: democratic resistance against the onslaught of totalitarian forces was bound to fail because its operational basis was the obsolete nation-state concept, while communism and fascism wielded the modern weapons of supranational action. The Spanish Civil War provided a case in point.

Personal experience and observation of these tragedies lead this author to conclude that *the future of Europe and indeed the fate of our Atlantic community will be decided in a neck-and-neck race between the forces of integration and those of disintegration.* The economic attractions of the Common Market and the joint economic strength of Western Europe and North America are positive factors but should by no means be relied upon to decide the issue.

You cannot introduce automation into the workings of history. The wheels of progress must still be turned by human brainpower and heartpower. This is particularly true of work in the headquarters of the Common Market organization in Brussels. There, a small body of dedicated men carries the main burden of unparalleled efforts. Many negotiations about secondary arrangements have lagged behind schedule because of shortages of trained personnel or sheer exhaustion of the negotiators. The problems that superficial press reporting interprets as an almost permanent crisis in Brussels are in fact the growing pains of a great human enterprise. Through years of trial and error, the foundation stones of a united Europe-to-come have been laid. For the first time in history, a nucleus of European administrators is being trained in supranational loyalty and supranational action. One of the great achievements of that spirit is the recent merger of the three agencies—the Common Market, the Coal and Steel Community and EURATOM. New problems are waiting round the corner.

In the meanwhile, it is highly desirable indeed to arrive at an overall agreement between the Europe of the Six and the Free Trade Area. Every ounce of energy at our command should be put into negotiations aiming at the closest possible cooperation of the Atlantic community in the fields of tariff policy, industrial partnership, monetary agreements, scientific research and, last but not least, an effective pooling of Western military strength within NATO.

Beyond this, the economic relationship between Western Europe and the European countries east of the Iron Curtain requires fresh thinking in West European capitals as well as joint initiatives of the six countries. There is danger that the so-called satellite countries, with the possible exception of Rumania, will become fully integrated into the economic structure of the Soviet empire within the next five years, unless Western Europe offers a workable alternative. There will be no way back to Europe, for Poland or Czechoslovakia or Hungary, once their whole economic life is geared to the requirements and plans of the Soviet giant. The dependency of these countries on Russian oil, cotton, iron ore and other deliveries is increasing. Conversely, the import demands of the Soviets have an almost prohibitive effect on the trade relations of Eastern Europe with the West. A well-calculated Western trade policy can provide the satellites with leverage for resisting Soviet pressure. Instead of writing abstract papers on all-European unity we must, therefore, find practical ways and means to preserve and develop a minimum of all-European contacts in matters of trade, transport, travel and cultural exchange across the Iron Curtain.

The battle for Europe, as it has developed, cannot be won with manifestos. It requires, to begin with, a new economic concept based on the structural needs of Europe as a whole. Twenty years after the communist take-over the economies of the countries of Eastern Europe are lagging sadly behind Western standards and even the standards of Soviet technology. There is a general shortage of capital, especially for new industrial equipment, power supply, modernization of transport, automation, motorization, housing programs and tourist accommodation. It is general knowledge in these countries that the Western standard of living is higher. The gulf is widening between official Eastern propaganda and the factual information that emerges as the dialogue with visitors from Western countries goes on.

Careful evaluation of numerous reports reveals a most important psychological change taking place in Eastern Europe. The German problem now appears to the peoples of that area in a different light. The German Federal Republic is at present the country having the largest measure of personal contact with the countries of Eastern Europe. Half a million Germans from the Rhine and the Ruhr spent their vacations in Yugoslavia last year. Nearly a quarter of a million went to Czechoslovakia. Hungary, Rumania and Bulgaria are now competing for higher quotas of German tourists, seven million of whom spend their money abroad each year. The number of German visitors to Poland is also increasing; these are mainly expellees who want to see their birth places in Silesia, Pomerania, Danzig or the southern half of East Prussia again. Contrary to widespread belief, the reappearance of expelled Germans in the German provinces east of Oder-Neisse or in the Sudetenland does not cause friction or anxiety. Many Poles and Czechs are pleased to see any visitors from the West and only too eager to measure the so-called socialist achievements of their governments by Western standards. In Hungary, Rumania and Slovakia the situation is better still. A new generation is emerging in these countries, one that does not look back to the horrors of Hitlerism and Stalinism but looks forward instead to a world free of party control—a world of free thought and free travel from continent to continent. While other issues may be in doubt, it is certain that the idea of a united Europe has many supporters in Eastern Europe. For the non-Communists in these countries, the effort to join Europe means the realization of "liberty, equality and fraternity." It is a defeatist policy to wait passively for new uprisings. Instead, the gradual approach of an anti-communist Fabianism offers itself. It is our task to look for ways and means to break holes in the Berlin wall and to undermine the Iron Curtain without giving up an inch of our own position. Meanwhile, we must think and act in terms of Europe as a whole, so as to keep the torch of hope burning for the captive nations.

The theory of an automatic polycentrism in Eastern Europe is not credible. Yet it may well be that the Communist parties of that area will be compelled to yield step-by-step to popular demands and historic necessities. If we want evolution in Eastern Europe and in the Soviet Union, we have to offer cooperative alternatives to the division of Germany and of Europe. Our next goal should be to balance Russian influence in Eastern Europe with a maximum of Western presence in those countries.

Meanwhile, we must be on guard against the forces of dissolution in our Western alliance. Moscow will consider it a sign of disintegration and dissipation of Western strength if economic relationships with the Soviet bloc are left to a wild scramble of Western moneylenders and competitors. Western economic initiatives toward Eastern Europe should not slip out of the hands of responsible governments. Only on the level of consultation and agreement between governments is a joint economic strategy feasible. This is indeed the test case for Western solidarity. If Great Britain and France think they can deal, each single-handed, with the bear and his cubs, then the United States and the German Federal Republic should enter into consultation about a coordinated policy toward Eastern Europe as soon as possible.

One more reflection about the danger of intellectual disintegration. There is room enough for speculation about the most convenient size of a united Europe-to-come. General de Gaulle is asking for disagreement, however, if he excludes Great Britain and claims Russia west of the Urals for a Europe to his own liking. In contrast to this narrow concept, Count Coudenhove has suggested a much wider interpretation in his recent lectures. He advocates the closest possible relationship with the Western Hemisphere, which he considers a daughter-continent of Europe. On the Eastern side Coudenhove wants to keep the door open for the whole of Soviet Russia, as far as Vladivostok.

A word of regret is to be added about the manner in which the German problem is approached in certain interallied deliberations about the future of Europe. The Germans are told in advance what contributions are expected of them, what rights they are not permitted to claim and with which boundaries they must be content. As one of the many Germans who fought communism and national socialism, each in turn, this author would remark to both European and American readers that whoever desires to promote European unity and an effective Atlantic partnership will need the good will of the German people and the stability of German democracy. It would be a fatal flaw in any constructive Western policy for Europe to deny to one particular nation the right of self-determination and the prospect of a just peace settlement. In Central and Eastern Europe the same bonds of partnership and cooperation have to be established as have been established in Western Europe. Clearly, the nations of Eastern Europe need a free and united Germany as a bridge if they want to join a European community of free peoples working in harmony for peace and prosperity.

Political science on both shores of the Atlantic could be of great help to statesmen, planners and legislators tracing a middle path between the worship of lofty ideals and the shortsighted pursuit of petty interests. As a pragmatic approach, the following actions looking toward European integration and Western unity should be undertaken within the next five years: (1) reaffirmation of the NATO agreement to harmonize the specific security interests of the European partners with North American commitments in Asia; (2) agreement between the six countries of the Common Market and the Free Trade Area aiming at the economic integration of all Western Europe; (3) treatment of the economic needs of Eastern Europe as an all-European responsibility—this requires special arrangements between the Common Market and East European countries with a view to long-range objectives of unhampered social progress, freedom of migration and all-European economic partnership; (4) realization of the full potential of Atlantic partnership to the best mutual advantage; and (5) eventual extension of European-American economic cooperation to the Soviet Union and other countries in exchange for a European peace settlement, coupled with an arms control program that affords adequate inspection without one-sided advantage to either side.

Finally, it is evident that we cannot achieve lasting economic integration of Europe without a directly elected European parliament and the nucleus of a European government. Future historians will measure the foresight and courage of the present generation by the diligence with which it undertakes this monumental task.

NOTES TO CHAPTER TWELVE

1. Richard Coudenhove-Kalergi, *Die Europäische Nation* (Stuttgart: 1953; English trans. *An Idea Conquers the World* [London: G. P. Putnam's Sons, 1953]).

2. Eugen Lemberg, "Eastern Europe: A Battleground of Contemporary Ideologies," in *Berlin and the Future of Eastern Europe*, ed. David S. Collier and Kurt Glaser (Chicago: Henry Regnery Co., 1963), pp. 160–82.

CHAPTER XIII

United Europe in French Perspective

JEAN DE FABRÈGUES

THE FIRST STEPS in the European effort to lay the foundation of a united Europe, in 1945 and thereafter, were experienced by this author with a sense of personal commitment, a passion born of hope. At the first great European conferences at Rome, at The Hague and at Luxembourg, we labored together to give form to Europe. Those were the days when we marched forward under the leadership of the Great Three: Adenauer, Schuman and De Gasperi. It is salutary to look back on this era, to see what we undertook and where we succeeded; this knowledge permits a fuller understanding of *what has not been done* and what still remains to be done.

What we have accomplished during the years 1948–50 and thereafter is self-evident. We have acquired a *consciousness of Europe*—an awareness of Europe's common destiny and of the common dangers that threaten it. Consciousness of a common destiny and of common perils is indeed the salient characteristic of the first stage in the building of Europe.

Among this author's recollections of these formative years, two events stand out in sharp perspective. The first of these took place at a meeting of the European Parliament* held at The Hague, at which England was not only represented but strongly represented. Winston Churchill was there; I still see him, remaining motionless in his chair after the rest of us had left the luncheon table, with a faraway look in his eyes, thinking inscrutable thoughts about British policy. Should this policy unfold *within* this Europe of which we

*This evidently refers to the European Parliament that is an organ of the Council of Europe, not the Parliament of the Coal and Steel Community, the Common Market and EURATOM.—*Eds.*

207

were seeking to achieve consciousness—or *outside* it? This hesitation was to last a long time. England was speaking the European language, but would she reach the point of thinking and acting correspondingly? No attack against our English friends is intended here, only a simple observation: it is not enough to talk about things; it is necessary to do them. Time works against those who have not acted. This lesson is still pertinent to the contemporary situation.

The second recollection from the days of European recovery from World War II that still has current relevance is that the United States followed the European effort closely at that time; it wanted that effort to succeed and it aided it. The United States and Europe found themselves facing a common danger posed by Soviet aggression, and this common danger united them. Today we are no longer very sure to what extent this unity has endured.

In the nineteenth and twentieth centuries the nations constituted as states possessed both a consciousness and a will. This self-awareness and this will nourished the patriotism of the citizens, motivating them to participate in the life of their fatherlands, up to and including the voluntary sacrifice of life in case of war. No political organism can ever be considered a mere machine, which the engineer momentarily at the controls can employ for this or that purpose as he sees fit. This fact has been and remains true of the national state. It is and will remain true for the prototype of a multinational state that is beginning to take charge of the structural development and public life of Europe, a process that should be intensified. If a consciousness of Europe indeed exists, not only as a cultural but as a political unity, then there must be a European will.

Those of us who, for fifteen or twenty years, have been experiencing the birth of European cultural and political consciousness and who have been bending our efforts to demonstrate awareness of a common European destiny are faced today with a tragic problem. We are seeking to find where the political will of Europe is being expressed; we are trying to discover the nature of that will; and we are having great difficulty in finding it.

André Philip, a non-Marxist French socialist theoretician—but more importantly a gifted historian of economics and social reality— once stated that submission to the same taxes and military duties had created the nation. The experience of recent years has shown that the constitution of Europe should contain the same prerequisites. The citizens of Germany, France and Italy do not yet pay the same taxes;

but they have become aware that unless the social charges that burden their respective economies are standardized or at least equalized to some extent, their countries can never achieve genuine economic unity. When the recent agreement on the price of wheat was signed, it was evident that a step was being taken to introduce Europe, not to a confederative form of existence, but to an irrevocable type of unity. The step forward to federalism cannot be reversed.

Is it not a paradox to assert that we have launched an economic integration without defining the terms for an integration of national defenses? Is it possible to accomplish one without the other, to separate the two? This question is asked because many believe that such an integration of national forces is in progress. But since the German rearmament program has for many years been conducted in association with non-European commands, is it possible to speak realistically of an integration of European defenses?

A realistic view of things is taking more and more the form of this threefold perception: there can be no genuine and permanent economic integration without a degree of political integration; a genuine political integration necessarily involves an integration of national defenses; and, finally, there can be neither lasting economic integration nor effective political integration without elements of a common foreign policy. The necessary unity in foreign policy cannot be achieved by mere periodic "consultations," since such consultations express the premise that each party is free to pursue his own road, a road different from that of others. The consequences of these truths require further examination.

Germany, France and Italy are all faced with more or less severe economic difficulties at the present time. If the conception that each of these countries has of its place in the world is not dominated by the idea of a common destiny more important and more basic than any divisive factors, each will permit itself to indulge in an economic policy of "everyone for himself." Each country will then be induced to follow economic and foreign policies that seek their points of support outside Europe. Extra-European powers, economic or political, find within Europe fulcrums that provide leverage for their own policies. In attempting to save itself individually, each European nation will actually be furthering the fragmentation of Europe and thus in the final analysis diminishing the strength of Europe and its role in world affairs. Certain recent political events within and outside Europe have already provided significant examples of this trend.

Some of us, indeed many of us, already seem to have conducted ourselves as though the common destiny of Europe could be conveniently ignored.

Those who express the wish that Europe should enjoy autonomy within the framework of the Atlantic alliance are on sound ground. But an autonomous European policy will not become possible until a common foreign policy for Europe has actually been achieved. This author does not share the contention of certain observers that a president of the united states of Europe or at least a firmly institutionalized single European executive is a prerequisite for such a policy. What appears certain, on the other hand, is that the inexorable logic of events has made necessary a unified foreign policy for Europe as an entity.

This need for an integrated foreign policy is not, however, merely an anticipated future development. On the contrary, the Treaty of Rome has already committed the nations of Europe to a common posture in relations with the outside world—that is, if we have really decided to make the treaty effective. One of the principal officials of the EEC, Michel Marjolin, wrote about two years ago:

> After economic questions have reached a certain stage of importance, they become political questions. It is hardly imaginable that states that decide to carry out a common economic policy should have different views in other fields, particularly in the areas of defense and foreign policy. *A common trade policy, such as is provided for by the Treaty of Rome, is inseparable from a common political policy toward the outside world.*[1]

Investigation of the bases for a common European foreign policy is thus no longer an academic exercise. On the contrary, it now belongs in the category of operational necessities. It is no exaggeration to say that this foreign policy research should logically precede analyses in the field of economic integration, since it is the entire European system—including, but not limited to, the economy—that would be paralyzed if a common foreign policy should prove impossible or should be rejected by the national states.

If what has been said seems to raise questions with regard to French policy, it also poses issues that must be faced by the German Federal Republic. These are illustrated in the question asked by

Edgar Faure in his address to the German Foreign Policy Association on June 3, 1964, at Bad Godesberg: "Are the Germans true Europeans, or are they free traders and citizens of the world?"

Does assertion of the need for a common foreign policy as a prerequisite for the realization of Europe mean an expansion of the European idea beyond its original dimensions? This author thinks not. It has already been observed that any truly mutual economic policy presupposes a common foreign policy. A fact that is probably of more fundamental importance is that ever since the beginning of European unification, responsible European politicians have sensed that their respective countries no longer afford a base of action ample enough and powerful enough to permit an independent posture in world affairs. It is precisely this feeling of national inadequacy that has led these statesmen to explore the modalities of common action.

In his press conference of January 14, 1962, President de Gaulle observed that the solidarity of the six members of the European Community is not limited to the common sources of their civilization, it is also rooted in the fact that they all inhabit the same continent and are all menaced by "the same threat from one end of their common territory to the other." This statement in itself constitutes recognition of the need for a common posture vis-à-vis the outside world in Europe.

Should this common posture be merely one of abstention—a kind of universalized neutralism? In this case, France would no longer seek to play a distinctive and autonomous role within NATO—but Europe as a whole would no longer have an Atlantic role. Germany would no longer generate ideas concerning Eastern Europe—but Europe would be equally devoid of such ideas. It must be admitted that such a concept lurks in a certain number of more or less confused minds. These people must be weaned from their illusions, for a neutralized Europe is a Europe condemned to death. It is even possible to predict the manner of death: it would take place through disintegration. One by one, each European country would fall under the tutelage of one of the extra-European "great powers," which would promise or guarantee it the fulfillment of its selfish desires.

Assertion of the need for a unified European foreign policy should in no way be construed as advocacy of a neutralization of Europe. Such a policy does, however, definitely presuppose that European decision-making in great continental questions—e.g., policy regarding Berlin, posture toward the East and Europe's role within the Atlantic community—will move beyond the stage of free consultations, however regularly these may be held. It is necessary to accept the consequences of a solidarity that has been affirmed once and for all and that can no longer be rejected without throwing Europe back into a state of anarchy and internal schism, in which the impotence of the community entails the impotence of each member.

In a world dominated by two hostile blocs, each possessing weapons of total destruction, a third world or a third power cannot disengage itself and exert a genuine influence unless it pledges itself to the strictest discipline in translating its solidarity into action. A French nationalist writer of the early twentieth century stated that France owed its unity to the fact that the French monarchy had labored ceaselessly to this end for a thousand years and that the monarchy would never have succeeded in its task had it not reminded the French on every occasion of the peril represented by the power of the House of Austria. His conclusion was that, in order to cement together a political union, it is necessary to have an "external federator," a threat that through both objective danger and the idea of danger catalyzes unity, which otherwise tends to dissipate.

The location of the peril that currently plays the role of external federator for Europe is self-evident. It may, however, be asked why such stress is laid on the necessity of European political autonomy and whether such emphasis does not actually diminish the weight of the Atlantic community. On this score, there are two points to be made, which have special relevance for Americans.

First, the prospect that Moscow and Peking may some day constitute two distinct centers of influence suggests that Washington will be increasingly tempted to make an "arrangement" with Moscow. If Europe will by that time have acquired its own weight and its autonomy of policy, this should not prove an embarrassment for Washington but rather a supplementary trump and an additional asset in discussion and in securing attention.

Second, if Europe must be required not only to take cognizance of its common destiny but to reinforce its self-awareness with a will, then it would be absurd and shameful politics to demand in the same breath that it renounce its autonomous existence and the expression of its own will.

Either Europe exists or it does not. If it does not exist, then let us drop the subject and consent immediately to a new Yalta. If Europe does exist—and we Europeans are as convinced of this as of our personal existence—then it is neither logical nor even possible to deny it its own will.

These things are said by a Christian to Christian America. If one day a new Yalta should appear on the horizon, the initial reason would be that Europe had neglected to raise its own voice, which is a Christian voice.

When this author recently visited an old mentor and friend, Robert Schuman, in his modest apartment on a side street in Paris, that elder statesman declared repeatedly that his zeal for the building of Europe stemmed more from his traditional Lorraine Christianity than from his commitment to democracy. The Europe we are building will have ample power to reconcile families of the spirit. All that is necessary is that we have the will to build it strongly.

NOTES TO CHAPTER THIRTEEN

1. Michel Drancourt, "Quinze ans de prospérité pour la France—un entretien avec Robert Marjolin," *Réalitiés* (Paris), No. 210, July, 1963, p. 5.

CHAPTER XIV

A Coordinated Policy Toward Eastern Europe

KARL THEODOR BARON VON GUTTENBERG

IN ONE OF HIS speeches in Berlin in June, 1963, President Kennedy referred to "winds of change" blowing across the Iron Curtain. That these winds are blowing, no one can doubt; the question is, how are we in the West to trim our sails? How are we to pilot our respective ships of state? And perhaps most important of all, how are we to sail in convoy, navigating the perilous waters of history according to a single, carefully drawn chart?

There have been a number of theories advanced in recent years about the best way to work toward a beneficial change in Europe, the best way to solve the dilemma presented by the current highly unsatisfactory situation on the continent. Despite an almost infinite variety of detail, these theories can be classified into three general types: (1) policies designed to loosen the ties that bind the East European satellites to their Soviet master; (2) policies of *détente*, of relaxation of tensions between East and West; and (3) policies designed to encourage a more liberal attitude on the part of Eastern leaders toward their own peoples.

Each type of theory requires examination in turn. Each has been much discussed, and when scrutinized under the magnifying glass of political realism, each seems likely to display some serious deficiencies and inconsistencies.

The idea of taking every opportunity to woo individual satellite states away from their dependence on the Soviet megalith is an attractive one, and its proponents point to presumed progress in Poland and Yugoslavia. But let us examine the situation in these na-

214

tions. Is the slight liberalization discernible there the result of Western policy? Of course not. With great competence, Gomułka has slowly tamed the revolutionary spirit of his people and brought them back into the Soviet fold. Tito mouths a neutralist line; but despite massive injections of Western aid, his nation is a member of COMECON. If, therefore, any real weakening of the ties between the Soviet Union and her satellites has taken place, it has been brought about by the nations concerned, not by any carefully aimed policy of the West. The defection of Albania and China from the Soviet-controlled bloc and the trip to Paris by Rumania's Maurer are remarkable developments of far-reaching importance. But Western policy cannot take credit for these developments any more than a drought-stricken farmer can boast of a heavy rainfall. Like the farmer, the most we can do is admire some of the new green shoots springing up in the mud and plan a bit for the harvest.

There is another factor that must be stressed when we contemplate a policy of working toward a lessening of the ties that bind the Eastern bloc together. The only instruments available to exploit the cracks and stresses observable in the bloc are economic ones; their employment necessarily implies our entering into at least a temporary partnership with the communist governments of Eastern Europe; they imply a Western contribution to the stability of these regimes. And what of the effect of this on the captured peoples of these lands? Is there not now a growing bitterness among the people of Rumania when they see their hated leaders received in Paris and Washington? This writer's father, who was imprisoned by the Nazis for political opposition to their policies, could not understand the attitude of the Western allies toward Hitler before the war. "Don't they realize," he would say, "that their efforts to reach an accommodation with Hitler have dignified him? Don't they realize that their failure to oppose him destroys the spirit of resistance in Germany?" How many would-be freedom fighters in Eastern Europe will feel the same way? Will they feel as though they and their hopes have been sold down the river of political expediency?

A final criticism of this policy of wooing the Eastern bloc away from the Russians is derived from close-range observation of communist behavior, for which the Germans have had ample opportunity since 1945. Experience indicates that the more any given satellite is successfully pulled out of the bloc, the more pressure will be exerted to keep the others in. The Soviet leaders are not fools. If the

Poles seem to be wavering, if Western pressures and enticements break a few of the fetters between Moscow and Warsaw, a tightening of the ties between Moscow and East Berlin will follow almost automatically. The Iron Curtain may take on a certain flexibility, but all that really means is that if external pressure forces it to bend inward in one place, it is bound to bend outward in another.

So much for the theory of alienation of affections. Let us now turn the magnifying glass of political realism to the idea of *détente,* the relaxation of tensions. This is another one of those glittering generalities so frequently offered as political wisdom. It is almost as if the world were a mildly neurotic patient in a psychiatrist's office, and the psychiatrist, too busy to get at the root of the patient's trouble, prescribes a bottle of tranquilizers. They don't cure anything, these little pills; but they make one feel a lot better about not being cured.

The present situation in Europe is analogous. Because no one—except along the rather short border between the German Federal Republic and the Soviet Zone, or along the Berlin wall—is shooting at anyone else, there is the illusion of a relaxation of tension. There is indeed a welcome measure of quiet in Europe, and it stems from two major causes. First, America's firm and courageous rejection of Soviet adventurism in Europe, along with her continuing determination to face up to communist expansionism in Vietnam and elsewhere, has obviously forced the Russians to think a little more carefully before they undertake any new adventures. Second, the serious ideological and political differences with the Chinese have led the Russians to consider most carefully the implications of their long and poorly defended border with the Red colossus to the south. But here again, this superficial *détente* in Europe is not something the Soviets have offered us as a result of some masterful political trick we have played; it is rather the result of Soviet inability to win the competition with the West that they started. The Russians have permitted a measure of *détente* purely and solely because it suits Russian purposes—at this moment. Real *détente,* a real relaxation of tensions, will come only when the sources of tension have been removed; the current situation merely preserves a rather unsatisfactory status quo, which redounds far more to the benefit of the East than to that of the West.

But merely because there is a measure of quiet in Europe, peace-loving people hasten to make the simple preservation of this uneasy and superficial peace the end-all and be-all of foreign policy. We Westerners are in the position of the poor unfortunate who died, went to Hell and found himself standing with a number of others on tiptoe in a great pool of nauseous liquid so deep that they were just barely able to keep their mouths and noses free. Frightened, he asked another: "Can't we do something about this?" "Yes, of course," said his companion. "Don't make waves."

In point of fact, the current calm in Europe indicates no real change in the situation. The calm was not of Western origin, and if the Russian orchestra strikes up again, we shall all have to dance whether we want to or not. Our blind acceptance of this calm as a thing worth preserving in itself simply allows the Russians to retain the initiative. We may think that time is on our side, that the superficial *détente* now in evidence will allow the forces of evolution in Eastern Europe time to work. But this is illusion; the Soviets have embraced *détente* because it affords them and their puppet regimes a breathing spell in which to stabilize their administrations and consolidate the political and economic gains they have made during the past twenty years.

In the realm of practical politics—and any other kind of politics is a misnomer—the soft-pedaling of the German reunification issue in order to preserve "the spirit of *détente*" is symptomatic of the kind of dangerous errors into which the West is being lulled. During the period of high tension in Europe, there was no possibility of discussing the reunification of Germany; now, during the period of apparent *détente*, the Germans are told, "Don't make waves." But the German question is symbolic of, and an integral part of, the overall European problem. The line that divides Germany also divides Europe. A neglect of the German issue is an automatic neglect of the issue of a divided Europe. Efforts to find a solution to the problem of German reunification are efforts to achieve the freedom and unity of the entire continent.

If the foregoing critical examination has focused attention on the defects of these first two theories for dealing with the Eastern bloc, it is because this author is convinced that the only almost guaranteed chance for the West lies in the long slow process of evolution within the bloc. The communist revolution is losing steam, and it is clear that the leaky vessel of communist ideology will eventually founder on the rock of human nature. But this process is a very long one. It progresses only by fits and starts. No one can say whether the immediate future will bring an improvement or a deterioration in the situation.

Above all else, however, the motivating power behind this evolution lies in the will of the people who are oppressed by the communist machine to resist. This is the drive, the restless energy, that will someday overcome those who have overcome; and that is why, for example, the reaction of the Rumanian people to the reception of their leaders in Western capitals was singled out as an event worth particular notice. Those in the West who are too ready to strike agreements with the East—particularly when there is often no compelling political need for such agreements—run the great danger of discouraging the very people they would help, depriving the evolutionary engine of fuel. There can be no denial of the necessity for maintaining business relations on a government-to-government basis, even with arch enemies; but politics, in the last analysis, is the translation of human will into effective mass action; and while the peoples of Eastern Europe cannot now make their political will felt, it is urgent for the West to lay up there a store of psychological readiness that can be drawn upon when evolutionary forces have prepared the way.

When the conversation turns to "liberalization" within the Eastern bloc, it must be determined just who is to become more liberal— the Hungarians, the Poles, the Bulgarians, the Czechs, the Slovaks? These people understand perfectly well the freedoms they lack— understand them better, perhaps, than do many people in the West who fail to take full advantage of the freedom they possess. If the evolutionary process is to be effective, it must take place within the ranks of the rulers of these nations, the *apparatchiks* who, once convinced that a change toward greater liberalism is necessary, are in a position to do something about it. This idea requires particular emphasis in order to counter the notion voiced by Lord Home that "a well-fed Communist is less dangerous than a hungry one." This is a remarkable statement to come from an English lord. Carefully examined, it contains a patently Marxian premise, that is, the priority of the economic in politics. The fallacy in the noble gentleman's remarks is evident when it is paraphrased in terms of recent German experience: was a well-fed Nazi less dangerous than a hungry one? Of course not. In this respect, disputing political honor between the Communists and the Nazis is about as fruitful as disputing relative virginity.

All this does not mean that the West should lessen the ties that now exist with the Eastern bloc. On the contrary, an increase in cultural exchanges is highly desirable, as are any and all means for broadening people-to-people contact. Any suggestion, any scheme that will serve the cause of a united Europe, of an increase in economic cooperation, is to be welcomed. The sterile slogan "All or nothing" represents the horns of an artificial dilemma. What is necessary is a policy of realism, a policy that does not reject economic opportunity but takes advantage of it for the achievement of political goals. The freedom of East Germany cannot be purchased, but is it not possible to insist that the destruction of the Berlin wall be part of the *quid pro quo* when Eastern states are granted credit for the delivery of Western goods?

This last theory, the idea of nudging the forces of evolution along while gaining what we can for the West, seems to involve fewer disadvantages than the others or rather to pose greater obstacles to the fulfillment of long-range Soviet objectives. What, indeed, are the weaknesses within the Soviet system that are open to exploitation? (1) the conflict with the Red Chinese; (2) the growing ferment within the satellite bloc; (3) Russia's own growing problems of national security—including seven hundred million Chinese who are regaining awareness of the irredentas formerly in the Chinese Empire that were annexed by the Czars during the nineteenth century and that have been retained by the Soviets; (4) profound economic problems in the motherland herself and ferment in the Kremlin leadership; (5) the economic and manpower strain of the arms race—the Soviets continue to concentrate on putting astronauts in orbit instead of "a chicken in every pot and a car in every garage"; (6) the problem of feeding a growing population with a bankrupt and ill-conceived agricultural policy—a definition of Russian magic might well be: Khrushchev sowed in Kazakhstan and reaped in Canada.

How do we exploit these weaknesses? Do we send aid? Do we minister at our enemy's bedside? Do we give him—free of charge—the relaxation of tensions he so desperately needs? Or do we exact a price for it, sending him a bill for guaranteeing his rear in his conflict with China?

As a German, naturally, this writer would like to charge the Soviets a German price, although he can see some other places, such as Cyprus, for example, where a bit of Russian *quid pro quo* would be useful. Every visitor to Germany who is more than a casual tourist is aware of the shootings along the Berlin wall and of the barbed wire and minefields along the zonal borders. There seems no good reason for not requiring the elimination of these bestialities as a condition of the delivery contracts and instruments of credit that are essential for the completion of communist economic plans. In any case, the West must strive for more than simply preserving what it already has. At an early age this writer learned a lesson on the streets that all little boys must learn: the quickest way to get beaten by a bully is to say: "Leave me alone, don't hit me!" Nothing in twenty years of political life has suggested that that early lesson was invalid.

What this all boils down to is that a policy of good, practical horse-trading, of swapping economic for political concessions, while at the same time being prepared to take advantage of evolutionary changes, is the best of the three ideas we have been discussing. But a major problem remains: what good is a workable policy if its execution is subjected to differing interpretations by the fifteen nations that make up the Western alliance? The success of NATO has been surprising at times. With painstaking care and great effort we have occasionally managed to come up with a joint policy. But the present system within the Atlantic alliance makes it very difficult indeed to come up with such a policy, fully coordinated and timely enough to be effective. Too many cooks don't necessarily spoil the soup; but it's likely to grow pretty cold before they can all sample it for salt and serve it up at the table.

There is only one practical solution: an effective, workable Atlantic partnership. Such a partnership has never been achieved, since America still lacks a genuine partner. Only the unification and strengthening of Europe can give her one. Coordination in the full sense of the word, including the equitable sharing of tasks in all phases of world politics and in all parts of the world, might be possible between America and a united Europe; such a partnership could marshal the common strength of the peoples of both continents to preserve peace and fight aggression anywhere in the globe where it was to the interest of the alliance to do so. But trying to produce effective action based upon agreements between the American giant and the individualistic European dwarfs is like trying to bail out Lake Michigan with a sieve: little is produced but sweat and splashing.

The integration and strengthening of Europe is even more important in the whole problem of developing a joint policy toward Eastern Europe, and it is more than just a matter of power politics.

It is a question of creating a Western Europe so powerful and so prosperous that it will act as a magnet, drawing the Iron Curtain away, drawing the wills and hopes of even the most recalcitrant *apparatchiks* toward the lodestar of Western success. The concept of a voluntary integration of the free peoples of Europe is no exclusionist doctrine. While Western Europe can make no accommodation to the political system of the East, the door to Eastern participation in a greater Europe must always stand open; and we who stand behind that door must express our welcome in every way possible. The boundaries of Europe extend far beyond the lands of Western Europe; they encompass all those on the continent who consider themselves Europeans.

Closely interlocked with the problem of European unity and security is the problem of German reunification. The interrelationship of these issues is illustrated by the following self-evident propositions:

1. German freedom is integral with European freedom; just as free West Germany and free Western Europe are mutually dependent, so do the liberation of East Germany and that of Eastern Europe constitute parts of a single objective.

2. Only a strong and unified Europe can play an effective role in bringing about the reunion of seventy million Germans in freedom.

3. Only the continuance of the American presence in Europe—the undiminished might of four hundred thousand American troops committed to the guarantee of European independence—can furnish the secure milieu within which Europe's destiny can be realized.

Summing up all these statements is this conclusion: it is highly unrealistic to see the problem of German reunification as isolated from or independent of the problem of the integration of free Europe, the problem of bringing Eastern Europe back into the European fold and the problem of creating an Atlantic partnership capable of leading the spread of freedom into every corner of the globe.

But there are men who serve the purposes of our enemies by claiming that the solution of the German problem can occur only as the last act in a long and slow process. Such people owe us an answer to the question "How do you know this?" Did the Hungarians see what was coming three months before the 1956 uprising? Could we in Germany foresee the uprising of June, 1953? Had we foreseen it and been prepared, could we not have taken better advantage of it? Politics is at best an uncertain science, poor at predicting the future and full of surprises, both pleasant and unpleasant. There is one thing that every politician has to learn: opportunities for sudden progress toward political goals do not come to those who are satisfied with things the way they are, those who are not at home when opportunity knocks. No suggestion is made that we should foment new armed up-risings behind the Iron Curtain; this would be attempting to relive the past, to seize initiatives that have long since passed. Such pro-posals remind one of the speculator who bought up all the 1964 cal-endars at the end of that year. "Sure, it's a long shot," he said; "but just think what a killing I'll make if 1964 ever comes back." Well, 1956 is never coming back, nor is 1953. But what will 1965 bring? And will we be prepared to take advantage of it when it comes?

A thought that has often been expressed—but in the opinion of this author cannot be repeated often enough—is that the concept of a unified Europe is meaningless without America's help. For us in Ger-many, therefore, there are two parallel courses we must pursue: one is Atlantic, the other European. Those who would separate Ger-many's fortunes from those of America threaten the security of Eu-rope. Those who would drive a wedge between Germany and France threaten the unity of Europe. And those who threaten the security and unity of Europe threaten the peace—which is, after all is said and done, the ultimate goal of Western policy.

Part Four

IN SUMMARY

CHAPTER XV

Toward a Strategy of Freedom

KURT GLASER

THE ESSAYS IN this collection, by both European and American authors representing various points on the political spectra of their respective countries, show a degree of coherence that indicates that European and Atlantic unity are no longer simply wishes for the future but also intellectual phenomena. Most Americans are Europeans, if not by virtue of having lived in Europe themselves then at least by heritage. Americans of European descent enjoy a certain authority to speak about Europe, precisely because of their personal, traditional or inherited experience as former Europeans. America has played and is playing the role of a catalyst of European unity, as demonstrated by, among other things, the Marshall Plan negotiations, in which the Americans insisted on planning for Europe as an economic unity and not for the recovery of small Rhode Island-sized autarkic economies.

The American experience in building a nation out of varied elements—experience that has produced the art of compromise that characterizes American politics—has created certain mental habits; one of these is an experimental attitude that may be helpful in solving European problems as well as common problems of security and freedom. Out of such experimentation, which is evident in the European as well as the American contributions, emerges the framework of a common intellectual structure. It is therefore the task of the summarizer, not merely to give a catalog of the subject matter of the individual essays—which the reader should have little difficulty in remembering—but rather to reemphasize a few main themes that reappeared with sufficient frequency to indicate a consensus and to point out what are at times conclusions, at times methods of approach to problems suggested by these themes.

Part I deals with currents of social and intellectual change behind the Iron Curtain, particularly in East-Central Europe. It is evident from the presentations of Doctors Campbell and Strobel and Professor Meissner, as well as by inference from some of the others, that communism is breaking down as a monolithic political-social structure controlled from the top. There seem, rather, to be autonomous forces of social development that the leaders are unable to control and that generate widespread attitudes of antagonism toward and conflict with those leaders who feel unable to function any longer as absolute dictators of the Stalin type. The forces of revolt take various forms, running from the nonpolitical or anti-political youth of Poland to the highly political intellectuals and writers of the Slovak Communist party. The responses of the leadership are varied; they include suppression, as in Poland; compromise within the party, as in Czechoslovakia; or compromise with non-party forces, as in Hungary. The ideological revolt against the Kremlin is accompanied by nationalist overtones that may strengthen trends toward autonomy within the Communist bloc. At the same time, however, these nationalist overtones may hamper the rapprochement between nations necessary for deep or permanent structural change.

The problem facing West Europeans and Americans is how best to take advantage of these trends in pursuing Western objectives. It is evident from both European and American contributions that the Western objectives are multiplex; only a few of them can be mentioned here. One major short-range objective is military security against the nuclear or conventional attack the Communists might launch if the Western guard were down and if the risk seemed small enough. And, as Professors Possony and Kintner have pointed out, the hard-line Communists, if they return to power, would judge the risk more optimistically than does the current coexistentialist leadership in Moscow.[1] While Professor Meissner's discussion of the Russian-Chinese dispute makes it evident that this conflict has a bearing on European security, this is peripheral to the main subject of this volume and is therefore passed over with a warning against being too optimistic about the utility of Russo-Chinese antagonism in terms of Western strategy.

Another major short-range goal is the restoration of European unity as far as possible while East-Central Europe is still under communist rule. One phase of this goal is the expansion of the freedom of East Europeans as much as feasible under present overall structural conditions. The limitations of what can be done in this regard seem generally recognized. The feasibility of such gradual liberation is based on the assumption that trade, aid and cultural exchange can be used to erode the communist system; the truth of this assumption depends on how these means are used. A third short-range objective is the economic and military unity of Western Europe.

An objective that may be listed as semi-long-range is the political unity of Western Europe—the establishment of a West European parliament and government. Some Europeans may be inclined to feel that this is now moving into the category of immediate objectives, a position to which Americans would hardly be inclined to take exception.

Among the long-range objectives the most important is the political unification of Europe as a whole, either through elimination of the present Russian hegemony or through evolution or revolution to abolish at least the totalitarian phases of the communist system. Finally, Westerners are committed to the ultimate objective of liberation, though perhaps not in the sense that certain politicians have used that word as a vote-getting slogan in connection with election campaigns.

The contributors to this volume did not undertake to lay out a specific strategy for achieving these goals, and it would be inappropriate to attempt it here. (A number of scholars associated with the work of the Foundation for Foreign Affairs have been concerned with this problem individually, as illustrated by the book *Peace and Freedom Through Cold War Victory*, to which Professors Possony, Dobriansky and Niemeyer contributed.[2]) The present work does, however, provide insights about both the nature of the communist system and Western tradition, insights that afford essential guidance for strategic planning.

As Dr. Strobel demonstrates in his chapter, communist societies have certain cultural problems that are common to industrial societies. The economic bases of these problems are rooted in Western culture rather than in any particular ideology or economic system. The significance of this fact becomes evident in Strobel's discussion of attempts to find a socialist morality, attempts that have met with universal failure. Communist theorists have tried to solve the problem indirectly by developing occupational moralities but in so doing find themselves obliged to draw on more conventional morals. This failure of the attempt to find a socialist morality indicates that the moral values reflected in Western society have a universal validity going beyond the economic system of capitalism or the political system of liberal democracy. In other words, the Socialists are obliged to return to Judeo-Christian morality in the area dealing with human personality, precisely because there is no other. All else that exists is a moral vacuum, which is exactly what the Communists find themselves facing, even though they are not ready to recognize it as such. It is interesting to note in this connection that the criterion of success of the cultural revolution the Socialists would like to bring about is its effect on the individual; precisely here is where the vacuum leads to a return to the moral bases of Western culture. The experience of communist ideologists in their search for a socialist morality seems to point to the conclusion that the intellectual and philosophical platform on which we will meet the younger generation of Eastern Europe—both the nonpolitical younger generation, the anti-political generation and the young Marxists—is that of Western Judeo-Christian ethics insofar as they deal with the human personality. The Marxists may contribute certain behavioral insights, but they do not have a basic philosophy; therefore they must borrow ours.

The next point, which is brought out by Professor Mosely in his contribution, concerns the functions of ideology. Of these he lists three: a picture of the past, present and future; a justification of communist rule; and a justification for extending the Soviet system over East-Central Europe. Mosely notes, as do others, evidences of decay in the ideology of the Soviet system and hence a decline in its vigor. This leads of course to hesitation in liberalization or de-Stalinization. There is still "dangerous literature" that communist bosses do not dare let circulate, and the party is hesitant to carry de-Stalinization to its logical conclusion. A certain loosening of controls can, of course, be observed. The Soviets give less guidance than they did before to East-Central Europe, sometimes even when the local Communist parties ask for it. At the same time the satellite Communist parties have demanded a right to choose their own policy—within communist ideology, of course.

There is a loss in faith in Marxism or in Marxism-Leninism as a pseudo-religion. The question asked in Eastern Europe, however, is not are we going to return to the past, but where do we go from here? Again, though, there is a return to basic ethics—such as the ideas of truth and honesty and respect for people who call things what they are—which as suggested here are not purely Western but are shown by experience beyond the Iron Curtain to be in fact universal. This is a value that even the young Marxists are finding they need, because without it the breakdown of communication produces an intellectual vacuum. However, a paradox may be observed: while this ideological breakdown is going on, the economic as well as political ties to Russia are nevertheless being at least maintained and somewhat strengthened. Although the communist governments don't need the active interference of the Kremlin, they do need Moscow's support in reserve. The motive is rather clearly that of self-preservation. Professor Eric Waldman of Marquette has referred to what he calls revolutionary pragmatism, which is the guidance system of the Communist who no longer really believes in Marxist ideology.[3]

At this juncture we are faced with the question of how far these social, structural and intellectual changes are going to go. Professor Niemeyer has warned against projecting the Western concept of evolution into situations where it does not necessarily apply. In other words, since our own society is highly evolutionary, we are inclined to assume that other societies are equally dynamic, which may not be the case. Communist society, in particular, seems to have inherited, through the Russian model, the static quality characteristic of Byzantine culture. And as Niemeyer suggests, one of the main questions is who controls human energy behind the Iron Curtain—how does the ruling minority relate to and utilize the rest of society? Although Marxism is weakened as a philosophy or ideology, it is still intact as an operational system.

There is, of course, a revolutionary potential against communism in Eastern Europe. This was pointed out by Christopher Emmet, among others. The regimes require the support of the Soviet Army to exist, and there is a limit to the degree of independence a communist government is able to seek. The discussion on this subject brought out very clearly the difference between the philosophical or ideological decay of Marxism, of which there is no doubt at all, and operational decay, which is an entirely different question. It seems evident that the distinction between religion and the Church that came out in one phase of the discussion also seems to apply to Marxist pseudoreligion. The ideology may no longer be believed in, but the organization as a power system not only continues but may even expand.

A lot has been said about methodology. This writer would like to take the liberty of introducing a little bit of his own methodology, which may perhaps serve a certain clarifying function. This methodological invention is called the *Ziehharmonika-Theorie* or accordion theory of totalitarian power. It is simply this: totalitarian power, like an accordion, must be alternately tightened and liberalized, pulled in and out. The inner limit represents a maximum of power and terror, a minimum of freedom. But, as Charles E. Merriam suggested in his book *Political Power*, power carried to an excess is self-defeating.[4] In other words, if the music is to go on, the totalitarian ruler must pull the accordion out again; he cannot keep it at a maximum of repression. Certainly Stalinism reached a dead center, from which Stalin's successors simply had to get away. This was inherent in the whole structure of communism.

Then the dictator (or collective dictatorship) can pull the accordion out. The result is relaxation, the thaw, liberalization, more freedom. But, again, there is an outer limit; if the accordion is pulled out too far, the whole instrument may break apart. That is evidently what happened in Hungary.

The point of this accordion theory is that there is an outer limit and therefore a limit to the expectations that can legitimately be placed in liberalization. There is a possibility of relaxation within the limits of the communist system. But when the outer limit is reached, the trend is going to stop and will probably go the other way, as has happened recently in Poland. These inner and outer limits are of course changeable, and one thing that needs to be explored is the possibility of exercising outside influence from the West so as to propel the Communists in the direction of greater freedom.

The articles in Part II address themselves, directly or indirectly, to the subject of images, a discussion that necessarily introduces the phenomenon of nationalism. There is no need to repeat here what is said about nationalism and its various forms in the preceding articles, particularly those that touch on German-Slavic relations. The following observation, however, seems in order. After World War I the Treaty of Versailles produced a peace settlement. There was much to criticize in it, but at least it was a treaty valid in international law. World War II, on the other hand, ended without a peace settlement with the principal belligerent on the Axis side: Germany. There have, of course, been the minor Paris treaties with Italy, Rumania, Bulgaria, Hungary and Finland, and the Austrian Treaty—but no treaty with Germany. What this means is that politics today has a dual purpose. The West faces the short-range task of defending against the spread of totalitarianism and securing the maximum freedom now possible. But over and above the communist issue there is a long-range challenge: to develop the principles for a peace settlement. It needs to be emphasized again that a permanent peace settlement does not exist today. There is, of course, a status quo that has lasted for some time; but this is a provisorium, not a permanent peace. This is a basic fact that shapes the framework in which the free nations must operate.

One of the differences in determining the shape of the future peace is that while at Versailles the Germans were kept behind barbed wire until the treaty was ready for signature, now they have something to say about it. The advantages of this are too obvious to require elucidation. Germany, as the Hamburg editor Axel Seeberg observes, no longer seeks to be a world power. Even when it is reunified, the German potential will not support *Weltmacht* after the manner of the Kaiser's or Hitler's aspirations. The new nationalism present in Germany is aware that the existence of one people depends on the others. The Germans now see their role as a member of a society of peoples.

Facing the incursion from Eastern Europe, this new German nationalism and the nationalisms of other European countries confront a communism that has been brought to Europe on the vehicle of Russian imperialism. Quite apart from communism, there exists a traditional Russian imperialism that has been mentioned repeatedly. While communist and Russian expansionism exert continuous pressure, the West is disturbed by periodic Berlin crises—which, as Herr Seeberg points out, the Soviets deliberately provoke to distract attention from the reunification problem.

On this score, it may be commented that Western aspirations, which of course include German aspirations, conflict in no way with the legitimate aspirations and rights of the Great Russian people or of any other people of the Soviet Union. They very definitely do conflict with Russian imperialism and colonialism. It is, in this connection, somewhat illogical that the Assembly of Captive European Nations, which enjoys some official support in this country, includes only some of the captive nations; it does not include the Ukrainians, Georgians, Slovaks or Croats. Some Americans might be inclined to ask the State Department, "Why not? Why should we advocate liberty for one group of nations and not for another?"

Another phase of German policy outlined by Herr Seeberg is the question of the Hallstein Doctrine. While there is little doubt that the Federal Republic's policy of refusing to have diplomatic relations with any government that also recognizes the Soviet Zone (except in the special case of the Soviet Union) is an effective diplomatic weapon, there has recently been criticism that the Hallstein Doctrine, as this rule is called, is unrealistic. Such criticism may be answered with the statement that the Hallstein Doctrine is not only effective diplomatically, it is also realistic, because it is an expression of a fact. This fact is that only one German state, the Federal Republic, possesses the essential constituent element of a state: the will of the people it represents. We may indeed have operational contacts with the so-called German Democratic Republic, but these are administrative. The G.D.R. is not a government but an administration, with which contacts occur on the operational level as they do with other local administrations that do not exercise sovereignty.

Part III examines the economic field. Professor Gross points out that the Soviets use economic policy as an instrument of politics. This is a fact that must be taken into account in developing Western trade policy. Soviet tactics require a coordinated Western response. The Soviets' maxim of "the primacy of the political over the economic" is clearly reflected in their policy. This strategy must be recognized and an appropriate counterstrategy developed—a strategy that not only hampers the achievement of Soviet political objectives but also advances positive Western goals. Professor Gross suggests, among other things, the use of incentives to induce the communist states to abandon their state-trade monopolies, which lend themselves all too easily to political manipulation. In planning a trade policy—the economic details of which are too voluminous to be reviewed here—it is necessary to avoid one-sided advantages to the communist countries, which threaten to develop if Western states do not exercise the greatest caution in planning our relations with them. As Mr. Emmet has pointed out, the Soviet Union would benefit from the extension of credit beyond the Berne agreement. We may become involved in what, although we may think it innocent civilian trade, nevertheless finds its way indirectly into the communist military machine. The Soviets are engaged in the foreign aid battle; and it is necessary to exercise some precautions lest the articles we send them as trade or possibly aid become military materiel for the enemy in Southeast Asia, Latin America or other areas where Western forces, Americans in particular, find themselves on the firing line.

Trade can be employed for political purposes. It can be employed as an instrument of freedom, but it must be guided. The point does not need to be argued that mere trade will not in itself accomplish anything positive—there is no sense in expanding trade for the sake of trade, except the advantage of immediate profit, against which Dr. Jaksch and others have warned. No one who has thought seriously about this problem will have forgotten Lenin's saying: "The capitalists will stumble over one another's toes to sell us the rope with which we shall hang them."

There are various ways in which trade can be channeled for positive purposes. Dr. Jaksch and Professor Possony, among others, have suggested that trade be used to stimulate consumer goods demand. For instance, if automobiles are sold to communist countries, the Communists will then need highways, filling stations and spare parts. The tactic is to sell things that provoke further demand.

There is, however, a basic limitation in the economic approach to East-West relations. The main problem in East-Central Europe is not economic—it is not the existence of a socialist system or even the degree of economic coordination with the Soviet Union. The problem is, rather, essentially political: control by totalitarian dictatorships, which may practice varying degrees of liberalization and which perhaps enjoy *de facto* toleration by the people, in the sense that there is no active revolt at present, but which ultimately depend upon foreign power. What may, if we do not observe carefully, be taken for the consent or assent of the people may be simply an attitude of resignation, characterized by the paraphrase of a French saying: *"Faut de mieux on couche avec les Russes."*

Both Dr. Jaksch and M. de Fabrègues point out the necessity of European unity and the progress that has been achieved in that direction. Americans, of course, feel strongly the need for European unity; President Kennedy looked toward "a Europe speaking with one voice." Americans hope that a united Europe will not hide behind a tariff curtain or a currency curtain. M. de Fabrègues cites a question asked by M. Faure at a meeting of the German Society for Foreign Affairs on June 3, 1964, at Bad Godesberg: "Are the Germans true Europeans, or are they free traders and citizens of the world?" Most Americans would hope that these two alternatives are not mutually exclusive.

A point Dr. Jaksch brings out in this connection is the degree of unity that derives its existence from the growing European administrative corps employed by the Common Market, the Coal and Steel Community and EURATOM. Those familiar with administrative behavior will appreciate that the existence of a bureaucracy frequently serves to build up a social force—to give a movement or an idea stability. This has been pointed out by Max Weber and other sociologists. It is, of course, the academic version of the saying *"Wes Brot ich ess, des Lied ich sing!"* A growing group of European administrators and officials on the European payroll can be counted on to spread the message of a politically united Europe and to lend their influence in that direction.

In conclusion, it is possible to indicate certain points of philosophy that form the implicit basis for the consensus reflected in this book and that are essential guidelines for those who seek solutions to the problems of Germany and Europe. Again, it is not the purpose of this book to indicate a specific strategy but simply to point out certain ideas that can be used in our further explorations. Baron von Guttenberg has called attention to the need for a just settlement—a just peace—to fill the vacuum caused by the lack of a permanent peace. The acceptance of injustice would undo all that has been accomplished in creating a firm foundation for constitutional democracy in Germany. As the Baron pointed out, the Germans have no intention whatever of conducting a new expulsion. Rather, it has been recognized, and will in all probability become a principle of international law sooner or later, that a mass forced expulsion is morally wrong—it is an offense against basic human rights, even when undertaken to "undo" the results of a past expulsion. The Polish-German settlement, therefore, as well as the Bohemian settlement and all other phases of the settlement, must be based on mutual agreement. That certainly will be their basis if the ideas of European unity and freedom, for which we are struggling, prevail.

It has been argued that the Germans should sacrifice some of their rights, such as territories east of the Oder-Neisse line, in order to achieve reunification. As has been pointed out, however, this is not a genuine issue; the Germans have not been asked to do so. When such a question arises, an answer will probably be given. But as things stand now, as Professor Kulski has pointed out, the Soviet Union has not the least interest in unification. To make an offer of the eastern territories would be giving something away without getting anything in return. To expect the Germans to do so would be entirely unreasonable.

It is not necessary to emphasize here that the German struggle for reunification is part of the overall struggle for human freedom. This, of course, is a struggle that includes both reunification with the Soviet Zone or so-called G.D.R., unification with other parts of Germany and eventually the creation of a united Europe in which people are able to move about freely, to live in their traditional homes or to move somewhere else, with the rights that free peoples regard as essential—rights that many countries have put down in the Universal Declaration of Human Rights and that are perhaps even better stated—if a bit of national pride may be permitted—in the British Declaration of 1689, which we Americans borrowed to make our own Bill of Rights.

The ideological approach is essential, since we are dealing with philosophies and ideologies; but it is not enough. As Professor Kintner and others have pointed out, some powers can maintain themselves with very poor ideologies; the Ottoman Empire is a case in point. The Soviets today, now that their ideology is losing much of its appeal, base their power on technology. A tilting of the military balance to the Soviet side would, therefore, be very risky. Cuba, of course, is a case in point, and the confrontation there a preview of what might follow. There is a technological buildup taking place in the Soviet Union, which remains a power-oriented society. These are facts that must be kept in mind in planning Western trade relations with the communist bloc; as indicated before, there seems to be general agreement that they should be planned on a multilateral basis rather than being allowed to result from the spontaneous quest for profits of individual enterprises. It is, in other words, necessary to maintain the technological base of Western security.

Professor Possony has pointed out the chance that the communist "hard-liners" will come back. When they do, they may be prepared to take calculated risks. There is a need in the United States for emphasis on modern weapons systems, and in the Western alliance as a whole there is a need for greater European effort. There has been much talk about *quid pro quo*. Perhaps we need *quid pro quos*, not only with the East, but also to some extent within our own Western community. It may, for instance, be felt that Americans are not active enough on the Berlin question and not active enough on the question of German unification. Agreement might be possible on a *quid pro quo* whereby Americans would undertake such activity in return for a greater European contribution to the joint defense effort. The United States may be Atlas, but Atlas is swaying a little under the strain. We are feeling economic and financial difficulties, and it is evident that nowadays our European partners are able to shoulder a larger share of the burden than they have in the past.

Conversely, a warning must be repeated against the assumption that weakness in the West would encourage softness among the Communists, an illusion cherished by many people on both sides of the Atlantic. Without criticism of other countries, mention may be made of certain Washington "peace planners," whose continuance in business is based, not on national security, but on Parkinson's Law: bureaucrats will not only find themselves something to do, they will expand their activities as much as they can manage. Such bureaucrats, in our "disarmament agencies," take risks with American security on the thesis that being weak would promote a soft element in the Soviet Union and perhaps even in China. The exact opposite, however, is more likely. To assume that the Communists would respond to such unilateral disarmament or gestures of friendliness is a projection of Western assumptions into an area where they do not apply.

What this all adds up to is that we need a policy of cautious realism. We need to expand our contacts with Eastern Europe through trade, aid and cultural exchange; but we need to recognize at the same time that these things are weapons: they are two sided and may be used against us as well as for us.

While we are exercising this policy of cautious realism, we need to work together to build up the unity and power—the potential power, economic, political, diplomatic and ideological—of Europe and of the Atlantic community.

NOTES TO CHAPTER FIFTEEN

1. Throughout this chapter references such as this, quoting views of individuals other than the authors of this book without citation of published works, indicate contributions to the discussions at the Chicago Conference in March, 1965, where the papers on which the chapters of this book are based were originally delivered.

2. *Peace and Freedom Through Cold War Victory: Guidelines for Cold War Victory* (Chicago: American Security Council Press, 1964).

3. This concept was explained to the author by Professor Waldman in a personal conversation.

4. Charles E. Merriam, *Political Power* (New York: Whittlesey House, 1934), especially chaps. vi and ix.

Index

Index